Failure
Is NOT an
Option

This book is dedicated to the memory of my grandmother,
Sarah Lobell,
who believed in me at a time when others would not or could not.
For Grandma Sarah, the idea of allowing her only grandson to fail
truly was not an option.

Failure
Is NOT an
Option

Six Principles That Guide

Student Achievement in

High-Performing Schools

Alan M. Blankstein
Foreword by Michael Fullan

A Joint Publication of

CORWIN PRESS
A Sage Publications Company
Thousand Oaks, California

HOPE
Harnessing Optimism and Potential Through Education
Foundation

For information:

Corwin Press
A Sage Publications Company
2455 Teller Road
Thousand Oaks, California 91320
www.corwinpress.com

Sage Publications Ltd.
1 Oliver's Yard
55 City Road
London EC1Y 1SP
United Kingdom

Sage Publications India Pvt. Ltd.
B-42, Panchsheel Enclave
Post Box 4109
New Delhi 110 017 India

Printed in the United States of America

Library of Congress Cataloging-in-Publication Data

Blankstein, Alan M., 1959-
Failure is not an option : 6 principles that guide student achievement in high-performing schools / Alan M. Blankstein.
    p. cm.
"A copublication of Corwin Press and The Hope Foundation."
Includes bibliographical references and index.
ISBN 1-4129-0933-3 (cloth)—ISBN 1-4129-0934-1 (paper)
    1. School improvement programs—United States. 2. Academic achievement—United States. 3. Educational leadership—United States. I. Title.
LB2822.82.B53 2004
371.2—dc22   2003020053

This book is printed on acid-free paper.

04 05 06 07 08 10 9 8 7 6 5 4 3 2 1

Acquisitions Editor:	Faye Zucker
Editorial Assistant:	Stacy Wagner
Production Editor:	Julia Parnell
Typesetter:	C&M Digitals (P) Ltd.
Proofreader:	Theresa Kay
Indexer:	Pamela Van Huss
Cover Designer:	Anthony Paular

Contents

Appendices

Foreword

This powerful book, *Failure Is Not an Option*, addresses all of the elements that are absolutely necessary for effective and enduring educational reform. Alan Blankstein takes the key pieces of strategic reform ideas and weaves them into a coherent whole. In the first four chapters, he clearly and convincingly establishes the foundation for courageous action—why failure is not an option, why courageous leadership is crucial and what it looks like, ten common routes to failure and what to do about them, and why and how professional learning communities are central to successful reform.

Having established the philosophical and values base for reform, Blankstein proceeds to tackle the very difficult how-to questions. He does this through six principles, with a chapter on each. The six principles again also cover the waterfront of effective reform: mission, achievement for all, collaborative teaching, using data, active engagement of the community, and sustained leadership for continuous improvement.

In addition to getting the content right and doing it in a comprehensive way, *Failure Is Not an Option* is chock-full of interesting vignettes, case studies, and tested techniques for addressing difficult issues. The techniques in the appendices are invaluable in their own right. Particularly powerful is how Blankstein provides both sides of all key points. He describes what is wrong, and then *what right looks like*. He systematically poses challenging questions, and then proceeds to outline solutions to each challenge. All through the book there are ideas and strategies for pursuing practical applications to perplexing problems.

Failure Is Not an Option is a deeply passionate call to arms, combined with an entire arsenal of information—from the worlds of both research and classroom practice—to enable the reader to take systematic, continuous, and effective action. This book is absolutely a *must* read for all those interested in reform because it is simultaneously inspiring and practical.

Michael Fullan
University of Toronto

Acknowledgments

W riting a book like this can be a lonely endeavor at times. The support and encouragement of friends and colleagues, however, made it survivable! First, picking up in the encouragement department where my grandmother left off, is Nancy Shin, a true friend and executive director of the HOPE Foundation.

Michael Fullan and Andy Hargreaves have been longtime supporters, and both have contributed tangibly to this work. I am grateful for their written contributions and what each is doing to improve the lives of children worldwide.

Several extraordinary practitioners provided written contributions to *Failure Is Not an Option* in the form of "case stories." They include James Baiter, Alan Boyle, Steve Edwards, Debra Pitts, James Scaife, Mary Pat Venardos, and Deborah Wortham.

Many colleagues have helped to shape and edit this book. Three of my favorite and most incisive thinkers and editors, Robert W. Cole, Maurice Elias, and Fredrika Harper, dedicated many hours to refining the message and enhancing this overall work.

I had the good fortune of receiving feedback on various parts of this work from a number of bright, talented, and committed colleagues, including Richard Ackerman, Ryan Champeau, Linda D'Acquisto, Kris Hipp, Shirley Hord, Gwen Lee, Jay McTighe, Dennis Sparks, Patty Taylor, and Kathleen Van Antwerp.

Members of the HOPE Foundation provided crucial support necessary to bring this work to fruition. In particular, the diligence of Esther Vargas in her research, Robin Lori administratively, and Shawna Brynildssen in copyediting was key to completing this book.

Maggie Mangini and Tom Koerner have each been on the cheerleading squad for more than fifteen years. Their advice and support have been invaluable. I also appreciate the efforts of the tireless Faye Zucker and her excellent assistant, Stacy Wagner. Their diligence has led to a timely and polished release of this work.

**CORWIN
PRESS**

The Corwin Press logo—a raven striding across an open book—represents the union of courage and learning. Corwin Press is committed to improving education for all learners by publishing books and other professional development resources for those serving the field of K–12 education. By providing practical, hands-on materials, Corwin Press continues to carry out the promise of its motto: **"Helping Educators Do Their Work Better."**

The HOPE Foundation logo stands for Harnessing Optimism and Potential Through Education. The HOPE Foundation helps to develop and support educational leaders over time at district- and state-wide levels to create school cultures that sustain all students' achievement, especially low-performing students.

About the Author

Alan M. Blankstein has worked within youth-serving organizations for twenty years, beginning as a music teacher. He subsequently worked for such organizations as the March of Dimes, Phi Delta Kappa, and the National Educational Service (NES), which he founded in 1987 and ran for twelve years. He has created award-winning publications and video staff development programs, including *Reclaiming Youth At Risk* and *Discipline With Dignity*; and produced the PBS-ALSS and C-Span productions *Breaking the Cycle of Violence* and *Creating Learning Organizations: Growth Through Quality.*

Alan began the HOPE Foundation (Harnessing Optimism and Potential through Education) as a nonprofit organization whose Honorary Chair is Archbishop Desmond Tutu. HOPE supports educational leaders *over time* in creating school cultures in which *all* students succeed, especially underserved students. Alan and the HOPE staff began their work around "quality" and "professional learning communities" in 1988 by bringing W. Edwards Deming and his work to light in educational circles through a series of Shaping America's Future forums and videoconferences that involved Al Shanker, Peter Senge, Mary Futrell, Linda Darling-Hammond, Ed Zigler, the CEOs of Firestone, GM, and Ford, and scores of other leaders. The HOPE Foundation provides support for some 10,000 leaders annually through Courageous Leadership Institutes, Courageous Leadership Academies, and Comprehensive School Reform based on the Failure Is Not an Option Learning Communities of HOPE.

Based on his own background as a "youth at-risk" growing up in New York and on his professional career in education, Alan has authored the *Reaching Today's Youth Curriculum*, now provided as a course in sixteen states; and he has written articles for *Educational Leadership, The School Administrator, Executive Educator, High School Magazine*, and *Reaching Today's Youth*. Additionally, Alan provides keynote presentations and staff development, reaching tens of thousands of professionals annually through organizations including ASCD, NASSP, National Association of Private Schools for Exceptional Children, Illinois Council of Administrators for Exceptional Children, and the International Association of Special Educators.

CHAPTER ONE

Why Failure Is Not an Option

In times of drastic change, it is the learners who inherit the future. The learned usually find themselves beautifully equipped to live in a world that no longer exists.

—Eric Hoffer, *Reflections on the Human Condition*
(New York: HarperCollins, 1972, p. 32)

In the spring of 1970, the *Apollo 13* spaceship faced repeated crises as it circled the moon. Most Americans, including many of those working at NASA's ground control center, gave up hope for the survival of the *Apollo 13* crew. Newscaster Walter Cronkite described the challenge: "Perhaps never in human history has the entire world been so united by such a global drama."

At one point, when the ground control team became aware of the ship's inability to reach Earth with its current power supply, the director of flight operations, Gene Kranz, assembled the NASA team. He had been told that they had only 45 hours to get the astronauts home before the power ran out. Marking a point on the chalkboard halfway between their current position and Earth, he stated, "That's not acceptable!"

The group exploded into a cacophony of reasons for their assessments and explanations of the limitations they faced. Then the voice of one team member rose above the rest to point out that everything

1

depended on power. Without power the astronauts would not be able to communicate with the ground crews, they couldn't correct their trajectory or turn their heat shields around. Everything would have to be turned off. Otherwise the craft would never make it to reentry.

When asked what he meant by "everything," he replied "At the current rate, in sixteen hours the battery is dead; so is the crew. We have to get them down to 12 amps."

The crowd erupted at this idea. "you can't even run a vacuum cleaner on 12 amps," said one. Another objected to the idea of shutting down everything, as he felt that the guidance system at least must be kept running. Another NASA scientist was concerned that this course of action had "never been tried before," and still another added that it had "never even been simulated."

Scientific data eventually prevailed over the fear of the unknown and the untried nature of the proposal to turn off the power. Kranz was adamant in response to his crew's fear of the many unknowns, telling them they had to figure it out, that the teams in the simulators would have to work out scenarios for reentry to Earth. He ordered them to find all the engineers and assembly workers who had designed and put together all the switches, circuits, light bulbs, everything connected to the power supply, and to work out a way to reduce the use of every amp possible in the spacecraft. Pointing at the mark he had made on the chalkboard, he said, "I want this mark to go all the way back to Earth with time to spare. We never lost a man in space, and we're sure as hell not going to do so on my watch!"

Gene Kranz's motto was "failure is not an option." And he led his crew to success by bringing the astronauts safely back to Earth.

Failure Is *Not* an Educational Option

Many educators would intuitively agree: Failure is not an option for today's students—at least not one we would conceivably choose. Although clearly students *may* fail, and indeed many do, the consequences are generally too dire to *allow* for such an option (Springfield, 1995). Students who don't make it through high school earn substantially less in wages (Springfield, 1995) and have far greater rates of incarceration and drug abuse than do their peers (Woods, 2000).

Rosa Smith, former superintendent of the Columbus, Ohio, schools, had an epiphany one morning when she read some statistics about the U.S. prison population. Some 75% of the prison population, she found, is Latino or African-American, and 80% are functionally illiterate. She felt a new sense of purpose: Her work was no longer about teaching math or science, but about saving lives!

The ability to articulate such a clear and compelling message to all educational stakeholders—inside and outside of the school building—is the beginning of defining what Michael Fullan (2001a) refers to as "moral purpose." Leaders who tap this clear sense of purpose in themselves and others are addressing the beginning of what we refer to in this book as the Courageous Leadership Imperative.

Many leaders have yet to discover their moral purpose or develop their courageous leadership abilities. One former superintendent, Rick DuFour, recounts his reaction to a superintendent who challenged the importance of educating *all* children to *high* standards. The superintendent told DuFour, "This isn't brain surgery. No one is going to die here! Some kids advance a little, some a lot. Isn't that the way it goes?" DuFour retorted that this cavalier attitude reminds him of a little office building he once saw in a small town. On the office door were posted two signs: "Veterinarian" and "Taxidermist." Underneath was printed these words: "Either way you get your dog back!"

Failure is not an option for public schooling, either.

Leaders in Western society have long articulated the close tie between a strong public education system and democracy itself (Dewey, 1927; Glickman, 2003; Goodlad, 2001; Putnam, 2000; Putnam, Leonardi, & Nanetti, 1993). Schools are clearly for the common good, and they serve as the gateway to, and potential equalizer for, economic and life success for millions of under-served children.

As Michael Fullan states, "A high-quality public school system is essential, not only for parents who send their children to these schools but also for the public good as a whole" (2003a, p. 4). Failure is no more an option for the *institution* of public education than it is for the children within that institution (Glickman, 2003; Goodlad, 2001).

Yet we have seen countless threats to public schools in recent years. They include the rise of vouchers—even for religious schools (Walsh, 2002)—as well as the concerted entry of large, for-profit corporations into the public education arena. Moreover, it often appears that *public* policy itself is harmful to *public* education. Although public officials call for "leaving no child behind," they rarely accompany that call with adequate resources to meet the challenge. A greater level of courage and commitment are needed now—more than ever before, it seems—to meet these and other grave challenges.

THE AIM OF *FAILURE IS NOT AN OPTION*: HOW HIGH-ACHIEVING SCHOOLS SUCCEED WITH *ALL* STUDENTS

How did Gene Kranz persevere under such dire circumstances and unrelenting odds during the *Apollo* crisis? What are the elements of this kind of courageous thinking and action, and how does one develop them? How could he harness the urgency of the situation, yet maintain his composure with three lives at stake and the whole world watching? What kind of organizational culture allows both for the open commentary from "naysayers" and for the ability to quickly move beyond those initial reactions to concerted teamwork?

This book addresses these questions with a unifying framework for action. Parker Palmer (1998) indicates that most professional development (and books like this) answer the "what" or "how" questions: *What* should I do, and *how* should I do it? This book answers these questions in detail. In addition, we address the two questions often ignored, yet crucial to success: *Why* am I doing this, and *who* do I need to be to succeed?

Perhaps more than in any other profession, educators have pursued their calling for a noble reason. Indeed, what could be more compelling than undertaking a profession that *literally* places the future of *children* in your hands?

Educators don't have the "distractions" of fame and furtune to cloud their thinking about *why* they are here! So there must be another reason—a more profound *why* that leads to all the hours of toil, the deep concerns for the success of young people, the countless evenings and weekends attending plays and ball games.

Reconnecting with this *why* is imperative to sustaining one's passion and focus in light of the barrage of attacks that *public* education, and all those involved with it, regularly endure. Standing up for why we are in this field is essential to our personal and professional well-being. Equally important, it is imperative for our very future—and that of our children. In this, failure is indeed not an option.

Ironically, the single most important element for success in any endeavor is often omitted from books such as this. While it is easy to focus on what *others* need to do, or on how to *structure* an organization, or on what *policies* need to be handed down to staff members, the *real* determinant of success will no doubt be *you*! You, the person reading this book. This book grapples—most notably in Chapter Two—with the thorny issue of *intro*-spection to assure *external* results. Make no mistake about it: Failure Is Not an Option begins with *you*!

THE STRUCTURE OF THIS BOOK

Failure Is Not an Option begins in this chapter with an overarching "moral purpose" (Fullan, 2001a) for schools: *sustaining success for all students so that failure is not an option.* This answers the *"Why are we in this profession?"* question and provides coherent direction for our work.

The following chapter addresses the "who?" question by formalizing what we have discovered to be the mental framework of thousands of highly successful leaders. We call it the Courageous Leadership Imperative. The components of this imperative are described in Chapter 2, and specific examples and processes for developing this kind of courageous leadership are provided. Leaders of every variety can produce short-term gains in student achievement. A Courageous Leadership Imperative, however, is necessary to sustain significant gains. This is especially true under challenging circumstances. Leaders who adopt the five axioms that comprise this imperative are more likely than others to successfully adapt to shifts in educational spending, priorities, personnel, and policies. Ultimately, it is the internal strength of the leader and the school community that will act as ballast, rudder, and engine for the ship during stormy weather.

Chapter 3 gives a realistic depiction of the common factors that have derailed many change efforts. More important, it provides specific processes and strategies for keeping initiatives on track.

Chapter 4 provides an extensive research base to answer the "what?" question. It offers six principles for creating and sustaining a professional learning community. These principles are drawn from more than a decade of research on the topic and 15 years of practical experience in the field. The research is clear: Building such a community is our best hope for sustained school success (Darling-Hammond, 1997; Drucker, 1992; Fullan, 1993; Joyce and Showers, 1995; Louis, Kruse, and Raywid, 1996; Newmann and Wehlage, 1995; Senge, 1990). How this community is defined, constructed, and sustained will be addressed beginning in Chapter 4.

Finally, we address the "how to?" question in Chapters 5 through 10. In these chapters we provide detailed, field-tested processes for creating professional learning communities in which failure is not an option.

In sum, this book builds on 15 years of intensive work with educational leaders to reshape school cultures for *sustained* student success. Our work began with W. Edwards Deming in 1988 and continued with the work of Peter Senge, Michael Fullan, Andy Hargreaves, Maurice Elias, Shirley Hord, Rick DuFour, Robert Eaker, Kris Hipp, Tom Sergiovanni, and thousands of school leader-practitioners who have been at the forefront of creating true learning communities (Figure 1.1).

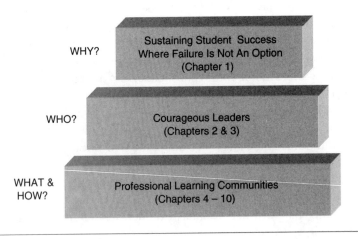

Figure 1.1

BACKGROUND OF *FAILURE IS NOT AN OPTION* (*FNO*)

This book is based on an extensive study of literature and practical research exploring high-performing schools and their ability to increase and sustain high student achievement. The "how to" section of this book focuses on six principles of professional learning communities. They were originally captured in 2001 in a video series titled *Failure Is Not an Option,* featuring Michael Fullan, Rick DuFour, Barbara Eason-Watkins, Jay McTighe, Mike Schmoker, Steven Edwards, Deborah Wortham, and six award-winning principals and their staff members.

Both the video and this book describe the "what?" and the "how?" of creating a professional learning community in which failure is not an option. In addition, this book details specific processes for building and sustaining student achievement. Included are "case stories" of both turnaround schools and high-performing schools that have successfully used these processes. Most important, this book clarifies the "why?" and the "who?" of successful school change.

WHY *FAILURE IS NOT AN OPTION* NOW? A NEW IMPERATIVE FOR A NEW CHALLENGE

In times of great challenge or dynamic change, such as schools are now experiencing, organizations must develop cultures that are significantly different than those needed in stable times. Schools, like most organizations, tend to seek consistency and equilibrium. Yet, according to Richard Pascale's (Pascale, Millemann, & Gioja, 2000) study of the life sciences, "Prolonged equilibrium is a precursor to disaster." Avoiding equilibrium enables living organisms to avoid extinction in periods of great change.

Michael Fullan (2003a) advises educators to "move toward the danger" instead of hunkering down in difficult times. It is better to face the danger with a proactive approach than to wait for the danger to surprise you.

However, this is not at all easy. Most people are not easily swayed to "move toward the danger." Schools facing the tremendous challenges posed by legislation that requires success for all children often end up using an array of approaches that actually prolong and even amplify the threats.

Two of the most common responses to the demands schools are facing are: avoiding the challenges at hand or, at the other extreme, embracing every possible solution to the point of losing focus. Others include:

1. Looking outside their own sphere of influence for reasons why students are not succeeding

2. Seeking a quick and easy solution

3. Avoiding or ignoring the data

4. Shooting the messenger

5. Total burnout and utter collapse

The Courageous Leadership Imperative described in the following chapter provides an alternative to these options. In unequivocal terms, it sets out the desired result and thus adds cohesion to change efforts with that aim. As such, it cuts through the many reasons to forestall *meaningful* action while minimizing less substantive, or even counterproductive, *hyper*action.

In short, the Courageous Leadership Imperative deeply roots a school's purpose and passions in ways that are enduring and stabilizing in the context of rapid change. At the same time, the professional learning community (proposed in Chapter 4) and processes for its implementation (Chapters 5–10) will help create a culture adaptable to extensive change. Knowing *who* we are as educators and leaders and *why* we are here provides an enduring source of strength. *How* we fulfill our individual and collective purpose, however, must be flexible and adaptable.

PEOPLE: THE TOUGH PART OF CHANGE

In *The Answer to How Is Yes*, Peter Block (2002) reflects on how so many of his major corporate clients refrain from committing to action, replacing action with an ingenious barrage of "how?" and "yeah, but . . ." questions and comments. Even when professionals know what to do and how to do it, they are often reluctant to take courageous action. Mark Twain once quipped: "Quitting smoking is easy—I've done it a thousand times!" Like the smoker who knows better or the gambler who occasionally wins, we can become wedded to what worked at one time or what works once in a while.

The human aspect of school change is the most difficult, yet essential, element for success. Perhaps because of this, it is often overlooked, minimized, or dismissed.

Without clearly addressing the human dimension of change—the "who?" and the "why?" of school reform—the outcomes of efforts to change will be disappointing. Tom Gregory (2001) encourages us to identify our barriers and proceed with courage:

> I see most of the apparently formidable challenges to structural change in education as illusory. Many obstacles—even some scary ones—tend to evaporate when we muster the courage (or the effrontery) to push them aside. Most of the real obstacles to change are not "out there" but inside us. We each have our own collection of educational bogeymen who we're afraid to confront. (p. 580)

Dennis Sparks, executive director of the National Staff Development Council, summarized the challenge in our schools:

> Only a small portion of what is known about quality staff development is regularly used in schools. The daily practice of teaching and leadership have been virtually untouched in most schools in spite of the investment of billions of dollars and a great deal of effort. (Sparks, 2002, p. 11–12)

Sparks (2002) goes on to describe the challenge as a human and emotional one as opposed to being mainly technical or cognitive.

This is true outside of education as well. Corporations now spend some $50 billion annually in fees for "change consultants" (Pascale, 1997–1999). And reports from the "changed" corporations indicate that a whopping 70% of those efforts fail (Pascale, 1998). Richard Pascale (Pascale, Millemann, & Gioja, 2000) attributes this to "social engineering."

> "Social" is coupled with "engineering" to denote that most managers today, in contrast to their nineteenth-century counterparts, recognize that people need to be brought on board. But they still go about it in a preordained fashion. Trouble arises because the "soft stuff" is really the hard stuff, and no one can really "engineer" it. (2000, p. 12)

This book provides direction and support for the difficult but essential "soft stuff." Clearly defining who you are as a person and as an organization, and why you are engaged in the endeavor of building and sustaining achievement for *all* students, provides the greatest hope for success.

LIMITATIONS OF THIS WORK

We approach the task of this book with both caveats and conviction. The first major caveat is that there is no *formula* for success.

The initial "formula" for success in the *Apollo 13* example above had to be entirely tossed aside. It was replaced with processes for creating *new* approaches to success using data, past experience, a willingness to reconsider all assumptions, and the climate for challenging one another's assumptions toward reaching a widely understood and commonly desired outcome.

Most important, this "case story" exemplifies the courageous leadership necessary—in the face of nearly certain failure—to maintain a sense of hope and optimism, composure and urgency. And to *act* on the best information possible toward what was ultimately a successful rescue of the three men in *Apollo 13*.

Formulas for success are suspect. As Peter Drucker stated, the reason we have so many *gurus* is because we can't spell *charlatan*!

That being said, we *do* share some convictions and experience regarding "best practices" for reculturing schools toward sustainable student achievement, guiding principles for success, and using time-tested truths about leadership and implementation of initiatives, while taking into account the complexity of change.

The trick is sorting all this out, being accurate and precise without oversimplifying, and providing specific steps for action in the face of intricate challenges. That's the balancing act this book aims to perform.

TAPPING GREAT WISDOM

Finally, we draw from an array of literature and practice from all areas, including organizational development technologies, educational change, professional learning communities, practice and research, enlightened corporate approaches to leadership development, youth psychology, and enduring wisdom of the past.

To that end, we fashion this book in terms described by last century's leading champion for young people's potential. Janusz Korczak directed a school for Jewish street children from 1912 to 1942, until Warsaw came under Nazi occupation, and Korczak voluntarily tied his fate with that of his street orphans:

> *This book is designed to be as short as possible because it is addressed primarily to a young colleague, who, suddenly thrown into the whirlpool of the most difficult educational problems, the most involved conditions of life, and now stunned and resentful, has sent out a cry for help.*
>
> *A fatigued person cannot study thick volumes on education at night. One who is unable to get enough sleep will be incapable of implementing the precious principles he has learned. This shall be brief so that your night's rest may not be disturbed.* (Korczak, 1967)

Courage may be the most important of all virtues, because without it one cannot practice any other virtue with consistency.

—Maya Angelou

Courage, the footstool of the virtues, upon which they stand.

—Robert Louis Stevenson

Leadership has for centuries been closely associated with courage. Richard I, King of England from 1189 to 1199, was renowned for his courage and dubbed by troubadours "Richard the Lionhearted." More recent Western interpretations of courage have associated it with war, battle, and fallen or surviving heroes, yet the word itself comes from the French root *coeur*, or "heart."

Having "heart" was among the greatest virtues in many early Native American societies, and courage was systematically developed in young men (who were, not coincidentally, called "braves"). "The greatest brave was he who could part with his cherished belongings and at the same time sing songs of joy and praise" (Standing Bear, 1933). Eastman (1902) recounts that his grandmother encouraged him to give away what he cherished most, his puppy, so that he would one day become "courageous and strong." These young braves were taught to face their inner fears of loss. Many would later extend this courage to the ultimate sacrifice of their life for those members of the tribe, especially children and their elders, who were unable to defend themselves. Such a sacrifice for children was natural and consistent with the Native American culture.

Eddie Belleroe, a Cree Elder from Alberta, Canada, recalled a conversation with his aging grandfather. He asked, "Grandfather, what is the purpose of life?" After a long time in thought, the old man looked up and said, "Grandson, children are the purpose of life. We were once children and someone cared for us; now it is our turn to care" (Brendtro et al., 1990, p. 45).

Many educators constantly make sacrifices and face fears on behalf of children. We at the HOPE Foundation work with them nationwide. We know, as just one example, a principal who fought with the bus driver's union to create an ever-changing, flexible bus schedule that serves itinerant and homeless children. We work with thousands of teachers who daily put their practice on the line in an unwavering commitment to children who are years behind grade level. Every day, these teachers, and their students, face the very real possibility of failure.

These professionals have a Courageous Leadership Imperative (CLI). The CLI is defined as acting in accordance with one's own values, beliefs, and mission—even in the face of fear, potential losses, failure.

Rudy, another courageous colleague, recently ran a big-city school district. One day he met with one of his principals to ask why the children in his school were consistently underperforming. The principal took Rudy to the window of his office, pointed to the children entering the school, and said, "You see those poor kids? Most of them have one parent, if that; they can't read; and they probably don't even speak the language. They just aren't going to make it!" Rudy fired the principal that day, although the political consequences were serious.

The courageous actions described above are not calculated in terms of personal risk. They are not designed for personal gain. These educators act in accordance with their heart. They do what they have to do because of who they are and what they value. They do it because of the young people whom they are charged to protect, nurture, and help develop into successful young men and women. Developing such courageous leadership individually and organizationally, and leveraging it to assure sustained student success, is the subject of this chapter.

WHEN FAILURE IS NOT AN OPTION

Following a conversation with Archbishop Desmond Tutu, Nobel Peace Prize laureate, we asked his personal assistant if fear of failure ever influenced them in their struggle against apartheid. Oupa Scene responded:

> We never considered failure. Even though we were under apartheid, we had some African neighbors who were doing even worse than us! We drew strength from one another; we would reminisce and conceive of a brighter future for our country . . . a day when everyone could eat, lodge, and have other basics of life; a day when we could create a space program that would

a growing body of research indicates that the belief system of teachers heavily influences their students' possibilities for success (Clark, 1988; Cole, 1989; Fenstermacher, 1986; Nespor, 1987; Pintrich, 1990; Weinstein, 1989; Wilson, 1990). In short, "Positive expectations yield positive results" (Kouzes and Posner, 1999, p. 68).

Research on highly reliable organizations (HRO's) takes this concept of positive expectations and belief systems a step further. These HRO's embrace the core concept that *failure is not even an option*. In fact, for these organizations failure would mean disaster, as they are responsible for such things as clean water, electrical power supplies, and air traffic control. One study of two types of HRO's—air traffic control towers and regional electrical power grids—considered applying "HRO response" to meeting the demand for high-quality instructional services for *all* students. This study indicated the strong likelihood that what was learned from HRO's can be applied to work in schools.

Rossi and Stringfield wrote, "We found much support for the HRO construct [for potential use in schools] and for its dependence on an established network of high-quality relationships among all stake-holders" (1997, p. 6). Among the cited principles of HRO's were:

1. The central goals are clear and widely shared.

2. All staff in HRO's share a belief that success is critical and that failure to achieve core tasks would be absolutely disastrous.

3. HRO's build interdependence among all staff. (Rossi and Stringfield, 1997, pp. 6–7)

Our interviews with thousands of school leaders over the past 15 years have yielded findings similar to those immediately above. We found that those administrators who hold an unshakable belief in the ultimate success of their staff and students have far better results than those who do not hold such belief. Moreover, leaders with a Courageous Leadership Imperative take that belief a step further. They are unwilling to conceive of failure in the long term. Setbacks along the way are rapidly turned into learning experiences that fuel advances toward future successes. As a result, these leaders are more likely to see projects through to completion, inspire others to high levels of performance, and commit to sustaining achievement for *all* students.

What are the elements of such a Courageous Leadership Imperative, and how can they be developed? The next section addresses these questions.

FOUNDATIONS FOR SUCCESS

The Courageous Leadership Imperative was distilled from an extensive literature review on educational leadership and conversations with thousands of leaders over the past 15 years. The most successful leaders demonstrated characteristics that mirror those of highly reliable organizations listed above. These leaders do not consider failure to be an option. Specifically, leaders who turn failing schools around and keep successful schools moving forward over time exhibit characteristics that can be summarized in the following five axioms:

1. Begin With Your Core

This axiom refers to first clarifying the driving *internal* core of the leadership and the school community. "Authentic leaders build their practice inward from their core commitments rather than outward from a management text" (Evans, 1996). The core is defined here as the intersection of one's purpose, values, and intention. Determining one's core is a profound and intensive process that provides the enduring roots necessary to sustain efforts in the face of opposing forces.

School leadership often requires balancing the interests of varying groups. For example, parents on the "right" may want to reduce access to certain reading texts for their children, whereas parents on the "left" may highly value those same texts as well as the concept of free access to information. How can leaders attend to the many disparate interests that tug at them without losing their own center? As one high school principal puts it:

> The non-negotiable that I come back to most often is being true to myself—heeding the call of my heart, *my core*, for better or worse. Sooner or later a great leader is going to stir the pot and, if great things happen as a result, is going to get splattered and slopped on. (Hallowell, 1997, p. 55; italics added)

Although mission statements address why schools exist (e.g., to assure that all students learn), the axiom of "beginning with your core" goes a level deeper. It answers the questions "Why do I care?" and "What am I willing to do about it?"

Clarifying one's core as a person and a leader is perhaps the most difficult and most fundamental of all acts (Bennis, 1989). We should not be surprised that it is also rarely undertaken. In fact, one could find many understandable reasons for passing over this critical axiom, and there are many reasons why such practices are seen as unnecessary or impractical among modern-day educational leaders:

a. There is too little time to do *anything*, much less "getting to one's core"! Donaldson (2001) refers to the "leadership-resistant architecture" of schools in which there is a "conspiracy of busyness" (p. 11) that leaves little time to convene people to plan, organize, and follow through. Although most leaders find this leaves them with little time for reflection, the most effective among them make allocating their time properly a priority nonetheless.

b. There is an impression that "self-discovery" is "soft" or an otherwise unnecessary aspect of leadership. Our work with leaders indicates otherwise and more closely concurs with Warren Bennis' pioneering work in the field. "'Know thyself' is the inscription over the oracle at Delphi. And it's still the most difficult task any of us faces. But until you truly know yourself, your strengths and weaknesses, know what you want to do and why you want to do it, you cannot succeed in any but the most superficial sense of the word" (Bennis, 1989, p. 40).

c. Acting on aspirations and ideals can be painful. Such actions expose leaders to what Ackerman and Maslin-Ostrowski refer to as the inevitable "wounding" that true leaders inevitably experience (2002). It becomes easier and less risky, therefore, to just do what is mandated by the district, state department, or province.

d. Leadership is a lonely role to begin with. This isolation is compounded by the sense many leaders have that it is not safe to be themselves, even with their staff. They can become a "prisoner to their roles" and suffer from what Kets de Vries refers to as the "impostor syndrome" (1993).

e. In almost every society we researched there have been, or still are, mentors, spiritual guides, elders, and others who systematically assist people in self-development and self-discovery. Many African societies we visited still use rites of passage with their young boys and girls. Several Native American societies use "vision quests" to help prospective leaders uncover their purpose in life. Such practices have been seen as essential to leading a meaningful life, and especially to leading others to do the same. This is no longer the case in most Western societies, and many people simply don't know where to begin such a search for self.

There are many ways that educational leaders can reach their core. Livsey and Palmer suggest answering the following questions in pairs to get to "the heart of our life as a teacher":

1. Why did I become a teacher?

2. What do I stand for as an educator?

3. What are the gifts that I bring to my work?

4. What do I want my legacy as a teacher to be?

5. What can I do to keep track of myself—to remember my own heart? (1999)

Another way to get individuals to discover what lies at their core is through an activity that can be undertaken in groups of about 8–15. One group or several can do this activity at the same time within a room.

Ask everyone to begin by sitting in a circle while the activity is explained, and then break into groups of three (triads). Each member of the triad recounts a story from his or her own life that captures the essence of the person in some way. For example: "When I was a young teenager, I saw a couple of other teenagers robbing an elderly woman, and I intervened."

The person telling the story then draws out the elements that describe some of his or her essential personal characteristics. In the above example, the storyteller might say: "This shows the essence of who I am and what I value because I protect those who need help, and I am not afraid of the consequences." Others in the triad may add to the list of characteristics and see if the storyteller agrees with them.

Someone else in the triad can write down each personal characteristic to share with the larger group. It is also possible to build an affinity diagram from everyone's notes in order to discover the "common core" of the group. This, in turn, can be used as part of the development of the school's mission or values (to be described in Chapter 5). The full group is re-formed at the end of this sharing session, and everyone has the opportunity to briefly share their story and corresponding "essential" or "core" characteristics.

Educators can also get to their core by reflecting alone on these critical questions:

1. What do I *value* most? Another way to ask this might be, "What behaviors can I *not* tolerate and why?"

2. What do my past life patterns, strong interests, and passions tell me about my *purpose* in life?

3. How do my values and purpose in life overlap with what I am doing *here* in my current role? What are my *intentions* relative to the work I am now doing?

Defining the answers to questions 1 and 2 above, and ensuring alignment between this and the intentions of one's current work as a leader, will help to maximize the effectiveness of such an exercise. This process takes time, yet it builds a feeling of personal authenticity and therefore enhances trust within the organization.

"Leaders who are followed are authentic. Integrity is a fundamental consistency between personal beliefs, organizational aims, and working behavior" (Evans, 1996, p. 184). Defined in slightly different terms, leaders with the greatest credibility and moral sway know who they are. Their *purpose, values,* and *intentions* relative to their work are aligned. The next four axioms deal with leaders' *actions.*

2. Create Organizational Meaning

What's really important to being our best is concentration and focus on something that is meaningful to us.

—Kouzes and Posner (1999, p. 53)

Victor Frankl (1959) wrote persuasively about people's fundamental need for meaning in their lives. Despite the current focus on testing and standards, educators need more than incremental gains on their students' test scores to establish a motivating connection to their work. Similarly, students need to see the relevance of schoolwork in their lives. This is essential to gaining sustainable achievement or anything more than short-term results on tests. As one 14-year-old student shared with us, "What do I care about Romeo and Juliet? I ain't goin' to college . . . an' most of my friends ain't even made it to be 20 years old!"

The drive to create meaning guides the creation and communication of deeper meaning in the lives of all stakeholders, which in turn unleashes energy toward substantive school improvement. It also provides a sense of hope to those in despair. Such hope is a vitally important ingredient for success (Evans, 1996; Fullan, 2001a; Fullan and Hargreaves, 1996).

One way to create organizational meaning is through reframing. Although a budget cut may demoralize a school community, for example, it could also be an impetus for change and an opportunity to rally the troops. It could be seen, therefore, as an opportunity to gather people together to discuss how the community can collectively make their current work more effective, drop things that are not working, and learn about how other schools are dealing with similar challenges. It could even be the impetus for a school community that was otherwise isolated to undertake action research on "best practices" for dealing with budgetary constraints.

Reframing in Action

One savvy street worker for the Boys and Girls Clubs was recently faced with a brutal gang war between the Deuces and the Latin Kings on the South Side of Chicago. The death of one young Deuces member had touched off the battle, and our friend, Nicky, soon afterward met the boy's former girlfriend at the funeral. He used the crisis as an opportunity, another form of reframing, when he saw her:

Angie, I know you're broken up over this. I am too. But this is what you have signed up for by dating members of the gang and by being in it yourself. You will see this every

> *week, every month, and every year until it's you. But I can*
> *help you get out of the gang . . .*
>
> Nicky probably saved this girl's life. She followed his path
> and left the gang. He, in effect, did two things to achieve this:
> (1) He gave her a reality check during the crisis. Some call this
> "tough love." (2) But the reality check alone was not sufficient.
> He also gave her a viable alternative to her current reality—a
> bridge to a higher ground.

All leaders are faced with crises at some point. Leaders are also
regularly faced with challenges. A leader's most productive reaction
to such situations is to create a positive meaning of these situations
for themselves and for the people in their organizations.

3. Maintain Constancy and Clarity of Purpose

Sometime in the 1970's, advertisers must have quietly signed
a pact: *All products should now and henceforth be deemed "new and
improved"!* Educators, like most of us, gleefully bought the "latest"
and most "improved" lawnmower, car, and soap. As a profession, we
have also adopted this same regrettable concept—creating, consum-
ing, and abandoning the latest educational fad every few years.

But the educator who purchases a quick and convenient "initiative du jour" is buying a mirage. Most of these new initiatives are
later deemed ineffective and evaporate—or worse, they are kept
indefinitely without further evaluation. In the latter case, the educational "bookshelf" is filled with a confusing array of possible ways
to proceed. This approach is disjointed at best, and demoralizing for
an already overburdened staff.

This axiom—to maintain consistency and clarity of purpose—
moves us toward a disciplined approach to both clarifying and holding fast to organizational purpose. It saves time that would otherwise
be spent changing directions and filling vacancies for departing,
dispirited staff.

The "constancy of purpose" portion of this axiom (Deming,
1986) is made possible by first *clarifying* that purpose. In the
Apollo 13 example, the purpose was clear: Bring the astronauts

back alive. Had the purpose been vague (e.g., at one point there was still question as to whether they should attempt a moon walk) or the constancy of that pursuit wavering (e.g., had ground control given in to the pessimism surrounding their superhuman mission), the astronauts would never have made it home.

Maintaining clarity and constancy of purpose accomplishes two major goals. First, it helps reduce stress among staff—stress that arises from multiple priorities, coupled with insufficient time to accomplish them. Tom Williams (2001) surveyed current elementary and secondary principals in Ontario and found that more than 80% will retire by 2009. Three of five of their top "dissatisfiers" had to do with lack of time to perform their jobs properly.

As one principal told us, "I feel like I need to be all things to all people. And district priorities shift like the desert sands. It can be overwhelming at times." Adhering to this axiom helps provide continuity and coherence in an otherwise ever-changing landscape.

Second, maintaining clarity and constancy of purpose leads to greater success within those areas of focus. Evans (1996) explains: "Studies of high-performing systems show that their leaders provide direction that is clear, strong, and unambivalent. . . . Clarity brings many advantages. The first is to foster trust" (p. 213).

Evans goes on to advocate that any given team or individual considering a multifaceted project undertake "one thing at a time" (1996, p. 218). There are several ways to accomplish this:

1. Be fanatical about the positives of a project. Continually point out the milestones that are being reached along the way. Celebrate success. Encourage experimentation and refinements where necessary. Empower people to continue the efforts on their own in order to build momentum.

2. Systematically drop what should *not* be pursued. Involve stakeholders in creating a list of such activities or projects to determine "What needs to be done that is not being done now, and what can we quit doing so we can do what we need to do?" (Schlechty, 1992, p. 106).

3. Provide a sense of urgency to the area of desired focus. In Chapter 1, we described a superintendent who determined that she and her staff were not teaching math and science, but saving lives! Such "reframing" in compelling and urgent terms helps to focus people on desired outcomes.

4. Provide continuous feedback using data. Ensuring that pertinent data flow directly to those involved with a project (as opposed to being filtered through the leader) is even more powerful and focusing.

5. When necessary, stretch out time lines to meet the goal. It is better to provide the time needed for success than it is to have several half-completed projects.

Effective leaders help their school community succeed by first personally defining their core, making meaning for their organization around core values and core purpose, and continually clarifying and focusing on priorities that are aligned with that purpose.

4. Confront the Data and Your Fears

In *Good to Great* (2001), Jim Collins observes that successful companies consistently and accurately assess current performance with an eye toward improvement. "Facing the brutal facts" is often difficult; they can be unflattering! In addition, educators tend to correlate certain types of assessment with personal and critical evaluation by administration (Fullan and Hargreaves, 1996, 1997, 1998).

Naming and facing fears constructively can be the first step to overcoming them, thereby expanding the range of possible actions. Take these recent world events, for example:

1. The May 13, 2003, issue of the *New York Times* reported: "Scientists . . . said yesterday that the existing public health measures had been effective in containing the [SARS] disease in many countries and should work eventually in China and Taiwan, where the disease is now concentrated" (p. 13). Ironically, SARS reportedly began in China but was contained in places as near as Hong Kong and as far away as Toronto, Canada, before it was under control in China. This is likely due to the Chinese government's initial denial of the problem. Unlike Hong Kong, China was unwilling to confront the data and face the fears associated with this epidemic. As this article indicated: "The New China News Agency reported that 31 officials in the capital were disciplined for poor performances in carrying out measures to combat the epidemic."

2. In February 2003, the space shuttle *Columbia* burst into flames upon reentry into the earth's atmosphere, killing all seven astronauts aboard.

   The subsequent investigation revealed that a suitcase-sized chunk of foam smashed into the *Columbia*'s left wing and damaged a critical heat shield, causing the *Columbia* space shuttle disaster.

   According to the Associated Press (July 3, 2003): "During *Columbia*'s flight, shuttle managers rejected engineers' request for spy satellite images to ascertain the extent of damage to the left wing."

Although it is impossible to know what the fate of this flight mission might have been had scientists confronted the data (and their fears) early on, it is clear that they did not take this approach. By contrast, confronting the data and facing fears were critical to saving the lives of the three men on *Apollo 13,* as described in Chapter 1.

Like other organizations, school communities tend to avoid certain facts and related fears. We have entered many fine schools, for example, that pride themselves on an 85% passing rate on standardized tests, without examining who is in the 15% that are failing.

It is essential to develop the organizational norms and the personal "habits of mind" (Costa and Kallick, 2000) to dispassionately and regularly evaluate one's position relative to the ideal, and to use data-based assessments as fuel for continued improvements, hope, optimism, and action.

5. Build Sustainable Relationships

In the prior "A Test of Courage" section of this chapter, we noted that each of the more than 3,000 leaders surveyed emphatically said "yes" when asked if they would enter a burning shopping mall if their child were in it. Although the "moral imperative" (Fullan, 2003a) of potentially saving children was the same in both question #3 and #4 of this survey, the *relationship* was not. When the children in question were the *respondents'* children, there was no doubt as to whether they would risk their lives to save them.

Studies of courageous actions in war indicate that it is not so much moral purpose that lies behind putting your life on the line (although that can be a part of it), but the more tangible impact of loyalty to your buddies. "Quality relationships, in other words, are even more powerful than moral purpose" (Fullan, *Moral Imperative,* 2003, p. 35).

Clearly, in this book we are not advocating that leaders or their staff put their lives on the line. The research is clear, however, that relationships are a crucial element of student achievement and school success (Barth, 2001; Bryk and Schneider, 2003). They also support courageous leadership.

The relationships we refer to are myriad and multifaceted. They include relationships among staff, between staff and students, among students, between the school personnel and the community—among everyone touched by the work of the school.

Kouzes and Posner wrote:

Leaders create relationships, and one of those relationships is between individuals and their work. Ultimately we all work for a purpose, and that purpose has to be served if we are to feel encouraged. Encouraging the heart only works if there's a fit between person, the work, and the organization. (1999, p. xv)

It is important to understand that all of the axioms above interact with one another. Relationships serve to weave them together into a unified whole. Relationships support a leader in taking the risk to act from his or her *core* to create *organizational meaning.* Relationships allow leaders to maintain *clarity and constancy of purpose* and to *face the data and the fears,* though this might otherwise be too stressful, threatening, and disheartening.

In every district in which we worked toward long-term school reform, we have spent the first year on nonacademic items such as the development of mission and vision in ways that were collaborative and relationship-enhancing. It is interesting to note that although we did not focus on academics in the first year, in every instance academic achievement improved significantly during that same year. The "case story" in the next chapter on the Alton, Illinois, school district provides corroborating details.

Throughout this book, we share ways to enhance affinity among those in the school community. In Chapter 4, we also advocate the creation of learning communities based on relational trust. These sections provide specific strategies for developing relationships critical to the success of schools.

DEVELOP COURAGEOUS LEADERSHIP FOR ACTION

This culture, and we as members of it, have yielded too easily to what is doable and practical. . . . We have sacrificed the pursuit of what is in our hearts. We find ourselves giving in to doubts and settling for what we know how to do, or can learn to do, instead of pursuing what matters most to us and living with the adventure and anxiety that this requires. (Block, 2002, p. 1)

There is frequently a chasm between what we know to be the best action and what we do. The connecting tissue is often the courage to act.

In this book we appeal to the *heart* (as well as the mind) in order to find the courage to increase and sustain levels of student achievement. Given the challenges for staff, students, and the larger community in today's environment of accountability, there is much at stake.

As mentioned earlier, courage comes from the French word *coeur,* or heart. Effective leaders act with heart. In the final analysis, their decisions are informed by judgment but emanate from their core purpose, values, and intention. Leaders who act in this manner transcend fears of failure that would otherwise impede them; they act with a Courageous Leadership Imperative.

When courageous leadership permeates the school community, the "how to" questions of school improvement become easier to determine and implement. Where there's a will, there is indeed a way. When the will is lacking, questions about specific techniques and tools can become an obstacle to action or any real change. Developing the Courageous Leadership Imperative goes a long way toward ensuring sustained student achievement. The next chapter looks in detail at 10 other common obstacles to school change and how to overcome each.

CHAPTER THREE

Ten Common Routes to Failure, and How to Avoid Each

Educational change is technically simple and socially complex.

—Michael Fullan (2001a, p. 69)

Slow is smooth and smooth is fast.

—Jeff Pascal, Bicentennial East
Coast Weapons Champion,
U.S. Martial Arts Association Kung Fu
Instructor of the Year 2000

After years of behavior modification strategies with even the brightest children, any diaper-changing parent will agree: Change is messy business. Chang*ing* is even messier!

Although people may like eventual *change,* they often don't like chang*ing* because the *process* can be uncomfortable. The new golf course in your backyard may be convenient and desirable, but the months of drilling, tree-splitting, and constant noise involved with the change process are not.

Teachers are often less than enthusiastic about embracing change that affects their daily routine. Although they may agree with the overall *concept* of enhanced student achievement, getting there can create feelings of insecurity and fear. This is especially true for practitioners who have taught in relative isolation for years and have not been asked to question their current practice. Questions emerge: "Why do *I* have to change?" "Haven't we done this before?" and "How exactly do you want me to find time for *this*?" If left unanswered, they can thwart any change initiative.

The following case story provides an example of how one school district is grappling with fundamental changes.

CASE STORY #1: A STRUGGLING SCHOOL DISTRICT CHOOSES A NEW DIRECTION

Alton Community School District 11, Alton, Illinois
James Baiter, superintendent:

On July 1, 2000, I became superintendent of Alton Community School District #11. Having been employed in the district for 30 years, I felt I had a clear understanding of the challenges and opportunities ahead of us. In the spring of 2000, the board of education approved a plan for reconfiguring the district to reduce operational costs. The plan included the closing of four elementary schools, the consolidation of three middle schools into two buildings, and the reassignment of several employees to become effective in August 2000.

The district also needed to address the need to improve the academic achievement levels for all students. It became our goal for each of our schools to strive for continuous improvement.

James Scaife, principal, Lovejoy School:

"We've heard a lot of this before." "This is the same old thing presented differently."

The reactions were negative at first. This was what I expected to hear from veteran staff when we started a new comprehensive school reform model called *Professional Learning Communities of HOPE (PLCH)*. We had just begun to create some momentum in improvement of test scores the year before and were faced with an ultimatum from the state and the district to improve our low scores on state standardized tests (ISAT).

Failure to meet specific targets for these scores would result in our being placed on the Academic Watch List, with serious consequences for the school and district. We were forced to meet almost weekly to come up with effective strategies to improve our scores. Faculty had been required to attend these meetings and would not be happy about another initiative that would require additional time.

Debra Pitts, assistant principal, Alton High School:

"How can this model help our students . . . our school? . . . our community?" "How will our faculty react?" "How will we get the time?" I started thinking, "Is this our dream come true?"

My biggest challenge was getting my high school faculty to understand the PLCH model and to believe that it wouldn't be just another "here today, gone tomorrow" model. After 26 years in education, I had the same reservations myself.

Nancy Shin, executive director, HOPE Foundation

They were still recovering from a massive reorganization that had taken place the year before we arrived. Leadership and faculty were all rearranged. People were very upset. In addition, the staff were asked to undertake major school reform. I was asked: "How much time will it take? How will we get that time from the union? How will we convince others that *this* effort will work?" Within two years after we began our change effort, we lost the administrator who began this initiative and an additional six building principals, more than half of the entire group with whom we had begun the process.

Mary Pat Venardos, principal, Mark Twain School:

When the HOPE team showed up to do their initial on-site evaluation, I remember thinking, "Yes, this is what we have needed for a long time!" I was excited to be working toward common goals throughout the district. It is very exciting to be able to discuss similar topics concerning mission, vision, values, and goals with other administrators in the district and to have central office support along the way.

I had been involved in a previous school reform model that had not been successful in increasing academic achievement, and I had allowed a few individuals within the school to control decision making. Having gone through that experience, and knowing the attitudes of those in my building, I knew that getting the staff to buy into a model that included everyone in decision making would not be easy.

My biggest challenge was making the leaders of the previous reform model understand why we needed to look at something new.

Part #2: Responding to the Challenge

Mary Pat Venardos, principal, Mark Twain School:

I turned to the data and, before presenting them to the faculty, talked with a few key individuals about the PLCH model. We discussed how it would incorporate elements of the prior model, include all our stakeholders in collaborative teaming, and lead to increased student achievement. I wanted their support before I went to the whole faculty.

I then presented the data to the entire faculty for discussion. The data clearly showed that the previous model had not been effective in increasing student achievement. We discussed the new process and how we would be collaborating in grade-level teams involving all faculty, basing all decisions on data.

I called upon the resisters to join the leadership team. They declined. I asked for their advice on how to improve the process as we began to set up our teams and start looking at learning issues in the building. They continued to resist but as our leadership team and grade-level teams began to experience the process and understand how it would impact student achievement, building support began to grow.

James Scaife, principal, Lovejoy School:

Because I also had a large number of young staff and a large number of young teachers, I was concerned that bringing in a new model would create a division between "new" and "veteran" teachers. I recruited several veteran teachers to become a part of our leadership team. They were skeptical of "yet another program," so I set up a meeting with the HOPE representatives so they could ask all their questions face to face. When they were treated respectfully and believed that their input was truly going to be valued, they became advocates for the process. Surprisingly, other veterans whom I expected to actively block efforts to set up collaborative teams turned out not to be a problem. I believe that being given the opportunity to participate in the decision-making process satisfied their need to be "heard," and although they did not become cheerleaders for the initiative, they also did not oppose it.

Given the natural difficulty of change, there is a tendency to move toward topics that can be addressed quickly and easily. This often results in superficial changes rather than changes in the fundamentals of our actions.

We have seen the problem of superficial approaches to change. Excellent approaches to school improvement are enthusiastically adopted, soon pronounced a failure, and jettisoned in favor of the next hot program. One educational veteran wisely noted that by being in the field long enough, he gets hit twice by the same pendulum of educational reform—once coming, and again as it swings back the other way. In response to calls for change, some teachers knowingly recite: "This too shall pass."

PART #3: THE OUTCOMES . . . TWO YEARS LATER

James Scaife, principal, Lovejoy School:

As we began our leadership team meetings and our grade-level team meetings, teachers were forced to collaborate and plan together. After a few meetings, collaboration started to become accepted as commonplace and negative tension began to subside. The teachers started seeing some positive effects of this approach and they began to share with each other.

When the results of the ISAT came back at the beginning of the following year, our work and collaboration had paid off. We went from 38% of our students meeting expectations on the test to nearly 50%. We easily surpassed the percentage needed to keep us off the Watch List. We still had a lot of work to be done, but collaboration had put us on the right track.

Mary Pat Venardos, principal, Mark Twain School:

As the building leader, I was challenged to "walk the walk" and "talk the talk." Terms like data-driven, collaboration, research-based, mission, vision, values, and goals became second nature to me. I learned to guide the leadership team in decision making by using data-driven processes. The leadership team and I began to support one another. I feel more like an instructional leader in the building than I had prior, and I like that shift.

If you visit Mark Twain today, you will observe:

1. Leadership team members taking turns leading committee and school-wide meetings.

2. Grade-level teams all using the same format for meetings and minutes are distributed to the whole staff.

3. Meetings organized with timekeeper, recorder, and agenda.

4. Use of a "parking lot" helps keep meetings on agenda items.

5. Each staff member has a folder with sections for minutes from school-wide and grade-level meetings, as well as meetings of the MVVG (mission, vision, values, and goals) committee.

6. All decisions are data-based.

7. Our school improvement plan is aligned with the PLCH process model as well as the district's soon-to-be-finalized mission, vision, values, and goals.

8. We meet monthly with district principals to discuss PLCH issues/topics, challenges, and strategies to overcome them.

9. PLCH consultant meets regularly with principal and building staff.

10. Language arts curriculum is aligned to standards.

11. We have built a pyramid of interventions by the end of the school year to be used district-wide for all primary buildings. (*Note:* See Chapter 6 on how to build the pyramid.)

We know PLCH is working because we have seen that:

1. Language arts DRA scores significantly increase.

2. Discipline referrals are down.

3. Staff can be observed collaborating in grade-level and committee meetings.

4. Minutes of grade-level meetings reflect the PDSA (Shewhart cycle—plan, do, study, act) Plan.

5. We achieved our SMART goals (strategic and specific, measurable, attainable, results-oriented, and time-bound) for increasing student achievement at each grade level. (*Note:* See Chapter 5 on creating SMART goals.)

6. We can observe that teachers' respect for one another is reflected in the ways students, in turn, respect each other.

7. We are proud to have a warm, family atmosphere at school that promotes this climate with students, staff, and visitors.

We have now finished our second year of the model, and nearly everyone has "bought in" to the process.

Debra Pitts, assistant principal, Alton High School:

This is the first time in my 28 years in education that I have witnessed teachers collaborating and looking at data to determine where students are achieving and systematically looking at ways to move them forward. Since we began this process, I've noticed change from the top down, our superintendent, assistant superintendent, principals. We're all talking the same language: STUDENT ACHIEVEMENT!

Nancy Shin, executive director, HOPE Foundation:

We created a closely knit group of principals and leadership teams early on. This group, along with our support team, enabled us to endure the many leadership transitions and move forward toward increased student achievement. At the end of the biggest year of transition for us (year one), the Alton schools performed better than the state average on 10 of 13 indicators on state standardized achievement tests (ISAT).

James Baiter, superintendent:

Completing the second phase of our reconfiguration plan required the passage of a bond referendum by the voters. Our first attempt in April 2001 was unsuccessful. Shortly after the final results were in, the citizens' group announced they would begin planning for the next referendum in March 2002. This time, we were successful. The voters approved a $38.2 million bond issue.

Disaster struck again and the economy worsened, resulting in a loss of revenue in fiscal year 2003 in excess of $2 million. The board of education approved budget reductions of approximately $2.8 million for fiscal year 2004, resulting in the reduction of 81 certified and support positions.

We will be able to weather these difficulties because over the past two years the attitudes of our teachers, administrators, and support personnel at every location have changed. Leadership teams have emerged, and they are working in a spirit of collaboration to provide students with the best opportunity for academic success. The staff in each building have developed mission, vision, and value statements in support of continuous academic improvement.

Even in the wake of these devastating budget reductions, we have been able to remain focused on our goal for continuous improvement because of the strength the organization has gained by becoming a professional learning community.

THE LIFE AND DEATH OF AN EDUCATIONAL MOVEMENT

In the late 1980s, the HOPE Foundation began working with quality guru W. Edwards Deming, whose work formed the basis of all Japanese manufacturing processes after World War II. At that time it became clear that Deming's approach, often mistakenly titled Total Quality Management (TQM), was more effective in creating high-performing organizations than what was then being used in most U.S. corporations (Blankstein, 1992). Most important for us, Deming's work shed light on a potentially powerful new paradigm for education.

Not long afterward, we introduced Deming and, later, Peter Senge to the top educational leadership of the era through a series of Shaping America's Future forums, and PBS-ALSS programs. We proposed his concepts and those of total quality education (TQE) and learning communities for discussion in educational circles.

Lew Rhodes of the American Association of School Administrators asked to meet privately with Deming and a few months later began the Total Quality Network. At the same time, ASCD introduced *their* Total Quality Learning Network, with Jay Bonstingl leading the charge. Powerful business groups, including the Business Roundtable, added "total quality" approaches to their current site-based management initiatives. Prominent educational authors like William Glasser began writing about it (Glasser, 1992). One could hear a swelling chant from the ranks of educational leaders: "TQE! TQE! TQE!"

By the end of the 1990's, however, the "movement" was dead. Only a few remnants of some of the more technical aspects of Deming's work remain. The leaders of the HOPE Foundation went on to help catalyze the next educational leadership wave—professional learning communities (PLC)—through their publication of three works by DuFour and Eaker (DuFour, 1991; DuFour and Eaker, 1992, 1998). The cycle recommences.

Before looking at the possibilities and the perils that mark the current PLC movement, let us revisit the rise and fall cycle that marked the TQE/TQM leadership movement. The parallels between the two initiatives are striking, as are the misinterpretations in their implementation. A quick review of the pitfalls of adopting TQE/TQM begins our analysis and spells out the first six of the ten routes to failure, and how to avoid each. Understanding the recurring pitfalls of worthy educational change efforts will enable us to move beyond them. The following article, excerpted from *Executive Educator,* presaged the demise of TQE and TQM in education and begins us on our "road to success."

Is TQM Right for Schools?

A. M. Blankstein and H. Swain
(Excerpted with permission from *The Executive Educator*, 51, February 1994)

Everybody's talking about TQM, but do educators really understand the concept and the philosophy behind it? Most people who refer to Total Quality Management link it to the restructuring in U.S. businesses that grew out of the work of the late W. Edwards Deming in Japan. Deming is widely credited with the post–World War II economic recovery. Deming himself, however, decried TQM.

"My work is about transformation in management and the profound knowledge needed for that transformation," Deming said last year. "'Total quality' stops people from thinking."

Deming was speaking at Shaping America's Future II, one of a series of forums sponsored by our organization [now the HOPE Foundation], which convenes leaders from business, education, and government in the pursuit of education reform. "You can't manage quality—quality is an output," Deming told the participants. "You can only manage systems."

Can TQM work in education? This article looks at six reasons why it can't—and tells the story of one school that has overcome those obstacles by implementing Deming's quality principles.

1. *People do not like to change.* People are often wary of new ideas, and in schools, such resistance can present itself on many fronts. Teachers are tired of being asked to rethink their teaching styles. Parents want their children's school days to be just like their own and are often reluctant to endorse new and different approaches to education. Resistance to Deming's principles can be exceptionally fierce because of the philosophy underlying the traditional education system.

However, it is possible to overcome this reluctance to change. At Kate Sullivan Elementary School, Principal Nancy Duden dealt with such resistance by encouraging teachers, staff members, and parents to explore Deming's quality principles with her at their own pace. Duden did not force acceptance of these new ideas; rather, she provided workshops, reading materials, support groups, and community volunteers to help teachers and parents become familiar with Deming's work.

Duden also supported a great deal of dialogue with the teachers and parents, primarily through the PTA, which uncovered and helped to dispel anxieties about adopting quality principles. By taking her time and letting individuals voice their concerns, Duden quelled much of the fear that usually accompanies change.

2. *Leaders are supposed to take charge.* Through our experiences as students and employees, most of us have learned that leaders should make decisions and control outcomes. In education, principals might fear that relinquishing control over every aspect of the school could hinder its effective functioning. Other members of the staff often become comfortable in established roles as well and find it difficult to transcend years of experience as a "leader" or "follower."

The pursuit of quality requires that all individuals within an organization—administrators, teachers, staff members, parents, and students—work cooperatively for the benefit of everyone. In the long run, monopolizing power inhibits individuals in these groups from viewing themselves as contributing to the overall success of the larger system.

At Kate Sullivan, Nancy Duden reevaluated her own leadership style after she had begun studying Deming's work. Duden realized that her authoritarian role would not produce long-term commitment from her staff. Instead she decided to "diversify the leadership portfolio" by giving teachers and parents the opportunity to lead as well.

She now plays a support role and helps promote change by, for example, acting as a participant, rather than leader, in meetings; encouraging teachers and parents to explore new ideas, instead of moving them toward a predetermined agenda; and endorsing the changes teachers determine are beneficial for students.

By playing a supportive role with her staff, Duden has created a nurturing environment in which teachers are unafraid to take risks in leadership roles. Duden's commitment to changing her own leadership style allows individuals throughout the school community to reevaluate both their roles and the concept of leadership itself.

3. *People are lazy.* For many years, some educators have observed, the operation of American schools was modeled on the same assembly-line method that first permitted mass production of automobiles. In this fear-driven system, which requires employees to meet quotas and product specifications, workers compete with one another for promotions and bonuses that are parceled out to a few "winners." The internal strife and long-term *de*motivation this system causes is well documented. Yet educators persist in using grades, class ranks, and even merit pay to the same end.

This extrinsic approach to motivation implies that if individuals are not rewarded, punished, or pitted against one another in competition, they will fail to "perform." In fact, in our current system performance is the best possibility. Unfortunately, children learn to simply get the "right answer" instead of learning to make mistakes and learn from them.

Deming, in contrast, bases his philosophy on the opposite premise: that individuals have an *intrinsic* drive to learn and do well and that they do not want to fail. He maintains that if allowed to pursue this natural drive, people will strive to reach their potential without any need for external motivators such as competition or fear. The role of the education system, given such an assumption, is one of guidance and evaluation in an environment of continual learning.

At Kate Sullivan, Nancy Duden provided constructive alternatives to extrinsic rewards such as grades. Portfolios of students' work and parent/teacher conferences to help parents gauge their children's progress replaced report cards with self-evaluation. These and other processes have allowed teachers, parents, and students to work together for constant improvement, one of Deming's principles. Attaining the grade is no longer the goal. Now the goal is continually learning and growing.

Duden also replaced motivation by fear with motivation toward a common vision. Administrators, staff members, parents, and community volunteers developed this vision over three years. The school supports such a vision with a set of core values developed by a task force: Individuals are valued, teachers are professional educators, parents are partners, decision making is shared, and teachers are team members.

4. *We can't let go of grades.* Educators are often pressured by legislators and others outside the school system to use quantitative goals, such as standardized test scores, to measure children's progress. Parents can be even more insistent on the need for grades because, unlike legislators, they have the added fear that their children's future in higher education or the job market will depend on grades. But as many educators now realize, grades and test scores do not reflect what children are really learning, for several reasons.

- Grades are often based on factors other than academic work, such as attendance and behavior.
- Furthermore, teachers who are pressured to show increased test scores will teach to the test rather than being concerned with mastery of a subject. Therefore, external motivators fundamentally rob children of the natural desire to learn and do well.

Giving up external motivators is crucial to the successful application of Deming's principles in education; to that end, the Kate Sullivan staff has been struggling to let go of grades throughout its restructuring efforts. Three years ago, the teachers in kindergarten through second grade decided to stop using grades altogether. The results have been encouraging: Even without grades, standardized test scores remained high. What's more, parents now receive a more accurate picture of their children's progress.

However, the transition to a nongrading system has been difficult. Problems arise when children receive grades for the first time. One parent relates the devastating affect her daughter's first grade had on her learning style. Until third grade, the girl had been motivated and interested in learning, but since her first traditional report card, her mother says, she seems to be directed toward getting a good grade. This child's intrinsic motivation to learn and do well has been replaced by an external motivator: grades.

5. *State mandates get in the way.* Even if a school could successfully overcome all of the internal barriers to adopting Deming's principles, external barriers would still exist. State-legislated mandates, which often clash with new methods of teaching and managing, provide the final stumbling block to truly transforming a school.

According to Duden, an important part of focusing on quality is having the courage—and the data—to question state mandates. Duden objected to mandated teacher observation, for example, because it relies on inspection and top-down management. Instead, she obtained permission from her school district to provide data on teacher performance based on the school's principles of learning.

Finally, Duden spent years cultivating community support for Deming's quality principles, and she continues to involve the community as the school changes. For example, during each of the past three years, parents and community members have contributed more than 11,000 hours of volunteer work at Kate Sullivan. Duden has educated community members about Deming's concepts so they, too, understand the importance of making the changes necessary to ensure high-quality education.

6. *Using TQM will fail where high quality will succeed.* Even if a school surmounts these obstacles, using TQM will not significantly alter learning for students or improve the efficacy of the staff. Peter Senge, director of the Center for Organizational Learning at MIT's Sloan School of Management, puts it this way: "If we fail to grasp the deeper messages of the quality movement, we will one day awaken to discover ourselves chasing a receding target."

TQM is *not* synonymous with Deming's principles. Using the TQM tools and calling the outcome "quality" is like analyzing the contrapuntal motion of a Bach chorale and calling the resulting discoveries "music." In both cases, you're confusing tools with the reason for using them. Deploying mechanical techniques created to help implement Deming's philosophy should not become a substitute for understanding that philosophy. The outcome would simply be more of the same, with an "exciting" new label on it: TQM.

These challenges, and the responses to each, by one progressive leader point out the need to carefully build support and deep understanding for the change effort among all constituents. Dr. Duden took the necessary time to help her staff make a smooth transition. She even modeled the role of a learner alongside her staff. Perhaps most important, she built her base of support well beyond the school itself and created the capacity for additional leadership on all levels.

OTHER COMMON BARRIERS TO SCHOOL CHANGE

Four additional obstacles to success frequently threaten change efforts:

1. *Many schools don't know what they want, what they need, or the difference between the two.* This list of "ten roads to failure" will not apply equally to all schools—nor does *any* single approach to school improvement. For example, whereas some schools are "cruising" based on past successes and not yet willing to recognize and reveal their own areas for improvement, others have hit bottom and are desperate for *anything* that offers new hope.

Without a clear picture of the *needs* of the school community, it is easy to be like a kid in the candy store when pursuing the appropriate means of enhancing and sustaining student achievement. Whatever speaker or program is the most enjoyable, interesting, or popular in the neighboring school district wins!

A School District Determines Its Needs *Before* Shopping

After the Columbine, Colorado, school crisis, many schools around the nation purchased expensive and "fool-proof" metal detectors. One formerly dangerous district, in Poughkeepsie, New York, however, had already researched their violence issues. They knew, for example, that a major problem was fighting among boys, during classroom changes, in front of the boy's restroom on the second floor. Posting a guard there during those crucial times solved most of their problems. Developing an anti-bullying school culture took care of most of the rest.

The quick self-assessment provided in Appendix A will allow school teams to do a needs assessment and get a clearer picture of where they stand. Completing this assessment will help to focus all school efforts, guide the school improvement process, and maximize the benefits of this book.

2. *We have no time for this!* This statement is, on its face, completely legitimate. There is simply no way of getting around it— the process of creating mission, vision, values, and goals statements; completing needs assessments; collecting data; and planning for change will require an investment of time. Schools also need to make time in the daily schedule for teacher collaboration and continued professional development.

At the same time, this statement can also be a smokescreen for staff who resist change. This ruse can be uncovered by asking: "Is time the only issue? If I were to assure you that you will have sufficient time to do this, would you become actively involved in the process?" The change process must be seen as *worth* the time spent.

No nation requires teachers to teach more hours per day and year than the United States. In most European and Asian countries, teachers spend only 17 to 20 hours of the 40- to 45-hour workweek actually teaching. The remaining time is spent in

class preparation and joint planning; collegial work on curriculum and assessment development; one-on-one meetings with students, parents, and other colleagues; and learning through involvement in study groups, observation of other teachers, research, and demonstration lessons. (Darling-Hammond, 1999)

Rethinking the school culture and the importance of continual, embedded professional development is key for long-term success. Beyond this comes the practical issue of "finding" time. Here are some examples of how schools have addressed this issue:

- Provide common planning time. Schedule several classes for the same activity at the same time to free classroom teachers to work together (e.g., all third-grade art classes or seventh-grade P.E. classes meet simultaneously).
- Involve students in community service. At Central Park East Secondary School, eighth-, ninth-, and tenth-grade students spend one half-day of each week away from school, working

in various community-service programs. Teachers use the time for collaboration (Pardini, 1999).

- Create banks of time. Add a few minutes of teaching time to each class in a particular period daily for four days. On the fifth day, the class is cancelled or shortened by the number of extra minutes accumulated. Students are provided with an alternative activity, and teachers use that time to meet in teams.

There are many ways to deal with the issue of time. An additional 12 ideas can be found in Appendix B. We suggest that the ideas on this list be used as "starters" to stimulate brainstorming within your own school. Each teaching staff must develop approaches that *they* believe will work and that they are invested in implementing.

Making Time for Teaming

The Newport News elementary schools, in Newport News, Virginia, solved the problem of collaboration years ago—and though it wasn't an easy change at first, it has paid off. The school system extended its school day by 15 minutes on Monday, Tuesday, Thursday, and Friday, gaining an extra hour of instructional time. On Wednesdays, the students are released early—and the entire staff has collaborative planning time. The time is dedicated exclusively to collaboration and cannot be used for anything else.

Convincing the community to accept the new schedule was difficult; parents and other caregivers were unprepared for the Wednesday early dismissal. The school system had to work hard to build support for it, meeting with community agencies, parks and recreation representatives, and other leaders. Ultimately, however, the community not only accepted the new schedule, but actively embraced it, developing new programs and opportunities for kids to take advantage of on Wednesdays.

3. *Resistance.* Understanding and empathizing with people's legitimate concerns and fears goes a long way in helping to overcome them. At the same time, we often find too much attention paid

to a few holdouts to an overwhelming consensus for a particular school-wide reform effort. Gaining consensus on the definition of consensus is a critical first step. Here is one that may work for your school: (1) All points of view have been heard, and (2) the will of the group is evident, even to those who most oppose it (Eaker, DuFour, and Burnette, 2002). Once the school community has had ample time to reach consensus on an improvement initiative, it is better to spend time reinforcing those leading the change than on those trying to hold it back. "Water the flowers, not the rocks in your garden!" (See Appendix C for more strategies for dealing with resistance.)

4. *Waiting for the Dream Person or Program.* The many nuances of creating meaningful change defy formulaic approaches. What works in a wealthy Chicago suburb may not work in your urban or Appalachian school. Even if the processes are applicable, the implementation is sure to vary. School staff members would likely lack commitment to any "imported" initiative. And becoming too attached to a given charismatic speaker, buzzword, or program is inherently contrary to the successful use of any new initiative.

We have seen leaders *wait* to begin their new initiative until the sage of that particular program arrives to give a keynote speech or daylong workshop. Similarly, some school leaders, having had many of their past efforts thwarted by a new district leader, opt to wait two years before making changes so that their current superintendent can retire and the new one can set the new direction!

These kinds of "obstacles" to change were addressed courageously by Nancy Duden in the earlier article "Is TQM Right for Schools?" Being clear about who she was and why she was there made this possible. She carefully laid the foundation to sustain the changes and have them endure beyond her retirement. How to develop the kind of clarity, focus, and fortitude necessary to sustain student success was the thrust of Chapter 2.

The next chapter provides the research base for the rest of this book. It gives a synopsis of the professional learning communities movement, along with a vital definition for a true learning community: one that is likely to be sustained through many challenges, including change of leadership.

CHAPTER FOUR

Building a Professional Learning Community With Relational Trust

> School districts should not try to simply build a learning community that has as many definitions as there are people defining it. The emphasis should be on restructuring how people work together. That's what ultimately has an effect on the classroom.
>
> —Nelda Cambron-McCabe *(The School Administrator,* May 2003, p. 8)

DEFINING A TRUE "LEARNING COMMUNITY"

For more than a decade, a growing confluence of research and practice has indicated that our best hope for success in schools is through the creation of professional learning communities (Bryk et al., 1994; Darling-Hammond, 1996; Fullan, 1993; Louis, Kruse, & Marks, 1996; McLaughlin, 1993; Newmann and Wehlage, 1995). This is very good news indeed. It seems to provide clear direction for educators who are contemplating substantive school change. At the same time, it invites as many questions as it answers:

1. What is a learning community in practice?

2. What are the key elements for making such a community succeed?

3. How do I know if I have succeeded in creating such a community?

4. What are my next steps in the process of creating and sustaining a learning community?

There are many definitions of a "professional learning community." We include summary of these, as well as a brief background on the rise of interest in this area, in the next section.

How do you know if you are working in a professional learning community? Consider (with a smile) these possible indicators:

You know you are in a learning community when . . .

- You enter the school building and are warmly greeted by a parent volunteer.
- You see articles with highlights all over them posted in the teacher lounge.
- You are actually *happy* to see another teacher or an administrator visiting your classroom to observe instruction.
- Colleagues stop by your home on the weekend . . . to talk about work!
- Enhancing student learning is the primary focus of team meetings, and best practices for enhancing their achievement drive decisions.
- SMART goals (see Chapter 5) are set, regularly assessed, and achieved.
- Last year's worst-behaved fourth-grader is tutoring a second-grader this year.
- During professional development days, the *last* row of seats are the ones that are empty.
- The principal says "I don't know. Let's research this together."
- When the final bell rings, the teachers and principal aren't the first ones out the door!

More important than the use of one definition or another, however, is the common understanding of what such a community looks and feels like, how one behaves in this context, what the mutual commitments are, and how all of this affects students in general and academic achievement in particular. It is more common to find school professionals who say they are part of a "learning community" than it is to actually find a professional learning community in operation. In fact, a shadow version of true learning communities, "performance training sects" (Hargreaves, 2003, p. 176), provides intensive pressure and support for teachers in a limited number of instructional priority areas. While student performance is enhanced, it is rarely sustained and comes at the expense of other instructional areas (Hargreaves, 2003). Moreover, the research indicates that teachers dislike such highly prescriptive programs (Datnow and Castellano, 2000), which often diminish their long-term commitment to their work (Galton, 2000). There are many possible reasons for the disparity between the number of schools that *see* themselves as "professional learning communities" and those that actually are.

As we saw in the previous chapter, making fundamental changes and shifts in assumptions, beliefs, and actions is difficult. It is far easier to make slight modifications to old behaviors and then give the effort a new name. Moreover, this can be reinforcing, because some of these modifications actually *do* bring about modest changes. For example, it would be easier to create times when teams meet than to build a true collaborative culture in the school (see Chapter 7). One is structural, easily implemented, and *may* still have the benefits of creating a more motivated staff. The collaborative *culture,* however, would require more time, an effective school mission (defined in Chapter 5), and deeper conversations about the meaning and focus of the collaboration. This collaborative culture would also require discipline to maintain a focus on student learning.

Clarifying terminology *alone* requires time and effort. W. Edwards Deming wisely called for developing "operational definitions" (1986) before undertaking a new project. He would say, for example, "Is this table clean? How could one answer the question without knowing for what purpose or use the table would need to be clean?" (i.e., defining "clean" in operational terms). "If this is to be used to eat on, it may well be clean. Yet this would not be clean enough to place a patient upon for an operation" (Deming, in conversation with Blankstein, 1989).

Many schools striving to become professional learning communities, for example, are challenged to come to a common understanding of the word "community." This is particularly true of both moderately high-performing "cruising schools" and low-performing "sinking schools" (to determine your school's profile, see Appendix A, from Chapter 2). In these schools it is more likely to find changes occurring in *professional* structure (e.g., time for collaborative teaming) and even in a *learning* focus (focus on adult pedagogy and student learning). Richard Elmore (2002) describes the challenge:

> The schools that I have observed usually share a strong motivation to learn new teaching practices and a sense of urgency about improving learning for students and teachers. What they lack is a sense of individual and collective agency, or control, over the organizational conditions that affect the learning of students and adults in their schools. (p. 24)

This sense of *collective* urgency and control over *organizational* conditions is embodied in the *community* of professional learning communities. Many schools—especially high schools—lack these features. These schools do not often, however, benefit from the deeper meaning implied in the term "community."

Creating common understandings, therefore, is hard work. Getting commitment from the school community is even more difficult. And changing fundamental assumptions or beliefs is harder still. Yet these are the challenges inherent in building a true learning community, and the payoff for doing so is enormous. The chapters on building a Courageous Leadership Imperative and overcoming common pitfalls provide a foundation for beginning an enduring, sustainable learning community. The next sections of this chapter will help to clarify what such a community would look like, the key elements for success, and how to begin to develop it.

ORIGINS AND DEFINITIONS OF THE "LEARNING COMMUNITY"

Peter Senge first used the term "learning organization" in his 1990 best-seller, *The Fifth Discipline*. Though Senge was writing for the business community, soon thereafter the term made its way into the education literature. Thomas Sergiovanni translated one of Senge's five principles—"team learning"—to an educational context: "the idea of school as a learning community suggests a kind of connectedness among members that resembles what is found in a family, a neighborhood, or some other closely knit group" (Sergiovanni, 1992). This dimension, and that of "building shared vision," are two of Senge's original dimensions that have been embraced by the education community.

The concept of a "school-based learning community" was understood to include (Kruse, Louis, and Bryk, 1994):

1. Reflective dialogue among teachers

2. Deprivatization of practice

3. Collective focus on student learning

4. Collaboration

5. Shared norms and values

In their landmark study of school reform and restructuring, Newmann and Wehlage (1995) determined that there were four "circles of support" that determined successful outcomes for schools and students: student learning (focus); authentic pedagogy; school organizational capacity (including the creation of "professional communities" to support the first two items); and external support. The report stated that "The most successful schools were those that used restructuring tools to help them function as professional communities" (p. 3).

These communities were defined as having three general features:

1. Teachers pursue a clear, shared purpose for all students' learning.

2. Teachers engage in collaborative activity to achieve their stated purpose.

3. Teachers take collective responsibility for student learning.

In 1997, Shirley Hord coined the term "professional learning community" (Hord, 1997a and b). Her research through the Southwest Educational Development Laboratory (SEDL) led her to describe these communities as having five characteristics:

1. Supportive and shared leadership

2. Shared values and vision

3. Collective learning and application

4. Shared personal practice

5. Supportive conditions (including human and physical or structural capacity)

Another derivative of these earlier works, by DuFour and Eaker, also termed "professional learning community," borrows as well from business models to include shared mission, vision, values, goals; collective inquiry; collaborative teams; action orientation and experimentation; continuous improvement; and results orientation.

In a related area, the standards for leaders developed by the Interstate School Leaders Licensure Consortium (ISLLC) have become another guiding polestar for enhancing school effectiveness. Developed with the Council of Chief State School Officers, the standards are used throughout North America to influence leadership, development, licensure, and academic leadership. Its principles state, "A school administrator is an educational leader who promotes the success of all students by":

- Principle 1: Facilitating the development, articulation, implementation, and stewardship of a vision of learning that is shared and supported by the school community.
- Principle 2: Advocating, nurturing, and sustaining a school culture and instructional program conducive to student learning and staff professional growth.
- Principle 3: Ensuring management of the organization, operations, and resources for a safe, efficient, and effective learning environment.
- Principle 4: Collaborating with families and community members, responding to diverse community interests and needs, and mobilizing community resources.
- Principle 5: Acting with integrity, fairness, and in an ethical manner.
- Principle 6: Understanding, responding to, and influencing the larger political, social, economic, legal, and cultural context. (Murphy, Jost, and Shipman, 2000)

Figure 4.1 summarizes this history.

Date	Author	Terminology	Guiding Principles
1990	Peter M. Senge	Five Disciplines	1. Systems Thinking 2. Personal Mastery 3. Mental Models 4. Team Learning 5. Shared Vision
1994	Sharon D. Kruse & Karen Seashore Louis	School-based Learning Community	1. Reflective dialogue among teachers 2. De-privatization of practice 3. Collective focus on student learning 4. Collaboration 5. Shared norms and values
1995	Fred M. Newmann & Gary G. Wehlage	Circles of Support	1. Student Learning 2. Authentic Pedagogy 3. School Organizational Capacity 4. External Support
1997	Shirley Hord	Professional Learning Community	1. Supportive and shared leadership 2. Shared values and vision 3. Collective learning and application 4. Shared personal practice 5. Supportive conditions
1998	Richard DuFour & Robert Eaker	Professional Learning Community	1. Shared mission, vision, values, and goals 2. Collective inquiry 3. Collaborative teams 4. Action orientation and experimentation 5. Continuous improvement 6. Results-oriented
2000	Interstate School Leaders Licensure Consortium (ISLLC) Murphy, Jost, Shipman	Standards for Educational Administration	Promotes the success of all students by: 1. Facilitating the development, articulation, implementation, and stewardship of a vision of learning that is shared and supported by the school community. 2. Advocating, nurturing, and sustaining a school culture and instructional program conducive to student learning and staff professional growth. 3. Ensuring management of the organization, operations, and resources for a safe, efficient, and effective learning environment. 4. Collaborating with families and community members, responding to diverse community interests and needs, and mobilizing community resources. 5. Acting with integrity, fairness, and in an ethical manner. 6. Understanding, responding to, and influencing the larger political, social, economic, legal, and cultural context.

Figure 4.1   Development of the "Learning Community" Concept

Source: HOPE Foundation® *Failure Is Not an Option* Success Series

Synthesizing the research from the above sources, and factoring in research on effective schools, the U.S. Department of Education's criteria for excellent schools, and our own practice in the field, we have distilled the essence of professional learning communities into the following six principles:

- Principle 1—Common mission, vision, values, and goals
- Principle 2—Ensuring achievement for *all* students: creating systems for prevention and intervention
- Principle 3—Collaborative teaming focused on teaching and learning
- Principle 4—Using data to guide decision making and continuous improvement
- Principle 5—Gaining active engagement from family and community
- Principle 6—Building sustainable leadership capacity

These principles encompass the focus on student learning and collaboration emphasized in the above research. In addition, as with Shirley Hord's definition, the ISLLC standards, and the larger body of research of Newmann and Wehlage summarized earlier in this section, our sixth principle explicitly calls for the development of sustainable leadership capacity. Given the extraordinary rate of turnover in educational leadership, and the tendency toward "launching" versus "sustaining" learning communities, we have found this principle to be critical to the success of our work with schools throughout North America.

Similarly, as cited in Newmann and Wehlage's "circles of support" (1995) research and the ISLLC standards (2000), we have found that actively engaging family and communities (our fifth principle) is essential for long-term support and sustainability of school initiatives. This has been particularly true in times of great change, economic downturn, or intense media pressure on schools. Chapter 9 provides an abundance of research correlating enhanced student achievement and family support.

The prior synthesis of research and our own relevant experiences are presented as an explanation of how we arrived at these working principles for professional learning communities. Having "one best definition" for this or any other school improvement effort is counterproductive and defies all that we know about change efforts. In fact, there is danger in becoming too attached to one certain speaker, program, or set of principles. It is far more important that whatever is practiced is internally aligned, consistent with the research, and focused on student success.

Taking a cue from the medical profession, it is advisable to continually scan for new best practices and to stay current with changes in the research:

> Here on our first day of med. school, we were presented with the short white coats that proclaim us part of the mystery and the discipline of medicine. During that ceremony, the dean said something that was repeated throughout my education: "Half of what we teach you here is wrong—unfortunately, we don't know which half." (Sanders, 2003, p. 29)

In the past, the technical aspects of a given model (like TQM) or process for shaping cultures (like PLC) have gained widespread acceptance. The relationships and human side of change, however, are often left to chance (Barth, 2001; Kruse, Louis, and Bryk, 1994). The following section is focused on recent data that correlate "relational trust" with student success. In essence, every effective, sustainable, professional learning community that we have worked with in the past 15 years was founded on a consensus of what it meant to be such a community, and on relational trust. The next section addresses the meaning, importance, and development of "community" and "relational trust."

Cohesive Communities

Webster offers several definitions of the word "community." Here are two:

1. Common character, similarity, likeness, as, *community* of spirit.

2. The people living in the same district, city, etc., under the same laws.

The second definition is more commonly used. It is easier for a group of school professionals to achieve this definition since they generally work together, under the same rules, in the same location.

The first definition, however, is closer to how we would describe the ideal school community—one that leads to sustainable student achievement. "Community is concerned with the deep-structural fabric of interpersonal relations" (Gardner, 1991). "Soundly woven, this fabric permits a shared frame of reference and supports mutual expectations" (Rossi and Stringfield, 1997, p. 3).

Relationships and trust are the glue that holds this kind of community together. A professional community is built on more than a pay-for-service contract, in which adults and children run for the exits when the final school bell rings. It is built on more than common geography. It goes beyond symbiosis, common rules, or policies that bind all to *minimum* behaviors. This kind of community is founded on mutual respect, concern, caring, reliability, and commitment to a common, larger cause. In short, it is founded on relational trust.

Relational Trust

> The relationship among the adults in the schoolhouse has more impact on the quality and the character of the schoolhouse—and on the accomplishments of youngsters—than any other factor.
>
> —Roland Barth (2001, p. 105)

The report by the American Institutes for Research and the U.S. Office of Educational Research and Information (OERI), based on in-depth research on student success at 12 model and six replicate schools nation-wide, states:

> We noted several attributes of *interpersonal relations* in schools that were associated with effective programs or periods of program effectiveness. Students felt cared about and respected, teachers shared a vision and sense of purpose, teachers and students maintained free and *open communication,* and all parties shared a *deep sense of trust.* (Rossi and Stringfield, 1997, p. 3)

Relationships are at the core of successful learning communities as well as student success (Bryk and Schneider, 2002; Haynes, Emmons, and Woodruff, 1998; Kruse, Louis, and Bryk, 1994; Meier, 1995). In its *Set for Success* report of 2002, the Ewing Marion

Kauffman Foundation summarizes: "Stated simply, positive relationships are essential to a child's ability to grow up healthy and achieve later social, emotional, and academic success" (p. 2).

Those "positive relationships" begin with the adults in the school building and district. The personal rapport among teachers, students, and parents influences students' school attendance and their sustained efforts at difficult school tasks (Bryk and Driscoll, 1998; Bryk, Lee, and Holland, 1993; Bryk and Thum, 1989). The history of relations between the principal and the teaching staff determines teachers' willingness to undertake new reforms (Fullan, 1991). And the relationships among adults in the school greatly influence the extent to which students in that school will succeed academically (Barth, 2001; Bryk and Schneider, 2002).

The relationship among adults is an area for potential improvement in a great many schools. While it is relatively easy to install the technical aspects of a professional learning community—systems to collect data, time for teams to meet, etc.—the tough part is subtler, less scripted, and more human.

> Human resources—such as openness to improvement, trust and respect, teachers having knowledge and skills, supportive leadership, and socialization—are more critical to the development of professional community than structural conditions. . . . [T]he need to improve the culture, climate, and interpersonal relationships in schools has received too little attention. (Kruse, Louis, and Bryk, 1994, p. 8)

Building meaningful and productive relationships with people is much more complex than creating a new system or structure. People are less predictable, and their emotions can be scary! How many school leaders have been trained in the many nuances of dealing with an angry parent, a disgruntled staff member, or a crying teacher? Where is the how-to manual for these tasks? Moreover, who has time for these things when the "real" work of increasing student achievement awaits?

As stated earlier (and throughout this book), relationships *are* the real work of school improvement! Without people, whom exactly will administrators be leading, and how far will followers be willing to go?

Any project has three components (Figure 4.2): Content (what), Process (how), and People (who).

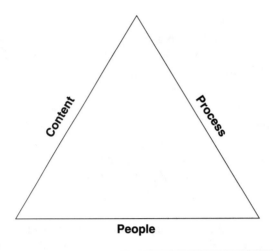

Figure 4.2

For schools, the "content" (what) would be the math curriculum, for example; the "process" (how), the teaching strategies and pedagogy. The "people" (who) would be all those involved with the process and content. Traditionally, schools have done fairly well in dealing with process, moderately well on content, and less well on people and relationships (Figure 4.3).

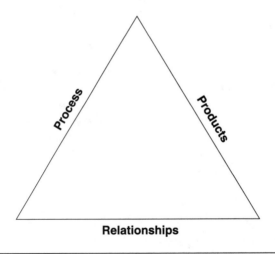

Figure 4.3

This understanding leaves even more questions to be answered. What *kind* of relationships lead to school and student success? How are they formed? How is our school currently faring in this arena? The rest of this section addresses these and other questions about relational trust.

The concept of "relational trust" came from a ten-year study of achievement in math and literacy in 12 Chicago public schools by the Center for School Improvement at the University of Chicago. These systematic case studies were augmented by researchers' clinical observations and field notes (Bryk and Schneider, 2002). The summary of research results is as follows:

> Schools reporting strong positive trust levels in 1994 were three times more likely to be categorized eventually as improving in reading and mathematics than those with very weak trust reports. . . . Schools with weak trust reports in 1994 and 1997 had virtually no chance of showing improvement in either reading or mathematics. (Bryk and Schneider, 2002, p. 111)

There are several preestablished bases of trust, including contractual trust, which focuses on material exchange. The concept of *relational* trust in schools, however, focuses on distinct role relationships and the obligations and expectations associated with each. When these expectations are met, trust is enhanced. When a person's expectations of another person are not met, trust is diminished.

For example, using our earlier proposed Principal #6 for a professional learning community, a principal may expect that the superintendent will prepare for leadership transitions so that any new district and building leader will be ready to move current initiatives forward. If the superintendent does not make such plans, the principal's trust in the superintendent may decrease. Even if the superintendent does make transition plans, the trust could be diminished if the principal views this as a means of getting positive strokes from the school board, as opposed to a true concern for student success (Figure 4.4).

As another example, let's say a superintendent announces his or her intention to undertake a new initiative to meet state standards. A teacher may hear this and think that the initiative is a good idea, but that the superintendent did it mainly for the public relations value, not to help students. The teacher may decide, therefore, not to support this initiative.

Figure 4.4

There are four components of relational trust (Bryk and Schneider, 2002, pp. 23–26):

1. *Respect* for the importance of person's role, as well as their viewpoint. Listening carefully augments a sense of respect and builds trust.

2. *Competence* to administer your role. This includes one's ability to act on what was heard (above). On the building level, it is also associated with having respectful discipline, an orderly and safe school, and meaningful instruction and assessment.

3. *Personal regard for others* is highly associated with reducing others' sense of vulnerability and with general caring. This is especially demonstrated by extending oneself beyond the requirement of one's role or normal duties—finding out about a staff member's personal challenges, helping teachers develop their careers, etc.

4. *Integrity* in this context means alignment of words, actions, and ethics. Does this person keep his or her word, and are the intentions ethical?

In general, the effective leader will create relational trust through showing a genuine regard for the professional role, interest in the concerns of others (respect), awareness of their personal interests (personal regard), and a willingness to act on those concerns (competence) toward an ethical outcome (integrity). If action on someone's concerns is not feasible, the leader will be truthful as to why such action will not be forthcoming (integrity).

When we combine this information with the chart above, we can see that the challenge often comes in *listening* to others (respect) and their beliefs about your behavior (competence, personal regard, and integrity). For this reason, it is best to check in with people.

On an organizational level, however, it is advisable to begin with a clear understanding of where the school is currently (Bryk and Schneider, 2002). See Appendix J for a brief survey used to gauge relational trust in the research cited above. In addition, in Chapter 6, we provide a powerful conceptual tool for enhancing affinity and communication through shared experiences. This can be used to begin discussion at your school.

This chapter was meant to serve as a final checkpoint. We have defined purpose as *sustaining student success where failure is not an option* (Chapter 1); anticipated and sidestepped common obstacles to success (Chapter 2); developed a Courageous Leadership Imperative (Chapter 3); and, in this chapter, determined the approach to take. Now you are prepared to begin and to take action. The rest of this book will emphasize specific processes for building such a professional learning community, beginning with the next chapter on creating common mission, vision, values, and goals.

CHAPTER FIVE

Principle #1—Common Mission, Vision, Values, and Goals

> The most important question in any organization has to be "What is the business of our business?" Answering this question is the first step in setting priorities.
>
> —Judith Bardwick (1996, p. 134)

> You cannot have a learning organization without shared vision.
>
> —Peter Senge (1990, p. 209)

The key to creating a school where failure is not an option is this: transforming the school culture. Some schools have productive cultures; others have problematic ones. But *every* school *has* a culture, whether one is aware of it or not. Does this sound familiar?

"Take a look at these test scores from my history class. They're just terrible. Quite a few F's . . . most of them got D's. We've been over and over this material, but they just don't seem to care. They don't do their homework, they don't participate in class, I have NO family support. I don't know what more to do!"

We have worked with many schools that have a culture of blame and hopelessness. One high school staff was asked to analyze a situation in which 25% of their students were not passing state tests. After much deliberation, the teaching staff reached a consensus: *It's that middle school! They were sending us students who were unprepared!*

A corollary to a culture of blame is a shift in responsibility for ensuring student learning. Consider the following often-heard statements:

- It's not *my* job to ensure that students *learned* the lesson—my job is to teach it!
- We believe all students can learn, but some learn better than others.
- In general, all students will learn, but *those* kids from *that* neighborhood aren't as smart or as motivated as the rest.
- If we had more _____ (discipline, resources, time, parental support, and so on), *then* I would be successful!

What these statements have in common is that they shift accountability *away* from school professionals. What could be more demotivating for a school community than to believe that they have no power and that what they do makes no difference?

In this chapter, we provide direction for transforming the school culture by addressing some often-held beliefs. We do this through a discussion of the four pillars of any organization: mission, vision, values, and goals. Together they establish the common base upon which all of our efforts will build (DuFour and Eaker, 1998).

The Mission

The mission of an organization is essential to its success. A mission statement should be created and published as a means of giving those involved with the organization a clear understanding of its purpose for existence.

Mission statements are found everywhere—in schools, big businesses, small businesses, nonprofit organizations, organized religion, and all levels of government. They are a popular management "tool" used by corporations to motivate stakeholders and keep everyone "on the same page." A quick survey of mission statements reveals a common pattern: They use superlatives and absolutes. Such an approach leaves people feeling as though they had cotton candy for lunch: happy but still hungry for the real meal! Phrases like "world's best," "premier," "largest," and "first choice of customers everywhere" abound. How "premier" status will be attained and how "best" will be measured are rarely clarified or discussed.

Schools and school districts also have mission statements—and they should. Unfortunately, education is not exempt from the tendency toward generic, vague, and meaningless mission statements.

> The typical mission statement of schools is going to sound very familiar, regardless of what part of the country or what part of North America we are talking about. In essence, we've all written the same mission statement. It's all based on this premise of learning for all. We want all of our students to become responsible, productive, and so on. I think what effective schools do is move beyond that sort of generic "here are our hopes for students," and they ask the critical corollary questions—that being to translate those hopes into reality. (DuFour, 2002)

The critical questions to be addressed in the mission statement are:

1. If we expect all students to learn, *what* is it we expect them to learn?

2. *How* will we know if they are learning it?

3. What will we do when they *don't*? (DuFour, 2002)

In addition to these three questions, we have often found it helpful to ask a fourth: How will we engage students in their own learning?

An effective mission statement must be specific enough to answer all four of these questions. If it does not, it will lack resonance for staff members, and it will quickly be forgotten or written off as meaningless. Because most schools already have a mission statement, it is best to review the statement in light of these criteria.

Case Study #2: Confidence, Commitment, and Culture

Having spent four years as a successful elementary principal in the inner city, I was excited about being assigned principal of an elementary/middle school. On July 7, I called the school to let the secretary know that I would be arriving soon. Perhaps I expected a welcoming committee. Perhaps a group of community members or even staff members would be there to greet the new leader. To my surprise, there was a welcoming committee. A group of students who wanted to meet their new principal awaited me by the curb. Was I happy!

As I walked from the curb down what seemed like a mile to the front door, they asked many questions. "Are you our new principal?" I knew the answer to that question. "Yes," I responded. "Have you been a principal before?" I knew that answer, too. "Yes." I guess, having successfully met their requirement, I qualified for the next series of questions.

A tall, handsome young man stepped forward. "Hi, I'm in the middle school. Can you have the middle school name added to the front of the building?" As I gazed at the top of the building, I realized this young man was absolutely right. The name of the school was incomplete. Three years ago, the elementary school was extended to include the middle grades. It was a matter of pride for the students to have "middle school" added to the existing elementary name. Feeling confident, I agreed to honor this request. Relieved, the student launched another question. This one caused me to pause, reflect, and think of the reason behind the question. He asked, "Am I in the slow class?" By this time, we were approaching the front door of the incompletely titled school.

The students had graciously carried my book bags, and we were already beginning to bond. I could not start off on the wrong foot. This precious jewel needed to know, in essence, if I could change the mission, vision, values, and goals of this school. "What makes you think that you are in the slow class?" When in doubt, I always answer a question with a question. This gives you time to think! "Well," he said, "I got into trouble a lot last year. I barely passed. I missed a lot of days from school. I didn't want to come to school because I would just get into trouble. My report card was not good. And, I'm in 08-03. That's the last class of the eighth grade. So, am I in the slow class?" Everything that he said made me think he definitely qualified to be in the "slow" class. Suspensions, poor grades, and poor attendance—any principal's nightmare.

I hadn't even entered the building and I'm holding an unofficial "press conference" with my most important constituents. What do I say? In an instant, my entire educational philosophy came to me. What is my mission? Why do I exist? The reason I entered the field of education hung in the balance. The student looked at me to see if I believed in his capacity to learn. He looked at me with hope in his eyes. He looked at me as if to say, "Are you the one for such a time as this?" Pausing, looking him face-to-face, eye-to-eye, I replied, "No, you're not in a slow class! In this school, everyone is smart! Everyone is a star! Whatever kept you from learning, whatever caused you to miss school, whatever made you get suspended, will change."

Were these just words filled with hot air? Were my words just another cliché? Did I believe? I asked for his help. "Will you help me? Will you help let everyone know that we are going to succeed?" With a smile on his face, he said, "Yeah, and by the way, what's your name?" I entered the school feeling empowered, directed, on a mission. He had given me a job to do.

That year was most unusual. It would be like no other year in my career. The year began with creating the mission statement and a clear vision of how we would get there. "Rising Stars, Reaching Academic Excellence" would be posted everywhere! Two thousand stars of all shapes, forms, and colors appeared almost overnight. We discussed and documented things that we valued as a school and how those commitments would change our behavior and define our steps to reach our mission. We committed ourselves to deny sorting and selecting as a way of determining who would succeed. We made commitments to succeed in improving the culture through collaboration. We used the budget to make our commitments a reality. Resource teachers were hired to provide team collaboration time during the day. Each grade-level team met twice a week for 45 minutes. Team leaders were identified and taught how to conduct team meetings. Team leaders completed team meeting log sheets and received feedback concerning issues raised. As the principal, I spent 50% of my day in the classrooms serving as the instructional leader. The secretaries could only call me to the office if it was one of the "Three B's." The "Three B's" meant:

1. Boss (Board)

2. Boys in Blue (fire, police, ambulance)

3. Beloved (family)

Adhering to the "Three B's" allowed me to focus on classroom instruction and ensure that we were "flowing mellifluously" and "honoring time." Flowing mellifluously and honoring time meant that teachers would be mindful of time wasters, i.e., late starts, transitions, etc. Teachers received daily feedback "love notes" concerning instructional strategies seen during the day. Intense job-embedded professional development was planned based on the "love notes." In addition to their regularly scheduled team meetings, teachers routinely collaborated about student work before school and during lunch. Conversations about evening socials were also the norm.

It took three months for the 750-member student body and 40-member teaching staff to realize that they were all smart and that they could get smarter through collaboration and hard work. Walking into classrooms, asking for the smart students to raise their hands grew from one student to ultimately everyone raising their hand! Adhering to the mission statement was a task. But it was a task that had to be done for everyone in the school. When your mission and vision are intact, then you can focus on goals for success. The entire school year was spent learning how to succeed, step-by-step, and celebrating every evidence of success.

By changing the belief system, we changed the way we operated and we changed student and staff expectations. No longer could students enter the building with a notebook rolled up in their back pocket. They now proudly walked through the neighborhood with a book bag, notebook, textbooks, and all the tools for success. Getting by was no longer the norm and "getting smart" perceived as being a nerd. No longer was lateness tolerated. No longer could students wear their shirts outside of their pants and their pants down to their knees. They had to dress for success: shirts in, belts on, pants up! No longer was fighting a response to every altercation: "Thoughts determine actions!" Through this step-by-step process, students and staff acquired the skills necessary to have a high quality of life. "Smart is what you get if you work hard!" The words "Never Say Never" were instilled through the school song. The key to success came in the form of an educational rebirth. Staff and students were taught to believe and succeed.

Individual success was transferred to the entire staff and student body. Because of the change in the culture (now collaborating and learning) the staff believed that they could succeed. An environment that was once marred with graffiti was transformed. The students believed that they could succeed. The physical plant received a face-lift. Students and parent volunteers helped to repaint the school. We instituted performance-based instruction, coach classes, and a Saturday academy. At the end of the year, the 435 suspensions of the previous year were reduced to 43. Student attendance increased from 94% to 95%, and staff attendance increased from 94% to 96%. Test scores? A three-year decline ended. State test scores increased from −24% to +34% of the students scoring 70% or better. Parents cried at year-end closing exercises. Students crossed the stage determined to move forward. They overcame a stigma, a label of inferiority that's placed on students early in life.

All of these changes only required confidence in the established mission vision, values, and goals of the school. Confidence in their capacity to believe that they had what it took to grow and develop. Teachers had confidence to believe that they had in their repertoire what it took to find the strategies for student success.

—Deborah L. Wortham, Ed.D.

WHAT IS MISSION?

In effective schools, the mission statement goes far beyond an expression of "wishful thinking." The mission statement can serve as the vital lifeblood of the school's daily activities and policies. It should be fundamental to every decision at every level. An effective mission statement expresses the school's purpose—its essential reason for educating in the first place. It expresses why a school *exists*.

The mission serves as a polestar, or guiding principle, for a school. Just as a ship sails toward but never actually reaches its guiding star, we too strive toward but never actually fulfill our mission. Why? Because as long as the world continues to change and evolve, our students' needs will change, and we will need to develop new ways to respond.

WHAT GOOD LOOKS LIKE

The best mission statements are clear about why the organization exists and what will be done to ensure that the purpose is met. The mission statement serves the organization by providing specifics about: (1) what we want to do, (2) how we will know if we are succeeding, and (3) what we will do to ensure success.

Given the three questions provided above regarding effective mission statements, which of the following would you consider effective? Mark each one with an "E" for effective or an "I" for ineffective, and note why you made the selection.

1. _____ The mission of this school district is to ensure that each and every student is prepared to succeed in life. This is accomplished in an environment of trust and respect that fosters positive attitudes toward self, others, work, and responsible citizenship. We are dedicated to maximizing individual potential and developing lifelong learners who will be contributing members in a global society.

2. _____ The mission of our school is to create and maintain an environment that ensures that every member of the school community reaches a high level of academic achievement as determined by state and national standards. We commit to a comprehensive system of support to assure this outcome.

3. _____ It is our mission as a school district to educate students to be creative, responsible, self-sufficient citizens who have the capacity and motivation for continued individual growth and who will have the ability to make a positive contribution in our society.

4. _____ We are committed to the academic excellence of every student by empowering them with the means for the successful completion of high educational standards and by challenging them to become productive members of society.

What's your analysis? Consider the following.

The examples numbered 1 and 3 above do not attempt to clearly define "success" in measurable ways. "Success in life" would demand that we wait too long for feedback on how a school community is doing in fulfilling its mission. Similarly, terms like "creative" and "responsible" are vague and hard to measure.

Example number 4 provides more specificity on both the definition of students' success and how it will be measured (by "high educational standards"). However, it lacks the clarity to answer the third question ("What will we do when students don't learn?"). Number 2 does answer this question.

Only the second example above addresses all three questions. But be aware: Photocopying this statement and hanging it underneath the office clock for all to see will not improve your school. It is the process of collaboratively creating a mission and spelling out all the specifics that are not provided in a generic mission statement that will lead to school improvements and cultural shifts. Figure 5.1 summarizes some of the differences between traditional and more effective mission statements. Another example of an effective mission statement can be found in Appendix D.

Traditional Mission Statements . . .	Effective Mission Statements . . .
• Are vague or generic	• Are clear
• Say all kids can learn	• Are specific (what exactly are students supposed to learn?)
• Do not define learning	• Are measurable (how do we know students have learned?)
• Do not address the possibility of failure	• Provide for failure (how do we respond when students don't learn?)

Figure 5.1

Source: Failure Is Not an Option video series, 2002

IMPLEMENTATION GUIDELINES

Most schools have no problem creating a mission statement. A small number of people can sit down at a restaurant and hammer one out before the food arrives. The discussions leading to the final document, however, are as important as the final document itself. It is critical that the process involve representatives from all stakeholder groups—teachers, para-educators, administrators, community members, students, and parents. It is equally important that those involved reflect ethnic and socioeconomic diversity, as well as diverse learning styles. A statement of mission has little meaning or impact unless it reflects the thoughts of the school community and is collectively embraced by those whom it affects.

There are various ways to collaboratively create a mission statement. The first step for any process should be to evaluate what already exists. Using the criteria that have been laid out, ask stakeholders to evaluate and revise the statement, using any of the following methods.

1. *Assemble a task force* made up of representatives from each stakeholder group. In this strategy, the representatives are responsible for soliciting feedback from and accurately representing the views of their constituencies. They are also responsible for sharing drafts of the evolving statements with their respective groups.

2. *Collect the views of each stakeholder group* in a more formal way, perhaps through a written survey instrument. Convene representative focus groups, then examine and discuss the views obtained through the survey. Ultimately, the focus groups report their findings to a task force, which is responsible for drafting the statement.

3. *Small-group work.* Still another approach, used successfully in Alton, Illinois, brings stakeholders together for small-group work around the three questions (see Chapter 3). In this approach, groups of representative stakeholders are first reminded of the three critical questions that their mission statement must answer. They then form small groups of 5–7 people, and each group drafts a complete mission statement. The groups' statements are posted on the walls around the room, and participants do a "gallery walk,"

reviewing each statement and offering feedback on notes. At the end of the session, the school's leadership team collects all the drafts and sticky notes and uses them to write a statement—which then goes out for more feedback from all stakeholders.

4. *A "snowball" method* can also yield good results. In this approach, all stakeholders are paired into groups of two. After each initial pair drafts a statement, two pairs join together to share their thoughts and merge their statements into one. That group of four joins with another group of four, then does the same. The process is repeated until there is one comprehensive statement that incorporates all stakeholder feedback. This statement is then reviewed by a representative group in light of the criteria for a good mission statement. The resulting statement is circulated for final approval.

In smaller schools, the above approaches can be, and ideally are, used with the entire school staff. Doing so takes longer, but it deepens the commitment to the outcome. In any case, it is vital to focus the discussion around the purpose and the three questions that ask for the necessary specifics. Collecting feedback from all stakeholder groups helps to ensure that the mission statement provides enough detail and is meaningful. Such an outcome requires plenty of time for thoughtful reflection and response—as well as time for writing, reviewing, and revising the statement. A step-by-step outline of the mission development process can be found in Appendix E.

Mission as a Guiding Principle

The mission statement should play an important role in any discussion of major issues. Dan Galloway, principal of Adlai Stevenson High School, experienced the power of having a strong mission during a faculty meeting discussion of grade waivers and dual enrollment. "Administratively, we spent a lot of time on this, and our discussion was going all over the place," he said. "Continuously, we had to reference: What is our mission? What is our vision? As we referenced that, our decision on what to do became clear."

SUSTAINING SUCCESS

Once you have developed an effective mission, your next challenge will be to establish it in action and keep it alive. In all schools, the entire student body is replaced every three to six years, and in a growing number of schools staff turnover is even more frequent. How can you ensure that your mission statement remains a living, integral part of the school experience? Here are some strategies:

- Display your mission statement prominently within the school and in places where the school presents itself to the public, e.g., on your Web site, press releases, letterhead, and the like.
- Make sure the mission is cited as a guide whenever staff meets to set goals, plan programs, make decisions, or discuss problems.
- Coach teacher leaders in using the mission as a guiding force in their team meetings. Teachers' understanding of their role in maintaining the mission is critical for success.
- Frequently evaluate the school's policies and procedures to ensure their adherence to the mission.
- Schedule time to familiarize new staff and students with the mission. This should include in-depth discussions about the implications for how the school operates.
- Respond quickly and correctively to any and all failures to act in accordance with the school's mission.

Think It Through . . .

Do you know your school's mission statement? Does it address what you want students to learn, how learning will be measured, and how you will respond when learning doesn't happen?

THE VISION

Like mission, creating a vision is another common part of the planning process in most organizations today. The word "vision" is used as an adjective (the visionary leader), a noun (a vision for the community), and even as a verb (visioning the future). But what exactly *is* this elusive vision—and where do you get one?

What Is Vision?

Whereas the mission statement reminds us of why we exist, a vision paints a picture of what we can become. Most of us employ vision in our personal lives. We strive toward a better, future version of ourselves that may be wealthier, smarter, better organized, healthier, and so forth. We use that vision to guide our behaviors on both a long-term and short-term basis.

A school's vision serves the same purpose—that is, it offers a realistic alternative for a better future. It says, "This is what we want to be." Just as our own vision guides the personal or professional course we follow, a school's vision should guide the collective direction of its stakeholders. It should provide a compelling sense of where the school is headed and, in broad terms, what must be accomplished in the future to fulfill the school's purpose. Every decision made, every program implemented, every policy instituted, and all goals should align with this vision.

Without a common vision, decisions are made randomly. At best, policies, procedures, and programs will lack unity and fail to adequately support one another. At worst, they will actually work at cross purposes. Virtually no school lacks for new initiatives or programs; *most* schools lack cohesion and a unified effort shared between various programs and initiatives. Whereas the mission statement answers the question "Why do we exist?" the vision explains where the school is *headed*.

Vision as a Unifying Force

Prior to developing a vision, one Indiana high school had a very fragmented approach to teaching writing. Some teachers used writing rubrics to evaluate writing, while others did not. They lacked a clear understanding of state standards and rubrics for evaluation. As a result, there was no consistency in writing instruction. The development of the school's vision, however, allowed faculty members to unify their message for students. All departments began to identify ways in which their teachers could reinforce and improve reading across all curricular areas. In essence, the vision ensured that all faculty, across all departments, were working toward the same end goal. (*The foregoing comes from Linda Jonaitis, principal of Highland High School in Highland, Indiana.*)

What Good Looks Like

Like mission statements, a good vision statement should be detailed enough to carry meaning. The most successful vision statements are vivid and compelling; they motivate us to strive for an improved future. They provide a foundation on which we can assess the areas for improvement—and then plan. Perhaps most important, an effective vision statement describes a *collective* vision and is shared by all stakeholders.

Below are two sets of evaluation criteria for vision statements. The first, derived from Kotter (1996), says that vision statements should be:

- Imaginable—they convey a picture of what the future will look like.
- Desirable—they appeal to the long-term interests of stakeholders.
- Feasible—they comprise realistic, attainable goals.
- Focused—they are clear enough to provide guidance in decision making.
- Flexible—they are general enough to allow for individual initiative and changing responses in light of changing conditions.
- Communicable—they are easy to communicate and explain.

The second, from Nanus (1992), provides a list of evaluative questions:

- To what extent is the vision statement future-oriented?
- To what extent is it likely to lead to a clearly better future for the organization?
- To what extent does it fit with the organization's history, culture, and values?
- To what extent does it set standards of excellence and reflect high ideals?
- To what extent does it clarify direction?
- To what extent does it inspire enthusiasm and encourage commitment?
- Is it ambitious enough?

Using these criteria, how would you rate the following vision statements? Mark each one with an "E" for effective or an "I" for ineffective, and note why you made the selection.

_____ *Vision 1:*

As you enter Highland High School, the level of pride and accomplishment is evident. The school is well maintained and has a safe environment, with current technology appropriate to a wide range of curricular and extracurricular activities. The learning atmosphere, which is exciting, stimulating, and success-oriented, also affords students the opportunity to learn from their mistakes.

Students have access to a wide spectrum of academic and extracurricular experiences and are encouraged to widen their worldview by taking full advantage of diverse offerings. They possess a greater freedom of choice in decisions affecting their school community. The school climate engenders respect; students feel free to accept and express ideas without fear or prejudice. Adults are compassionate, competent, committed, consistent, considerate, and enabled.

Students at Highland accept their roles in education. This is evident by the way students accept responsibility for their learning, possess positive attitudes, and maintain well-rounded participation in academics and extracurriculars. Their communication is open, friendly, and caring, not only between students but also with staff. This exists because of respect among students and the adults in their lives. The students are self-motivated and excited about learning. Students have a true sense of direction, with goals and career paths clearly established.

Students possess a high sense of responsibility. Through their sense of good values, positive behavior, and high moral conscience, they hold themselves accountable for their actions. They accept the consequences of the choices they make.

Open communication exists between students and adults through mentoring; the mastering of all levels of communication, including oral and written; and the fostering of positive relationships.

Students come to school prepared, eager to participate, and devoted to their learning. They complete learning projects and assignments without hesitation and are successful because they believe in who they are.

Finally, all students work to become productive adults and contributing members of society. They aspire to be lifelong learners as they prepare and plan for the future.

The entire community embraces involvement in the educational development of all students. The parents and other members of the community demonstrate respect for education through their availability to and support for all members of the school population.

Parents take an active role in their child's education by providing basic needs so their child is ready to learn. By learning values and good work ethics at home, the students are prepared to succeed at school. Mutually respectful and cooperative in school and community, parents and staff work together with the vision of helping students become productive members of Highland High School and society. Administrators and guidance counselors are visible and accessible to students.

_____ *Vision 2:*

We envision a school where children and adults work productively toward success for all students. This would involve mutual respect, cooperation, and responsibility on everyone's part.

_____*Vision 3:*

Our vision is increasing reading by 6% in the next three years.

What is your analysis of these vision statements? Ours follows. The second example fails to provide clarity. From our perspective, it is not compelling. The third example is very clear, understandable, and communicable. Yet it is not ambitious and likely won't galvanize the school community.

Although the first vision does not include any quantifiable data, it is very specific in describing a compelling future that is imaginable and feasible. This example, from Highland High School, is our preferred vision of the three.

Figure 5.2 provides a comparison of traditional and more effective vision statements.

Traditional Vision Statements . . .	Effective Vision Statments . . .
• Are vague or unimaginable	• Are realistic, clear, and compelling
• Are created by a select group	• Have broad-based buy-in
• State hopes and wishes	• Describe intended change
• Are soon forgotten	• Guide action

Figure 5.2

Source: Failure Is Not an Option video series, 2002

Implementation Guidelines

Roland Barth (2001) notes that there are eight ways by which an organization can come to have a vision. The following is an adaptation of his list of methods (pp. 197–204), along with associated advantages and disadvantages.

Inherit a Vision	Use what's already there.
Advantage	No need to go through the periodic, introspective turmoil of crafting a vision.
Disadvantage	Vision was engraved in the granite of the past, whereas faculty come from the present and the students must be prepared for the future.
Explicate a Vision	Make overt what has been covert by putting it in writing.
Advantage	Vision is comfortable, genuine, and already existing.
Disadvantage	Doesn't ask, "What would we like to be doing in the future?" Waking a sleeping baby often causes noise—we uncover what we don't want to hear.
Refine a Vision	Take inventory of past practice, present aspirations, and tune up for the 21st century.
Advantage	Pragmatic; has something in it for everyone.
Disadvantage	Can become an exercise in putting new patches on a defective tire.
Buy a Vision	Use one from a "model."
Advantage	Most are rich, coherent, and fundamentally different from business as usual; those who don't like it can "shoot" at the creator rather than each other.
Disadvantage	Looking outside reinforces the belief that those inside are unable to get their own house in order, perpetuating a sense of helplessness.
Inflict a Vision	A person or office outside the school supplies the vision.

| Advantage | Can come quickly and be uniformly and impressively portrayed throughout the district. |
| Disadvantage | Teachers and principals are gifted and talented at offering superficial compliance to an imposed ideology while at the same time thwarting it. |

Hire a Vision	When things aren't going well, get a new principal with a better vision.
Advantage	Change in leadership may bring a change in culture.
Disadvantage	The principal's vision equals the school's vision, which sustains the paternalistic feeling that "This is the principal's vision, not ours."

Homogenize a Vision	Invite major constituencies to reveal their personal mission; common elements become the school's mission.
Advantage	Little in the final vision not in the vision of each contributor; little is unfamiliar or threatening.
Disadvantage	People feel there is much in their personal vision that is not in the school vision and so lose interest; the least common denominator excludes "out of the box" thinking (often the fresh, innovative, and most promising ideas of a few individuals).

Grow a Vision	Members of the school community devise a process for examining their school, then create together a vision that provides a profound sense of purpose for each of its members. The collective vision emerges from the personal visions of each member.
Advantage	It enlists and reflects not the common thinking, but the *best* thinking, beliefs, ideals, and ideas of the entire school community.
Disadvantage	Time-consuming; individuals must dig deep to come to grips with personal vision.

Of the eight possible ways to come up with a vision, it is clearly the last one—growing a vision—that is most meaningful and effective. Like mission, vision is not something that can be handed down from on high. It must be cocreated by the entire learning community in order for it to have shared meaning.

Should the vision be developed at the school level or district level? Ideally, both the district leaders and the schools they oversee should have a role in the process.

Should the development process involve only school personnel, or should it involve the larger community? Hargreaves's research (2001) calls for: (1) getting (emotional) depth or connection to the effort, (2) breadth in terms of who is involved, and (3) sustainability in terms of leadership transition plans for best results. In light of this, school leaders gain the best long-term outcomes by deeply involving the broader school community in creating the vision.

The vision should also be rooted in research on best practices and reflect the school's history and existing culture. DuFour and Eaker (1998) suggest that the following information be gathered in preparation for creating a vision:

- Relevant information about the school or district, i.e., a history of the district or school, copies of prior vision or values statements, internal and external factors affecting the school or district, findings of visitation teams who evaluated the school/district for accreditation purposes, longitudinal achievement data, and community survey results
- Research on school culture
- Research on characteristics of effective schools
- Research on school restructuring
- Research on any other areas that will be addressed in the vision statement
- An honest assessment of the current conditions in the school or district

Once stakeholders have had an opportunity to review the background information referenced above, they or a subset of the school leadership team can begin drafting the vision. Vision statements tend to be thoughtful, fairly lengthy documents that encompass many aspects of a school. For example, a school's vision might be divided into such sections as "curriculum," "attention to individual students," "personnel," "leadership," "students," "climate," and "community partnerships." The organization of the statement is not important, but the vision should include the ideas of all stakeholders and should touch on all aspects of the school deemed significant to realizing the ideal.

One method, used successfully by Linda Jonaitis, principal of Highland High School in Highland, Indiana, involves having all stakeholders make lists of the things that they think are important for a good school. The stakeholders then form groups of 8–10 people, combine their lists, and collaboratively agree on the "top 10." The school improvement team takes the top 10 lists from all the groups and clusters the statements by common theme. The school improvement team divides into groups, with each group taking one of those common themes, and writes a paragraph that captures all the statements in that theme.

A similar approach requires participants to write their initial statements—as many as they wish — on sticky notes. Participants then work together to group the notes into clusters. Each cluster is assigned a name, which is used as a vision category. As with the previous method, small groups take the various categories and draft mini-visions. Ultimately, all the mini-visions are combined into a single statement and sent to stakeholders for feedback.

A step-by-step process for developing the vision statement may be found in Appendix E.

Think It Through . . .

Does your school have a vision statement? If so, is it detailed enough to paint a vivid picture of a better future? Does it capture a future that motivates all stakeholders? Who in the school community knows what your vision is?

THE VALUES

Research indicates that in both business and education, an established set of shared values is a key factor in an organization's success. Champy (1995) says that values are "the most important structural element" in any organization. And Sergiovanni (1994) emphasizes the need for schools in particular to come together around shared values and ideas.

What Are Values?

Values are the attitudes and behaviors an organization embraces. They represent commitments we make regarding how we will behave on a daily basis in order to become the school we want to be. They are established and articulated guidelines we live by.

> Values are best described in terms of behavior: If we operate as we should, what would an observer see us doing?
>
> —Senge et al. (1994)

Values endure. They do not fluctuate with staffing changes, funding shifts, or trends in instructional methodology. They are never compromised for a short-term gain or a quick solution to a problem. Values express a *shared* commitment to certain behaviors; they do not result from a top-down dictate—that is, they start with "*We* will," not "*You* will."

Ideally, values reflect the attitudes and beliefs of the school community. Ultimately, after they are created, value statements guide the behavior of everyone in the organization.

School leaders cannot read minds or respond to perceptions of what people in the organization *believe.* Leaders can inquire as to staff members' beliefs on a given topic, but the response may or may not be forthcoming. At the very least, however, after having collectively created values, it is the leader's role to hold people to *behaviors* that mirror those values (as opposed to *beliefs*). In high-performing schools, eventually the school staff will also help bring individuals' behaviors into line with stated values. Acting in accordance with these stated values becomes part of the culture.

Without a shared commitment to a core base of values, schools fall into the "my belief versus your belief" pattern. These schools may have certain individuals or factions that operate as "rogue agents," taking actions that run counter to the school's mission and vision. For example, imagine a school with a mission that states that all children can achieve at a high level and that it will provide an environment to make that happen. Yet many classrooms in that same school have long lists of prerequisite criteria—many of which are quite subjective—that students must meet in order to access the more rigorous curricular offerings. Clearly, such behaviors do not support the school's mission. Therefore, it lacks a *functional* set of values—a school-wide statement that dictates *all* behavior.

What Good Looks Like

A successful statement of values touches on the most pertinent, pervasive principles shared by a school's stakeholders. The statement goes to the core of our belief and the depth of our commitment. Note that this does not mean identifying what stakeholders *should* commit to; we cannot "set" values and insist that others embrace them. Jim Collins points out that "core values are not something people 'buy in' to. People must be predisposed to holding them" (1996, p. 19). He outlines an in-depth process for "getting to the core," which can help to create values that are enthusiastically endorsed by stakeholders.

A statement of values that captures only core beliefs should be relatively brief. It may contain as many as ten values—but five or six is a more manageable number. Each value should be simply stated, so that the general meaning is easy to grasp and remember. It should also relate directly to the vision statement.

The question to consider when articulating values is not just what values are appropriate for our school, but what values *specifically support* our vision statement and are aligned with our mission. For example, the value statement "We will give students multiple opportunities to learn and to demonstrate their accomplishments" is consistent with a mission that states "All students will learn at high levels, in accordance with state standards." If a teacher is failing half of the students in his or her classroom year after year, that behavior will not be in line with the school's values or mission.

Living by Values

In the late 1990's, Adlai Stevenson High School already had one of the best Advanced Placement programs in the nation. But rather than becoming complacent, Principal Dan Galloway took a hard look at the data—and realized that the extremely high AP test scores probably meant the school should relax its AP criteria. "There were some kids we were missing," he explained. "There was that middle group, the ones who would score in the mid-range, who were not in the AP program. So we decided we needed to get those kids involved as well, and open the doors of opportunity for them."

When asked to admit more students to their AP classes, teachers were at first apprehensive. They feared both that test scores would decline and that new students would struggle. To ease teacher apprehension, the school's administration made a bold statement. "We told the teachers directly that we knew that by bringing more students in, we might see the average exam scores drop," Galloway said. "And we told them that's okay with us. We don't have to have scores at the highest possible level—our concern is with giving as many kids as possible the opportunity." Once teachers understood that the school was living by its value of success for all students, they were much more supportive of the idea.

The values of a school articulate what "we will" *do* and how "we will" *behave* (i.e., "We will model," "We will support," "We will provide")—not what we *believe*. Although a statement of beliefs might be useful in some circumstances, it lacks the critical element of prescribing action—of telling us what we need to *do* to make our vision a reality.

Effective values are

- Few in number
- Direct and simply stated
- Focused on behaviors, not beliefs
- Linked to the vision statement

Implementation Guidelines

Some view the establishment of a set of values as the most challenging component of a school's foundation because it requires a commitment to changing behaviors. It can be difficult to convey the full significance of values to staff members and get them to truly grapple with their beliefs and their perceived roles in the teaching/learning process. We must all "live into" our values by evaluating our behaviors over time.

In order for serious discussions among stakeholders to be successful, schools must invest time. As with developing mission and vision, it is best to start the process by breaking up into small groups. This helps engage participants and fosters honest, genuine dialogue. One easy approach is simply to review the school's vision statement with participants and then ask, "How do we need to behave to make this happen?" Allow time to discuss and draft answers to such questions. Then continue to consolidate lists using the snowball technique described earlier, or have a task force collect the responses and use them to draft a statement of values.

Another approach is to have participants divide into pairs. Have the pairs ask each other, "What are some of the behaviors that we [some, or all of us] engage in that are not consistent with our mission and vision?" After they have identified what they would like to see changed, have them ask each other, "What will you commit to doing, starting today, to change that?" Have participants write down their list of commitments. The facilitator can then ask each person to report out as he or she consolidates the comments onto one sheet of paper. Or the facilitator might collect the lists and consolidate them into a master list. In either case, it is best to go back to the staff to ask for a collective commitment to the final list.

Whatever process you use, be sure participants know that it is not trivial. Although it may be easy to get a list of values that everyone says they agree to, it is far more difficult to arrive at a list of values everyone will actually be willing to *live* by. One way to partially safeguard against abuses of the collective values is to go down the list and pose scenarios that might lead to someone bypassing a given value. Discuss the scenario and then ask participants to propose alternatives to behaving counter to the values.

The more energy and time you put into the process, the more effective your values will be at guiding day-to-day decision making. More information about the development process can be found in Appendix E.

Think It Through . . .

What are the prevailing values in your school right now? Which of those values accord with your mission and vision? Do any detract from your mission and vision? Are other people's behaviors consistent with your value statement?

THE GOALS

The three components of a successful school's foundation discussed thus far are meant for long-range planning. A school's vision, for example, may take five years or longer to reach. Values are also ongoing; we commit to them for as long as we are part of the organization.

But we also need short-term successes to help us stay focused and motivated. It is very difficult to commit to and work toward something that has no definite "success point" or pre-identified benchmark that will allow us to take a deep breath, pat ourselves on the back, and look with pride at a job well done. Most of us need to feel that we are making progress and getting things done. It is through the judicious use of well-written goals—the fourth component of our foundation—that this need can be met.

Strong goals are particularly important in school cultures with little previous record of success. The process of setting, committing to, and accomplishing short-term goals builds credibility and trust. It can also serve as the beginning of positive momentum toward change.

What Are Goals?

If our vision is the grand target—a distant ideal that we are striving for—then our goals are the short-term mini-targets that we aim for along the way. They break our long, winding journey toward school improvement into manageable, measurable steps. Goals provide intermittent reinforcement for our efforts and provide us with feedback on our progress toward the larger vision.

Goals also serve a more pragmatic purpose. They provide a detailed, short-term orientation for us in relation to our vision. They identify priorities and establish a timeline for our process of change. Equally important, goals establish accountability for stakeholders, ensuring that what needs to happen actually *does* happen.

What Good Looks Like

Goals, like the other foundational components we've discussed, are often too vague. A goal that is too vague to be measured is, essentially, worthless. After all, how will you ever know if you reach it? How will you know when to set a new goal?

Effective goals are both specific and measurable. They clearly identify the evidence that must be monitored to assess progress. They also set a time frame for completion. For example, "We will increase our students' average state test score by 20% this academic year" is a good, specific goal. "We will help all kids become lifelong learners," on the other hand, is too vague to be useful.

Goals should also focus on the results rather than on the process or the task. It's not uncommon for a school to have task-oriented goals, such as "We will adopt a new curriculum" or "We will have team meetings weekly." Although these are perfectly legitimate *inputs,* a SMART goal specifies the desired *results* of these actions in terms that are aligned with the school's mission and vision. To be SMART goals, these subgoals must go a step further, to answer the "so that" question: "We will adopt a new curriculum *so that we . . .*" Ultimately, answering this additional question should get us to the *real* goal for student learning. Criteria for SMART goals are listed in Figure 5.3.

Goals in Action

Goals set by Thornton High Schools District 205 provide an excellent example of the SMART criteria. The district's five-year plan includes three broad improvement initiatives, each one with a set of highly specific, time-bound benchmarks. Take, for example, the first initiative: to increase the mathematical, science, communication, problem-solving, and technical achievement, as well as the application of learning for all college- and career-bound students in the district. Included in that aim are specific *yearly benchmarks* for every core area, identifying how students should be performing relative to state scores. Other benchmarks include graduation rate percentages, GPA, and percentages of students with grade C or higher—all, again, tied to specific time frames.

The second initiative—to continue to reduce the annual deficit, using measurable annual goals, with minimal impact on student activities—likewise has a set of measurable goals, which might include hitting specific numbers in cost-containment efforts, for example. By measuring itself against these specific, periodic goals over the course of the five-year plan, the district's stakeholders can see clearly whether or not they are on track to achieve their vision. They can also readily identify areas in which they are struggling, and respond accordingly.

Implementation Guidelines

Developing goals for a school requires asking, "What steps do we need to take, in what order, to create our ideal school?" After identifying these steps, we must set a timeframe or deadline for completion. To be most effective, every stakeholder in the school or district should help to set the goals for which he or she will be responsible. For example, third-grade teachers should set goals for the third-grade team.

SMART Goals are . . .

Specific and Strategic. In this sense, "specific" relates to clarity. "Strategic" relates to alignment with our mission and vision.

Measurable. In most cases, this means quantifiable.

Attainable. People must *believe*, based on past data and current capabilities, that success is realistic.

Results-Oriented. This means focusing on the outcome, not the process for getting there. This refers to our desired *end result*, versus inputs to the process.

Time-Bound. When will the goal be accomplished?

Figure 5.3

Source: Failure Is Not an Option video series, 2002

How do you choose a goal? How do you decide what will make it measurable, attainable, results-oriented, and time-bound? An earlier vision statement example cited a 6% increase in reading scores. One might ask, "Why 6%? Why not 10% or 20%? Are folks lazy? Are they overly ambitious?"

There are different ways to begin goal setting:

- A school may be in academic trouble and have a "bottom line" that must be achieved.
- A school may look at last year's outcomes and then estimate how much better the school or district can do this year, based on improved processes, technology, or pedagogy.
- A school may start with the long-term vision and determine what needs to be accomplished each year to reach it, then dedicate the resources necessary for the annual improvements.

Regardless of where you begin in the process, it is essential to look at past data, new circumstances, and processes that can be modified to improve results. What will be done *differently* this year from last? How and when will we evaluate whether we are on target? Heed the warning implied in the statement: "If you do what you've always done, you'll get what you've always got!"

After SMART goals are defined and implemented, they should be monitored continuously and evaluated over time. If clear evidence emerges revealing that the goal or means of achieving it is not bringing about the desired results, then one or both of these should be amended or abandoned. If goals are well chosen, and the means of achieving them are effective, then a careful analysis of the outcome should be made to determine how to continue and maintain the improvement over a longer period of time. More information about the goal-setting and monitoring process can be found in Appendix E.

Think It Through . . .

What goals are guiding your school's plans and actions right now? Are they consistent with your mission and vision? Are they SMART?

CELEBRATING SUCCESSES

Many schools are reluctant to avail themselves of one of the best strategies for building positive school culture: celebrating success. In addition to concerns about lacking time, some school leaders are reluctant to single out individual achievements. Indeed, some school cultures are committed to mediocrity or egalitarianism to the point of hiding or ignoring successes!

But regular celebrations have the power to make the school's overall values increasingly positive. Moreover, celebrations help mark milestones and build motivation in the long journey of school improvement.

Here are some guidelines for celebrating success:

- Take steps that help assure the celebrations are deemed fair. This involves clarifying in advance exactly what constitutes success for all involved. (See SMART goals for additional guidelines.)

- Tie celebrations explicitly to organizational vision, values, and goals. This provides an opportunity to reinforce these organizational pillars while providing more clarity, credibility, and rationale for the celebrations.
- Design celebrations that are attainable by all staff members. Having only one celebration with one winner per year can alienate a majority of your staff.
- For formal celebrations, communicate in advance the likely outcomes for success. This affirms the fairness of the approach.
- Make the celebration widely accessible. Involving more people heightens the impact of your school's values and goals for everybody.
- Arrange for both formal and informal celebrations. For example, simply using a staff meeting to congratulate a teacher on his or her excellent job in researching and recommending a new teaching methodology will go a long way toward encouraging others to do the same. Sometimes informal celebrations are needed to provide *timely* encouragement of people's efforts.
- Do not use celebrations to make direct or indirect comparisons between high- and low-achieving staff members. Focus on the positive results you are celebrating.
- Be specific about the nature of the success. "Eleanor actually took the time to visit the home of her most improved student, James," is far better than "Eleanor always helps her students."
- Use stories and be human.
- Build sustainability and community into the celebratory process by allowing staff and students to eventually take it over. Schools can begin early on by involving others in selection committees.

This chapter has outlined specific processes for building the foundation of a professional learning community. That foundation rests on four pillars: mission, vision, values, and goals. Creating a "product" for each of these pillars is technically simple. But the real gains in doing this come from the *process* and the *relationships* that are shaped along the way.

CHALLENGES

Challenge: "This has nothing to do with me and my classroom." Getting faculty engaged in and supportive of the process can be difficult if they don't perceive it as directly meaningful to them.

Solution: Broad stakeholder involvement at the drafting stage. A top-down dictate will have little effect on the commitment of those on the front lines. The notion of assigning a purpose and a vision for others without obtaining their input is counterproductive. Every stakeholder group needs the opportunity to engage in thinking about a preferred future, to consider what the school stands for and what needs to be done. It is through ownership in the process and the creation of the guiding statements that the plan will become truly meaningful.

Challenge: "I think we used to have a mission . . . or a vision . . . or something like that." Too often, the excitement that is generated by a new mission, vision, values, or goals statement is short-lived. School staffs become energized during the drafting and unveiling process but sometimes lose interest in the face of the challenges and pressures that are part of their daily routine.

Solution: Constant reinforcement. Keep your mission, vision, values, and goals at the forefront of everyone's mind by constant reiteration and references to them in staff meetings, professional development days, and celebrations. Discuss them in orientations with new staff and in introducing the school to new stakeholders. Refer to them during group decision-making sessions. Create posters and hang them on the school walls. Use every opportunity to clarify and reinforce what the school stands for and where it is headed. Most important is confronting behaviors that are inconsistent with these agreed-upon statements of purpose.

Challenge: "I don't have time for more meetings. I have real work to do!" Time is always at a premium—and it can be a real stumbling block for faculty and staff who are already overworked and exhausted.

Solution: Make the time, and uncover other reasons for resistance. This statement is, on its face, completely legitimate. There is simply no way of getting around it—the process of creating mission, vision, values, and goals will require an investment of time. More important, schools will need to make time in the daily schedule for continual professional development. The issue of time is covered in more detail in Chapter 2 and in Appendix B.

CONCLUSION

In this chapter, you have learned the specific processes involved in building the foundation of a professional learning community. Creating, or at least revisiting, mission, vision, values, and goals is fundamental to all that follows. The next chapter poses and helps resolve one of the greatest challenges schools face: "What happens when children *don't* learn?"

CHAPTER SIX

Principle #2—Ensuring Achievement for All Students: Systems for Prevention and Intervention

Not all of us are a mess, you know. . . . People often associate anyone who's been abused with "There's no hope for that child." . . . Tell people we can do it. That you can survive all that and be a fully functioning member of the community. Don't give up on that kid at age 7 and say, "Oh, he's been through so much; he's never going to amount to anything. . . ." The abused are labeled. But you can change somebody around.

—G. Higgins (1994, p. 318)

If we individually make the effort to ensure that each child is known in our system, our organization will be a caring learning community that knows and lifts each child.

—Les Ometani, Community School District
Superintendent, West Des Moines, Iowa
(quoted in LaFee, 2003, p. 7)

C onsider this exchange between two teachers.

Ella: "How are things going with your class, Jim?"

Jim: "Not well. I just gave my first test, and over half the class failed. I don't know how I'm supposed to teach these kids. They're all reading below grade level. They appear to have learned nothing in middle school. What am I supposed to do with them?"

How do we ensure successful learning for all students? Most educators are trying *very* hard and come to their work with a genuine desire to succeed with each of their students. However, there are undeniably numerous significant obstacles to learning. These include, but are not limited to, differing learning styles, need for additional time and repetition, low socioeconomic status, a language other than English spoken in the home, and parent/family situations that interfere with the learning process.

In high-performing schools, these variables are addressed in a proactive manner so they do not become barriers to the successful achievement of all students. Teachers are engaged in continuous study of educational research to learn how to prevent failure and how to provide effective interventions for each student in need. They actively seek alternatives to failure, and the concept of "throw-away" students is itself discarded.

Even the most abused and troubled children *self*-correct as they mature in age (Anthony, 1982, 1987; Garmezy, 1983, 1994; Werner and Smith, 1977). Werner and Smith (1977) summarized one part of their 30-year longitudinal study on high-risk youth this way: "We could not help being deeply impressed by the resiliency of the overwhelming majority of children and by their potential for positive change and personal growth" (p. 210).

Teachers are among the most likely mentors and positive influences for underachieving students. And schools can often be the only bastion of stability in a student's life. A committed school faculty, therefore, can do a great deal to enhance the life of every child. When acting in concert to create a reclaiming *environment* and to build *systems* to prevent failure, school communities dramatically enhance the likelihood for student success (Schorr, 1988).

The challenge is getting all staff members to believe in schools' ability to intervene positively in a student's life and to act on this information in a sustained, concerted, systematic manner. That is the focus of this chapter. Here we look at the research, the "end products" of successful schools, and the processes that high-performing schools undertake to succeed with even the toughest students.

Specifically, we look at three major aspects of assuring success for all students through comprehensive systems for prevention and intervention:

1. The school community's belief system regarding low-performing students

2. The overarching philosophy that unifies staff behavior

3. Comprehensive systems for assuring success

WHAT DOES THE SCHOOL COMMUNITY BELIEVE?

In most schools, the answer to this question is, "It depends." Beliefs about low-performing students often vary among teachers. A small number of classroom teachers often account for the majority of those students who are referred to the principal's office. At the same time, other teachers are able to succeed with those same students. This is generally not a case of the student's becoming more intelligent or a better person once he or she reaches the classroom of the successful teacher. It has more to do with the varying belief systems in operation within the school.

As we stated in Chapter 2, the link between student success or failure and teachers' and principals' expectations for those students is well documented (Bandura, 1986; Edmonds, 1979; Gardner, 1988; Goleman, 1995; Sternberg, 1996). Moreover, the research in Chapter 3 indicates that one of the keys to success for highly reliable organizations (HRO's) is both believing in and acting on this information. The difficulty lies in the challenge of getting the entire school community to understand this connection and take appropriate action. Simply reading the research—absent belief and action—is not sufficient to bring about change.

Changing the belief systems of people is an extremely difficult and complex process. Most texts don't address this issue, focusing instead on changing behavior. In the previous chapter, we endorsed this approach as a practical way of addressing behaviors that are inconsistent with organizational values.

It is imperative that a school's entire staff hold high expectations for students, and this chapter addresses some of the practical complexities in this effort. Gaining staff *compliance* alone is not enough. It takes total staff *commitment* to succeed in the thorny work of reaching low-achieving and under-served students.

Addressing the core *beliefs* of the entire school community is a lengthy process. Along the way, it is essential to be sure to hold the line on *behaviors* and *language* that may conflict with organizational values and mission. Doing otherwise creates an environment in which "anything goes." Without at *least* commitment to *behavior* that supports the school's values and mission, the fundamental aspect of almost any school's mission—that "*all* students will learn"—will become invalid. It is essential that the mission really means that *all* students—not *some* students—will learn.

Confronting Behaviors

After numerous discussions with Bob, the science teacher, regarding the poor grades his students consistently receive, the school principal meets with Bob:

Principal: Hi, Bob. Did you get those grade distributions I sent you?

Bob: Yes, I did.

Principal: Great, let's just go over them. It's obvious from these numbers, Bob, that students in your class consistently underperform, semester after semester. Something is clearly happening in your class to cause this discrepancy, and I'd welcome any explanations you might have.

Bob: This is the way I teach, Mr. Martin. It's the way I've always taught. I teach responsibility. I'm very tough on them. I'm not going to enable them like these other teachers do.

Principal: It's not our mission to make courses difficult for students, Bob. It's our mission to help them succeed. We need assessments that accurately reflect what they know, and we need approaches that are consistent with our value statement—which you helped create. I'm going to ask you to work with the two other teachers in your division, and with your director, to develop some new assessments that are more in keeping with what we're trying to accomplish. If, at the end of the next grading period, your students' scores aren't in line with those of the other classes, I'll work with you directly to assure the necessary improvements.

Think It Through . . .

Does it seem as if the teacher is being asked to lower his standards? How can we reconcile maintaining high standards and still ensuring success for all students? How do leaders respond to behaviors that conflict with vision, mission, and values?

High-performing schools realize that (1) What they do *matters* to the learning of each of their students, and (2) all children can indeed perform at high levels. Many school communities do not take direct responsibility for the learning of each of their students. Here are three common reasons why this might be the case, and some suggestions for addressing each:

1. The teachers may not believe that a school can succeed with all students.

Some members of the school community have had experiences that, to them, confirm the worst: Not all children *can* learn! Based on their own predispositions, initial bad experiences, or inabilities to reach all children themselves, some may understandably hold this view. In fact, it wasn't until relatively recently that schools were even *considered* a possible part of the solution to students' *non*academic life challenges (Bower, 1964; Clarizio and McCoy, 1970; Guetzloe, 1994, p. 3).

Most educators have had minimal experience and training in dealing with the kinds of problems that today's children present. Dealing with students' problems ineffectively or misinterpreting a student's inability to learn is common. The teachers described in the following sidebar, for example, mistook Sidiki's personal problems for an inability to learn.

Sidiki's Story

I was called to school for an appointment with the teachers of a 10-year-old boy, Sidiki, to whom I had become "big brother." When I inquired into the purpose of our meeting, one teacher's analysis of Sidiki's performance was: "Sidiki is not performing at the skill level of his classmates. He has difficulty paying attention and refuses to participate in class. His reading comprehension is well below grade level and his scores on our standardized tests indicate that his math skills are only at third-grade level."

The team leader provided a more succinct analysis: "He just doesn't get it! I think he may be learning-disabled."

I shared with Sidiki's teachers that he was an African immigrant who already spoke four languages, the last of which was English. I shared how enthusiastic and excited Sidiki could become once he was engaged in our evening tutoring sessions, remaining exclusively focused on his homework for hours at a time—often longer than I could! I also explained the tremendous tumult in his family life, and the pressure and abuse he received from his father.

As I spoke, it was clear that neither teacher had been aware of Sidiki's impressive multilingual abilities, his enthusiasm for learning and capacity for intense concentration, his father's status as an international scholar, or the abuse—physical and otherwise—which Sidiki received from him. As I revealed these facts, a look of empathy began to play on one of the teachers' faces. . . .

(Excerpted from Blankstein, 1997, pp. 2–3)

When Sidiki's teachers understood the situation, they redoubled their efforts, changed their approach, and Sidiki succeeded. If the challenge is one of school personnel truly questioning whether or not all students can learn at high levels, then this is more easily dealt with than the other challenges on this list. Teachers with a strong sense of self-efficacy can generally change their behaviors readily when faced with new information that calls for such a change. Similarly, professionals in a culture that focuses on continuous learning will be hungry to learn that there is a better way, and they will soon adopt that better approach.

If this is the situation, it is often possible to change behaviors (leading to changed beliefs) by introducing conclusions drawn from research. This will generally create cognitive dissonance for those questioning the possibility of creating a school in which low-performers can turn around. The dissonance, for those with strong self-efficacy, will be resolved in favor of a pilot project testing the new theory, or wholesale change, depending on the school's culture.

Leaders can also create this dissonance, as well as pathways to change. Modeling alternative behaviors, demonstrating success, and forcefully challenging assumptions are all part of good leadership.

It would be helpful, however, to check to see if "lack of information" is the only barrier to change. One could ask, "Do you really believe that you cannot educate all of your students to high levels of achievement? Does this mean that if you found out otherwise, you would try some new approaches and work with me and the team to assure all students' success?" If the answer to either of these questions is "no," the real hesitation may be something else mentioned below.

Options for addressing a true information gap include reading and sharing research and best practices. To this end, the Education Trust Fund has identified 2,770 schools that are high-ethnicity, high-poverty, and yet high-performing over time (1999, 2002). Countless other studies point out best practices and school successes in virtually any setting. (See the next chapter on maximizing research through collaboration.) You can also take a field trip to another school that succeeds or bring a speaker/practitioner from a school similar to your own. Most powerfully, discovering who within your own school succeeds with "low performers" opens up great possibilities for others to do the same.

2. The teachers may not feel personally competent to succeed with all students.

This will be harder to uncover than the first reason listed above. The idea here is that the student's failure is actually the teacher's failure once the teacher admits that all students *could* in fact succeed. The response to this becomes one of support, on one hand, and "creative tension" (Senge, 1990) on the other. The idea is to build a sense of self-efficacy among staff members by challenging them to do things they *can* do, while making inertia uncomfortable.

One principal in an urban high school explains:

> When I first got there it was bad—attendance, behavior, academics. . . . I decided we'd tackle them in that order, but that we would organize our efforts under one simple heading: "You Can Make a Difference."
> I worked to convince the faculty that they would succeed with these kids and that we had to convince the kids that they, too, could succeed. We began with attendance. Our message was "We want you in school." We called parents, sent them postcards about attendance, and had individual teachers follow up with each kid or parent after each absence. Attendance improved. The second year we started on behavior—just some basics about courtesy, language, some more consistency about how we handled discipline and so on. Now we're ready to start on achievement. (Evans, 1996, p. 214)

By collectively generating the motto "You Can Make a Difference" and providing definition with some clear and specific goals, this principal and his staff created an inherent tension, then addressed a means of resolving that tension through small steps and successes. These baby steps in turn built a sense of efficacy among the staff, which enabled them to take on more difficult tasks, which in turn led to enhanced student achievement.

Another way to build creative tension is to bring staff members into closer contact and affinity with the students whom they feel are unlikely to succeed. As affinity increases, it becomes more difficult to dismiss an individual's academic potential of the individual.

In her 12-year study of 120 organizations in 35 cities, Milbrey McLaughlin (Lewis, 2000) found that building relationships with young people as well as holding relation-building events that "allow youth and adults to see each other in new ways" were two of six guiding principles for success (p. 643). Creating opportunities for shared experiences in the form of social events, field trips, or experiential learning activities deepens the affinity and the communication among participants. Figure 6.1 below demonstrates the interaction among the elements.

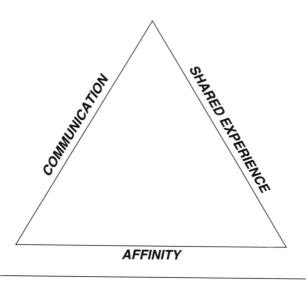

Figure 6.1

Any time one of the three sides of the triangle is enhanced, the other two sides are strengthened as well. This can also be applied to building support for students within the larger community. Having community members become mentors for students, for example, builds the communication, shared experience, and affinity for students and the school. Assigning students to research the history of community members has a similar effect while also providing an intellectual experience for the student.

This section presented a handful of ways to help educators overcome their fears of competency associated with committing to success for all students. The general principle is to provide both support and encouragement for the staff member while creating a cognitive dissonance or creative tension to spur movement.

3. Finally, it's not worth it!

Most veteran teachers have experienced disappointments at one time or another due to past waves of school reform. The idea of quickly embracing the next new reform seems foolish to some. Past failures may have been due to (1) a premature change of leadership; (2) lack of political, financial, or other capital necessary to ride out the storms involved with the change effort; or (3) a superficial attempt to get teachers to simply "buy in" when committed engagement is actually *required*. Whatever the past experience may have been, many teachers are understandably reluctant to jump into the waters of reform with both feet.

Understanding is required in such cases. It is also important to bring people's underlying assumptions to the surface so that they may be addressed: "Why do you feel this way? I'm interested in knowing what you have experienced in the past."

Shutting down people's inner concerns will lead only to increased outside conversations or gossip. It is better to hear legitimate concerns firsthand in order to deal directly with the situation, for example, "I see, you have been burned in the past and don't want to dive in again before you know this is 'for real.' That's understandable, and I accept and respect that. Moreover, I will make sure that your concerns are addressed, as you will see over time. However, in the meantime, I would like to ask a favor. Could you withhold any negative commentary or judgment of this initiative until you have watched it unfold for a while? Then if you have any suggestions, can you see me directly?"

Another increasingly common reason for the "Why bother?" mentality, especially among new personnel, is the time and effort involved. The idea of succeeding with every student may indeed seem overwhelming. The latter part of this chapter discusses relieving *individuals* of this task, and instead instituting a collaboratively created, system-wide approach. The following section is a necessary precursor to that approach.

WHAT IS THE SCHOOL COMMUNITY'S UNIFYING PHILOSOPHY?

One of the biggest challenges school leaders face is the tendency toward fragmentation of efforts and focus. Many demands are placed on educators, and those demands come from all directions. Often the demands from the state, district, parents, staff, unions, and students are at odds with one another. Good leaders, therefore, are called on to make organizational meaning out of apparent chaos. In this section, we provide a framework and philosophy for how the entire school community can deal with one of the most difficult challenges: student failure to meet high academic standards.

Traditionally, when a student did not comply with school policies, he or she was punished. If this punishment didn't work, the student was suspended or expelled. Whether or not the student succeeded academically or grew from the experience was not generally thought to be the school's concern.

Although there may be a place for this cut-and-dried approach to student "misbehavior," there have been many advances in the behavioral sciences. This new information has the power to lead us to different understandings of the complex *interactions* between students and teachers, students and the school environment, and students and their home. We now know that there is more that the school community can do to positively influence behaviors and the development of young people.

Most of the traditional approaches to dealing with student behavior were based on the Skinnerian philosophy of reward and punishment. But students are more complex than rats, and the fact that these traditional approaches often lead to more misbehavior attests to that complexity.

The traditional philosophy regarding student behavior has led to a mismatch between how some schools deal with students who don't comply and what those students actually need in order to improve their behaviors. The behaviors worsen in such cases. This leads to frustration on the part of many teachers and administrators as they sense that "what we are doing isn't working!" Without an alternative to traditional approaches, there is a tendency to see the inefficacy of the "treatment" as the fault of the "patient."

Banishment becomes a popular response to the problem. Some schools in which we work have literally hundreds of suspensions each year. The line to the principal's office looks like one for a rock concert! Labeling, then referring students to remedial programs, special education, and even alternative schools, seem to be the only answer for some beleaguered teachers. This has become so widespread that entire mini-industries, as well as billion-dollar pharmaceutical treatments, have sprung up to treat the latest "disorders" like ADHD. So many of these diagnoses for children happen to begin with the letter "D" that the Ten D's of Deviance were created to depict the label used and actions prescribed for each (Figure 6.2).

Perspective	Problem Label	Typical Responses
Primitive	Deviant	blame, attack, ostracize
Folk religion	Demonic	chastise, exorcise, banish
Biophysical	Diseased	diagnose, drug hospitalize
Psychoanalytical	Disturbed	analyze, treat, seclude
Behavioral	Disordered	assess, condition, time out
Correctional	Delinquent	adjudicate, punish, incarcerate
Sociological	Deprived	study, re-socialize, assimilate
Social Work	Dysfunctional	intake, case manage, discharge
Educational	Disobedient	reprimand, correct, expel
Special Education	Disabled	label, remediate, segregate

Figure 6.2   The Ten D's of Deviance in Approaches to "Difficult" Youth

Once there is a diagnosis for the disorder, the treatment becomes clear. Unfortunately, far less time has been spent creating diagnoses for young people's strengths.

A BETTER WAY

What we want to achieve in our work with young people is to find and strengthen the positive and healthy elements, no matter how deeply they are hidden.

—Karl Wilker (1920/1993, p. 69)

Over the past 100 years, a relatively small but growing number of leading child psychologists and youth professionals have developed a strengths-based approach to viewing and "treating" young people. They have been surprisingly consistent, in fact, in defining the basic needs that drive behavior (Figure 6.3).

The Community Circle of Caring synthesizes this body of research to provide a common framework and core philosophy (Figure 6.4) of action (Blankstein, DuFour, and Little, 1997).

THE BASIC NEEDS THAT DRIVE BEHAVIOR

Source	Basic Needs
William Glasser, M.D. *Control Theory in the Classroom* (1986)	1. Survival and reproduction 2. Belonging and love 3. Power 4. Freedom 5. Fun
Stanley Coopersmith *The Antecedents of Self-Esteem* (1967)	1. Significance to others 2. Competence 3. Power to control one's own behavior and gain respect 4. Virtue of worthiness in the eyes of others
Martin Brokenleg *Circle of Courage* (1990) Based on Sioux tradition	1. Belonging 2. Mastery 3. Independence 4. Generosity
Boys and Girls Clubs of America *Youth Development Strategy*	1. Belonging 2. Usefulness 3. Competence 4. Influence
Allen N. Medler *What Do I Do When . . . ?* (1992)	1. Success and being capable 2. Acceptance, belonging 3. Influence over people, events 4. Generosity and helping others 5. Stimulation and fun

Figure 6.3

COMMUNITY CIRCLE OF CARING

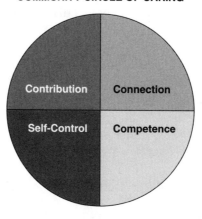

Figure 6.4

Young people will naturally attempt to meet each of these four basic needs in either a prosocial or antisocial manner. One of the gangs we studied, the Latin Kings, uses a very similar framework, for example, to recruit and retain youth whose needs for connection are not being met prosocially. Young people whose need for competence is not being met in a positive manner may turn to auto theft, for example, to gain a sense of competence. The ultimate goal of the school, then, becomes one of creating an environment and culture that meets students' basic needs. Figure 6.5 shows examples of practices in such an environment, as well as contrary practices.

The four C's of the Community Circle of Caring provide a framework for rethinking and coordinating the actions of the entire school community. Once the beliefs and philosophy are agreed upon, it is far easier to create a unifying system for action. The next section gives very specific examples of how two schools have done just that, as well as guidelines and steps to proceed on your own.

What Is the Comprehensive System for Assuring Success?

Ensuring achievement for *all* students means having an overarching strategy that encompasses the majority of learners—and then having specific strategies aimed at those who need extra support. Essential components of a plan for all students' success include:

- Having an improvement plan for all students
- Having systems for quickly identifying those in need
- Providing a continuum of support and targeted strategies for low-achievers
- Publishing results on closing the achievement gap

The following sections will discuss each of these components in detail. In addition, this section provides examples of intervention systems from two very different schools.

Having an Improvement Plan for All Students

The most effective schools provide a ladder of opportunities for struggling students, ranging from identification of students needing

Connection	*Disconnection*
Welcoming students even when they are late	Sending students to the principal's office, regardless of circumstances of late arrival
Greeting students warmly at classroom door	Working on paper at desk until all students are seated & the start bell rings
Systematically assuring every student is positively connected to an adult	Leaving personal connections to chance
Using extra-curricular engagement data of *all* students as a measure of school success	Assuming most students are involved in extra-curricular activities

Developing Competence	*Building Incompetence*
Allowing make up work	Having "One chance" policies
Demanding mastery of material	Averaging zeros into semester grades
Testing what is taught	"Surprise" tests and pop quizzes
Finding and emphasizing strengths	Focusing on weaknesses

Self-Control	*Compliance and Obedience*
Allowing students to help create class rules	Telling students what the rules are
Eliciting input on class projects and readings	Recycling prior year's projects
Teaching empathy, self-awareness, and other emotional intelligences	Keeping emotional learning apart from academics

Contribution	*Self-Centeredness*
Allowing older students to teach younger ones	No student-led mentoring
Creating Community service and learning opportunities	Holding learning within the school
Encouraging cooperative learning	Teacher directs all learning

Figure 6.5   Practices That Promote Connection vs. Disconnection

extra support before the school year begins to mandatory enrollment in remedial and/or skills classes. The effect of this range of interventions is to make clear to students that they may *not* fail. It tells students that the only choice is to learn and succeed.

An effective improvement plan for all students includes components of both prevention and intervention. Some prevention strategies are targeted; others apply to the entire student population. The latter include:

- Building relationships with students
- Systematically identifying and building on students' strengths
- Meeting with students each day
- Having staff be visible and available
- Involving students in the decision-making process (*Failure Is Not an Option Video Series*, 2002)

Intervention strategies target students who are not demonstrating learning at the level of expected performance. To be most effective, these strategies are graduated in their intensity. These types of graduated prevention and intervention systems take a pyramidal form; the prevention strategies at the bottom apply to all students, and the high-intensity interventions at the top apply to only a few. You will learn about two of these exemplary "pyramid of interventions" (Noer, 1993) systems: one from Adlai Stevenson High School, which is located in a wealthy suburb, and the other from a poor urban district in East Hartford, Connecticut. They are in the "What Good Looks Like" section of this chapter.

Intervention Strategies

One of the most successful interventions at D.R. Hill Middle School, in Duncan, South Carolina, has been its SOAR Reading Program. SOAR takes students who do not qualify for special education resources, and yet still struggle with reading, and helps them improve their reading skills through four strategies: (1) summarizing, (2) predicting, (3) questioning, and (4) clarifying. Each SOAR class lasts one semester and has a ratio of seven students to one teacher. Since its inception, the program has resulted in tremendous gains, with students generally improving their reading by three grade levels from pre- to posttest.

HAVING SYSTEMS FOR QUICKLY IDENTIFYING STUDENTS IN NEED

Effective schools do not follow the "sink or swim" approach. Nor do they wade in to rescue students only when they have proven that they can't swim. Schools that are committed to success for all students systematically identify struggling students. They identify problems as early as possible—well before students have a chance to fail. The timely identification of problems is what distinguishes intervention strategies from remediation strategies.

When prevention systems are already in place for all students, it becomes easy to identify those who are at risk for academic difficulties. Mechanisms for identifying struggling students should ideally be built on the programs already in place for supporting *all* students. For example, a high school that monitors *all* incoming freshmen by having staff members submit frequent progress reports automatically has a "net" in place for "catching" struggling students.

Identifying Students in Need

At Pelham Road Elementary, in Greenville, South Carolina, a special kindergarten class comes under the umbrella of the school's Special Education department. The children in the class are completely unaware that they are in a special program. The object of the class is to give children who have been identified as lacking necessary social or academic skills the boost they need before starting first grade *without* saddling them with the "special ed" label. The school chooses these students based on interviews with Head Start participants and places the identified students in a smaller-than-average class. The program's goal is to prepare participants for immediate mainstreaming into first-grade classrooms. In the great majority of cases, the program accomplishes that goal.

Think It Through . . .

How does your school identify students who need additional support? How early in those students' academic careers does such identification and intervention take place?

Providing a Continuum of Support and Targeted Strategies for Low-Achievers

Students who are moving from one level of schooling to another—from elementary to middle school or from middle school into high school—need a continuum of support that sees them smoothly through the transition. Schools provide the resources necessary to ensure that new students can "hit the ground running."

Schools use various mechanisms to facilitate a seamless transition for incoming students. One is collaboration between counselors in the feeder schools and in the receiving school. This allows counselors at the receiving school to become familiar with new students' needs and with what approaches have been successful at meeting those needs in the past.

Continuum of Support

A primary goal in developing a system of prevention and intervention is to catch struggling students as early as possible in their academic careers. In the Newport News Public Schools (Newport News, Virginia), this means catching them even *before* they get into the school system. The district uses all of its federal Title I money to fund a preschool intervention program called First Step.

"The biggest problem we were having was that kids coming into kindergarten were having a two- to three-year discrepancy in their levels of skills and readiness, based on their range of previous learning experiences," explains Harvey Perkins, the district's assistant superintendent.

The district now attempts to close this gap by enrolling eligible 4-year-olds in First Step. Eligibility is determined by a preschool screening, which is open to all families. The program accommodates 1,300 students—which is especially significant given that there are only 2,000 students in the district's kindergarten enrollment.

Other projects and programs include:

- Programs to prepare for the next school level, e.g., "Survival Skills for High School"
- Reviews of student records before school starts in order to provide extra supports for children in need
- Faculty mentor programs, in which every incoming student is closely monitored by an adult who gets to know him or her well

Once high-performing schools have identified those students who are at risk of failure, they find ways to bolster their weak areas to ensure success. The types of strategies used vary depending on the grade levels served by the school and the needs of the students.

Think It Through . . .

What systems are in place in your school for providing incoming students with a continuum of support?

PUBLISHING RESULTS

Making the achievement gaps an agenda item and publishing them for the stakeholder community to review adds focus to the staff's efforts. The schools in San Diego, California, used this strategy to help close their achievement gap.

What Good Looks Like

Effective systems of prevention and intervention ensure that no student slips through the cracks. They are designed so that the majority of students benefit from careful, continuous monitoring and low-level support strategies. They have mechanisms in place to ensure the early identification of struggling students. And they follow a prescribed order, so that higher-level strategies are implemented only after lower-level ones have failed to produce results.

Case Study: Pyramid of Interventions in a Wealthy Suburban High School

One highly developed example of such a system is Adlai Stevenson High School's "pyramid of interventions" (Noer, 1993). The pyramid has several levels, beginning with intensive monitoring of all incoming ninth-graders and ending with mandatory remediation for those who fail despite intermediate intervention (Figure 6.6).

Intensive Intervention—
> 9. Student Support Groups
> 8. Mentor Program w/Parent
>   Support Group

Targeted Intervention—
> 7. Guided Study Hall
> 6. Mandatory Tutoring

System-wide Intervention—
> 5. Progress Reports After 3 Weeks
> 4. Faculty Advisor & Upper classmen

Targeted Early Prevention & Strategies—
> 3. Good Friend Program
> 2. Summer Classes
> 1. Counselor Watch

Figure 6.6

Source: DuFour, *Failure Is Not an Option* video series, 2002

1. *Counselor Watch.* Counselors begin by meeting each spring with teachers and counselors at the feeder schools to identify incoming students who will require special support. Those students are "red flagged" and assigned to the counselor watch program.

2. *Summer Classes.* These same students are also invited to attend a preparation program held during the Stevenson summer

session, in which they are taught such success skills as time management, note taking, and reading in the content areas.

3. *Good Friend Program.* When school starts in the fall, students meet with their counselors weekly. Students needing extra support are also assigned a "good friend." The good friend is a teacher who sees that student daily in class and takes a few extra moments to get to know the student better and encourage him or her to open up about any problems. This program runs "behind the scenes"; the students themselves never realize that it exists or that they have a designated "good friend."

4. *Faculty Advisor and Upper-Class Mentoring.* Every ninth-grader is assigned to a faculty advisor, who meets with the students in groups of 25 four days a week for 25 minutes. The advisor is assisted by five older student mentors, who serve as "big brothers and sisters," helping the new students to transition smoothly. These student mentors are responsible for explaining school rules to the newcomers, encouraging them to join extra-curricular activities, answering questions, discussing common problems, and even helping with homework when students face difficulties.

Each ninth-grader is also assigneed to a counselor, who comes into the advisory group once a week. Although the counselor will meet less frequently with the students, he or she is expected to know each of them by name within the first two to three weeks of school.

5. *Progress Reports After Three Weeks.* The school issues progress reports on its freshmen three weeks into the school year. Teachers quickly consult with students who do poorly, along with the faculty advisor, the counselor, and the student mentor. Each of them encourages the student to work harder, to get extra help, or to attend voluntary tutoring. For example, if, at the three-week report, a ninth-grader were in danger of failing mathematics, his or her math teacher would point out the problem and ask that student to begin attending voluntary sessions at the math-tutoring center.

When the student attended the advisory, his or her advisor would also have a copy of the progress report. The advisor would again discuss the math problem, ask the student what he or she planned to do about it, and suggest spending some time each day reviewing math homework with an upper-class mentor. The student's counselor would also have a copy of the progress report and would schedule an individual meeting. Finally, parents receive the progress report, too, and will likely ask their children about the situation.

The outcome of this "quadruple teaming" is that most ninth-graders realize quickly that they will not be allowed to slide. The typical student recognizes that it will be easier simply to do the work.

6. *Mandatory Tutoring.* If a student continues to do poorly despite the help of staff and student mentors, the school may require the student to attend daily mandatory tutoring during study hall. Students in the mandatory tutoring program are monitored continuously and receive weekly progress reports.

7. *Guided Study Hall.* If students fail to make sufficient progress in the mandatory tutoring program, they will be taken out of the regular study hall—which has approximately 80 students—and put into a guided study hall, with no more than eight students. Students are required to spend 90 minutes a day in the guided study hall, under the close oversight of an adult supervisor who serves as a liaison with their teachers and oversees completion of assigned work. This liaison—typically a parent volunteer—talks with each student's teachers and therefore already knows the exact status of his or her assignments.

If a student claims that he or she has no work to do on a given day, the liaison will know if this is accurate. If not, the liaison will point out the assignments still to be completed. If the student says he or she has left a book at home, the supervisor produces a book from a stock of extras kept on hand in the classroom. Essentially, the supervisor "hovers" over the student, *insisting* that assignments be completed. For 95% of students, this level of intervention effectively addresses their academic problems.

8. *Mentor Program with Parent Support Group.* The very few students who fail to benefit from previous interventions

enroll in a program in which they receive extensive tutoring, close supervision of their work, and study skills practice. They spend two hours a day in this program. The big difference in this intervention is the mentor parents' support group that parents must attend. Designated parents attend monthly meetings designed to teach them how they can encourage their children's progress.

9. *Student Support Groups.* Students whose persistent low academic achievement is grounded in nonacademic problems such as substance abuse, family breakdown, or social problems are offered a support group in which they meet with students having similar problems and share ways to overcome them.

Case Story #2: Building a "Pyramid of Interventions" (Noer, 1993)

Steven Edwards, award-winning principal, East Hartford High School, East Hartford, Connecticut

The pyramid of interventions shown below is based on a foundation that addresses the needs of a broad population of students. Generally, the number of students decreases as one moves up the pyramid, and the interventions become tailored to meet the needs of a more focused population. The pyramid of interventions was the result of an intensive planning process. The process, as well as each element of the pyramid, will be explained in detail.

In developing a pyramid of interventions, a number of core components make up the planning process. *Ultimately, these results enabled our continuous student improvement.* They include:

- Identifying the problem
- Collecting relevant data
- Analyzing the data
- Implementing a plan
- Regularly reviewing and evaluating the intervention

Data Collection and Analysis

The importance of data collection and analysis cannot be overstated. It was essential that we accurately portray issues relating to low student performance to ensure that the root causes of the problem were clearly identified. Without accurate data collection and analysis, people tend to rely on their perceptions alone. But perception lacks a concrete foundation and is often based on opinion, with little or no data to support the conclusions.

When collecting and examining data, it was important to keep in mind the following points. Data had to be:

- Quantitative and qualitative
- Collected from multiple sources
- Relevant
- Timely
- Consistent over time
- Collected by users
- Disaggregated

(See Chapter 8 for more detail on the use of data.)

First Things First

After our school established clearly defined mission and vision statements, the next step was to set up a mission/vision oversight committee. The committee served as a check and balance system to ensure that decisions regarding direction of the school are consistent with our school's mission and vision. The makeup of this committee reflected a diverse set of stakeholders, including faculty and staff, parents, students, and community representatives. (The building principal should serve as a member of the committee, but not as the chair.) Membership on this committee was voluntary, through nominations by peers.

After establishing the oversight committee, we collected and analyzed data to be shared later with the entire school community. This allowed a greater number of school members to be engaged in the school improvement process.

Building in time for such planning to take place was an important issue. The initial stages of the planning process were accomplished off school grounds, where there are fewer interruptions and distractions. We worked during four Saturday mornings over a two-month period, from eight to noon each Saturday.

As principal, I emphasized to participants that this is a process; if the school attempts to shortcut the process, the results will be compromised. I also used an outside facilitator to oversee the planning sessions, to allow committee members to communicate openly with one another, and to develop the leadership ability of group members. Finally, using an outside facilitator helped ensure that the changes and decisions made were not viewed as the decision of only one person, the building administrator. As the group proceeded through the process, we kept nonparticipants thoroughly informed of our deliberations. We saturated the school community with information, and I emphasized that high-quality results take time and that quick fixes don't work.

First Meeting

After providing a brief explanation of our purpose, I turned the meeting over to the facilitator. Key elements of the first meeting were reviewing the data and determining the context in which they would be examined. Data typically fall into four areas that affect student achievement:

- Academics and standards
- School climate and student behavior
- Facilities/equipment/technology
- Community support/interactions

We then divided the planning team into four groups, one for each of the four categories identified above. Each group selected a team leader—a member of the staff to be trained by the facilitator. Once the group logistics were arranged, the facilitator focused on possible planning models. We used the Social

Reconnaissance Model, which focuses on the following elements of the planning process:

- Problem identification
- Prioritizing problems
- Barriers to addressing problems
- Solutions to identified problems
- Identification of resources

We analyzed the data, identified problems, and then voted on the top five problems in each category. After counting the votes, we selected the top two problems in each area for further investigation, i.e., with four groups, there were eight problems to be addressed. Although we uncovered many problem areas, it was essential to focus only on the top two in each category; when a school attempts to address too many issues at one time, usually nothing gets done. Figure 6.7 (see below) highlights the process thus far.

The role of the mission/vision oversight committee is to oversee the four teams, each of which focused on one specific area of student achievement. These teams brainstormed and developed solutions for the two identified problems in each area (represented by P-1 and P-2 in Figure 6.7), which then served as the basis for our pyramid of interventions (See Appendix H for a complete description of Figure 6.7.)

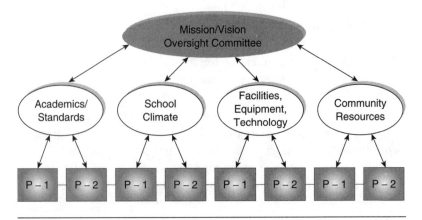

Figure 6.7

IMPLEMENTATION GUIDELINES

Developing a system of prevention and intervention is a major task. The approach you take will depend on both the culture of your school or district and the extent to which such strategies are already in place. Consider this approach as an example:

1. Get verbal commitment from faculty members and define "success."

   Schools that have undertaken the development of mission, vision, values, and goals have already gone a long way toward accomplishing this first step. In order for a system of prevention and intervention to work, every member of the school must accept responsibility and commit to ensuring that all students learn. Part of that commitment is a continual assessment so that students who are not learning can be helped immediately.

2. Provide examples of exemplary programs.

   Share with the staff successful programs that have been implemented at other schools (including those in this book from Adlai Stevenson and Hartford, Connecticut). Ask them to thoughtfully review these examples, with an eye toward how they could be adapted for use in your own school.

Developing a Plan

One school district, in Pixley, California, used Adlai Stevenson's "Pyramid of Interventions" (ibid.) as a jumping-off point for developing its own student improvement plan. The district used the following process.

1. Participants were introduced to the "Pyramid of Interventions."

2. Participants formed small groups and began to evaluate how existing strategies could be organized in such a pyramid, so that the broadest level of strategies captured the largest number of students.

3. Using color coding, participants identified some current strategies that were philosophically sound and didn't need

to change, strategies currently in place that needed to be changed to better fit the pyramid structure, and strategies that would have to be added to make the pyramid complete.

Note: A worksheet for this process is included in Appendix F.

3. Jointly develop a plan of action to be used when students don't learn.
Ask the staff to begin detailing a system of interventions. Aspects of the system that will need to be addressed include:

- Optional support opportunities for identified underachievers, e.g., tutoring, mentoring, intensive or review classes in core academic areas, and support groups
- Mandatory interventions for persistent low-achievers, e.g., required study hall or tutoring sessions
- High-level interventions for students who do not improve in lower-key programs, e.g., counseling/mentoring sessions with parents, support groups led by counselors, and daily check-ins with advisors

Be sure that your staff uses any existing programs as a starting point. Ask them to consider which existing programs need to be eliminated, modified, or retained in order to fit into the newly developed system.

4. Agree on criteria for identifying students in need of assistance and ensuring they enter the appropriate programs.
The referral of any student to a prevention or intervention program should be dependent on data that provide good evidence of his or her strengths, weaknesses, and root causes of learning difficulties. (Guidelines for the use of data are in Chapter 8.) In addition, make decisions in advance regarding what will be used as criteria for inclusion in each support program. Questions to ask include:

- What criteria, data, or information will be used to identify students who are eligible for each intervention program?
- Who will help provide the information?
- Who will be responsible for gathering and evaluating the data?

5. Surface objections and address resistance.
   Techniques for doing so are covered in detail in Chapter 2 and earlier in this chapter.

6. Pilot aspects of the new program.
   Start slowly, and implement just one easily implemented aspect of the pyramid. This will allow more complete monitoring of the effectiveness of the programs, allow schools to work out any kinks, and allow for an early success to motivate further reform.

7. Build a culture of success.
   As soon as any strategy is implemented, a system for regularly monitoring its effectiveness should be established. As data come in that indicate a positive outcome, celebrate your success. In addition, be alert to any positive actions by staff or students that lead to better performance and an improved school climate. Be sure to acknowledge and praise these efforts publicly. Such public celebrations and "pats on the back" help to build a culture that believes in, values, and expects success.

8. Refine and add to interventions.
   As you receive data on the results of your programs, use the information to refine existing strategies and to better develop new ones. Continue to phase in more intervention programs and strategies, as outcome and disciplinary data suggest a need.

GETTING STARTED

Work with your colleagues to sketch plans or procedures on separate sheets of paper for: (1) identifying students in need of extra support and attention; (2) monitoring these students intensively; (3) providing mentors, "good friends," or other adult support to these students; and (4) establishing intervention programs. List programs that already exist; note whether they need to be modified or expanded and, if so, in what ways. For new programs, state the specific goal and then address questions that arise.

See Appendix G for more specific guiding questions for getting started.

In this chapter, you have seen best practices in meeting the great challenge of providing for students who *don't* initially learn to standards. This has included gaining staff commitment to the task, developing a unifying philosophy, and creating systems of prevention and intervention. These are among the greatest challenges a school will face. How schools respond to the question "What do we do when students *don't* learn?" tells more about the values and collective commitment of that school than anything else. Although this chapter has provided a clear picture of, and direction for, how high-performing schools tackle this challenge, the subsequent chapters will help you develop the *capacity* to use these practices to address success for *all* students in your school.

CHAPTER SEVEN

Principle #3—Collaborative Teaming Focused on Teaching and Learning

I wonder how many children's lives might be saved if we educators disclosed what we know to each other.

—Roland Barth (2001, p. 60)

We had a group of teachers that didn't do very well. But we didn't share our ideas and we didn't share how we brought about the changes in our own classrooms. We just went in our classrooms and closed the doors. But we found out that's not the way to go. We found out that when teachers share with one another—if there's something you can't do that someone else is really good at doing, you can get them to help you. And if someone can't do something that you're great at, you can help him or her. In the end, the entire staff performs better

—Winifred Brown (2002)

Central to the success of high-achieving schools is a collaborative culture focused on teaching and learning (Barth, 2001; Driscoll, 1998; Fullan and Hargreaves, 1996; Hipp, 2003; Hord, 1997a and b; Kruse, Louis, & Bryk, 1994; Newmann and Wehlage, 1995). This

127

culture supports regular meetings of teachers who share responsibility for assessing needs and developing solutions that address all students' learning. DuFour and Eaker (1998) note that any school that hopes to function as a professional learning community must tackle the task of reshaping the school's culture. They write, "Unless collective inquiry, collaborative teams, an orientation toward action, and a focus on results become part of 'the way we do things around here,' the effort to create a professional learning community is likely to fail."

FOUR TYPES OF COLLABORATIVE CULTURES

According to Fullan and Hargreaves (1996), when it comes to collaboration, there are four main types of school cultures.

1. *Individualistic.* In this type of learning environment, teachers are accustomed to developing their own practices and techniques for classroom management and may not consider the relevant experience of colleagues. In fact, in traditional school cultures, teachers often regard the intrusion of other adults into their classrooms as an invasion of privacy. In these cultures, one might hear, "Why do I have to collaborate? I'm a good teacher, and my students are doing fine!"

2. *Balkanized.* This culture is characterized by the presence of deep-rooted cliques within the staff. In a balkanized school environment, small groups of people align themselves with a particular technique or ideology, pitting themselves against other groups that hold opposing ideas.

Inside a Balkanized Culture

In balkanized cultures, team members often spend their time taking sides and vying to achieve dominance, as in the following example.

Mr. Jones: Yesterday in my mailbox I received the final state scores. Looking at them, it's easy to see which members of our team accomplished certain skills and which kids are lacking in certain areas. As a team we should start talking about how to use these scores.

Ms. Rodriguez:	Well, I was thinking of not necessarily putting students in small groups, because there's not enough time to do that in one class period. They need to be divided according to their ability and placed in a classroom with all similar abilities.
Mr. Hamilton:	I agree—I think we should put them in separate classes.
Mr. Jones:	Sounds like tracking to me.
Ms. Rodriguez:	I don't think that's tracking, because they can always go into other classes depending on their level in that subject. We're not talking about every subject—we're only talking about instances in which students are struggling.
Mr. Hamilton:	I agree. I think we should put them in different classrooms.
Mr. Jones:	Sounds like another name for tracking to me.

Teachers may be intensely loyal to the members of their cliques and hold strongly to their ideologies, but they may have little loyalty for the school as a whole. The problem of exclusive cliques is particularly difficult to address because they can be deeply rooted in opposition to one another.

3. *Contrived Collegiality.* In this culture, teachers appear to be collaborating. They may spend time on committees and in meetings, but they actually don't focus on deeper issues related to teaching and learning. In these cases, the structure of the school may have changed (i.e., meetings now occur), yet the deeper culture has not changed. In this instance, teachers collaborate only on the surface without challenging their beliefs or approaches to teaching and learning. In this culture, one might hear: "How was your weekend?" or "Ronnie has presented some behavioral challenges for me. How about you?" or "Overall, test scores in my class are pretty good. How about yours?"

4. *Collaborative.* In a collaborative school culture, teams of highly skilled individuals comprise a teaching staff. Each of these individuals is fully committed to helping students learn by becoming active learners themselves. They work continuously with their colleagues to improve their teaching strategies and better manage their classrooms. They recognize their crucial role in the educational process and know that they can meet the challenges confronting them only by solving problems in concert with their professional colleagues. Teachers in a collaborative culture make specific analyses of the data to discover ways of improving teaching and learning. For example, one might hear: "I noticed your students are scoring higher on problems that test for reading comprehension. Can I watch you teach a class?"

Schools with a successful culture of collaboration are aware that not all collaboration is necessarily good. Collaboration must take place with the overall goals of the school in mind. The type of collaboration these schools foster is an open-ended inquiry that incorporates new ideas from both inside and outside the team. The team itself becomes a mini–learning community, actively seeking best practices from other members, as well as other schools and literature on best practice. Decisions are made using an approach similar to the one outlined in Figure 1.1.

THE AIM OF COLLABORATION

Collaboration among colleagues is a means to an end: enhancing teaching and learning. To accomplish this, team members work *interdependently* toward a common goal (see SMART goals in Chapter 5). This goal, in turn, supports the larger school vision and is aligned with the school's vision and values. As a result, the school's mission, vision, values, and goals provide context and direction for all team members.

Teams will invariably look at data to assess how they are doing relative to their SMART goals. Members collectively brainstorm ways to improve and celebrate successes. Being committed to constant improvement, these teams will always find ways to "raise the bar" once their current goals are accomplished.

Areas of Collaboration

In setting up collaborative teams, it is important to choose the appropriate members. Team members should share common students or common problems, and the issues they deal with should be of concern to all members. Following are some areas that may lend themselves to collaboration.

- *Professional practice forums:* Teachers who work with similar grade levels, or who teach related areas, should work together. They present colleagues with accounts of strategies that work for them, share concerns, describe challenges, research best practices, and plan new strategies.
- *Classroom observation:* Teachers observe classes of colleagues who are experimenting with new strategies or techniques. Through observation, they learn about new strategies and can help evaluate how well the innovation is working. Similarly, teachers can regularly observe classes of teachers having specific problems to provide constructive suggestions and support.

District-Wide Teaming

Teachers in the public schools of Newport News, Virginia, have been teaming for more than a dozen years. But now the school district wants to take collaboration to a new level. "We're interested in doing district-level reform," explains Assistant Superintendent Harvey Perkins. "We believe there are lots of opportunities for collaboration outside the building level."

The district is taking high-performing faculty members and teaming them with less successful schools, so they can share successful strategies from one school to another. For example, if a third-grade team in one school is having trouble, they might observe a successful meeting with their counterparts in their partner school. Principals could also collaborate, says Harvey, to define areas for further collaboration.

- *Curriculum planning.* Relevant groups or committees frequently meet to plan and monitor curriculum sequence and coordination. They may determine who teaches what, what content they teach, what skills they teach, which students they teach, and in what order. They synchronize knowledge and skills that students should have acquired at specific times and when they are supposed to have acquired them. They may also determine which assessments to use in order to gauge whether all students have successfully mastered core knowledge and skills in each academic area.

- *Professional study groups.* Teachers research and report to colleagues on articles and books containing matters of professional interest, or they share the information gained at workshops or conferences. They may occasionally invite speakers or guests from outside the school with expertise on matters of interest to them.

- *Grade-level or subject-area teams.* These teams can identify curricular outcomes, determine methods of assessing student progress, select instructional materials, plan and present professional development programs in support of team-identified issues, and participate in observation and monitoring programs for mutual support.

- *Interdisciplinary teams.* Such teams deal with the same groups of students (e.g., all teachers of ninth-graders) to focus on the curriculum and the needs of students.

- *Task forces.* These teams are drawn from all areas of the school to study and develop recommendations for dealing with a specific problem affecting the entire building, such as the best way to handle tardy students. Task forces dissolve when their task is completed.

- *Teaching strategy or professional interest teams.* Staff members who are interested in a specific approach or innovation (e.g., cooperative learning) form groups to research the approach; receive training; develop implementation strategies; and provide reciprocal observation, review, and evaluation. As with task forces, these teams are relatively short-lived.

Think It Through . . .

How frequently and in what ways do staff members in your school work together to solve problems or plan improvements?

What Good Looks Like

Schools where collaboration is the norm share some very distinct characteristics. They include the following:

- The staff is committed to a shared mission, vision, values, and goals, and recognizes its responsibility to work together to accomplish them.
- Strong leaders engage teachers in meaningful collaboration and support their activities and decisions.
- The school is characterized by a culture of trust and respect that permits open and willing sharing of ideas and respect for different approaches and teaching styles.
- The staff has real authority to make decisions about teaching and learning.
- Meetings are well managed and truly democratic, following established protocols for setting the agenda and making decisions.
- The functioning of teams is frequently discussed and reassessed.
- A plan is developed to provide meaningful time for teams to meet. (See Chapter 2 for strategies on making time to collaborate.)
- Each team has clear purposes and goals.
- Educators acquire and share training in effective teamwork strategies.

What Real Teaming Looks Like

At the seventh-grade teachers' weekly meeting, one of the science teachers proposes a problem with science and social studies teachers. She explains that although science and social studies are tested on the state tests this year, the class schedule allows much less time for those subjects than for math and language arts. She presents her concern with getting her students ready for the tests, given the limited teaching time.

The team leader acknowledges the legitimacy of the problem and opens the floor for other teachers to propose solutions. Soon, a collaborative strategy is formed:

Language Arts Teacher 1:	I realize that you have a lot of reading material in Science and Social Studies that is difficult. And Mr. Evans and I would be glad to take some of that material and use it for our self-selected reading periods.
Language Arts Teacher 2:	And maybe if you could get us information about what you were going to do during the following week, Ms. Shaw and I could collaborate to make sure that the questions we propose are similar to the kinds of questions asked on the state test. That way, you're not only reinforcing your Science and Social Studies skills, but also working on how to answer the questions.
Math Teacher:	Regarding the mathematics aspect, Mrs. Atterman and I could help to teach measuring skills. I know that in science one does a lot of measuring—and I know from my student teaching experience last year that a lot of students really need help with that. Also, if you had a set of data, we could use graphing calculators—especially with the gifted class—and let them do a presentation on that data.
Science Teacher:	Okay . . . well, let's sit down and bounce these ideas off some other people in our department and see what we can come up with in the way of a schedule. We'll also want to determine what a "success" will look like in terms of student learning and how we'll know if this effort *is* successful. Let's get input on these questions and discuss this again next Friday.

The preceding scenario shows one aspect of true teaming. The teachers jointly accept responsibility for student learning—*across* subjects, not just in their own classrooms—and work together to overcome an obstacle. They also commit to defining "success" before trying this new approach and assessing their efforts toward that success.

Think It Through . . .

How would you describe collaboration among staff members in your school? Do you work together for a common aim like the teachers in the example above, or is it "every man for himself"? Are instruction and student learning the focus of your meetings?

Implementation Guidelines

> What you want to do is put teachers together, give them a common area of difficulty students are currently facing, and ask them as a team to first dredge up the best strategies they can think of with respect to that area of difficulty. Then to choose the best strategy that's going to have the best result on the greatest number of kids. Then talk about how you're going to beat out a lesson plan or strategy that's going to get the results you want.
>
> —Mike Schmoker (quoted in
> HOPE Foundation, *FNO Video Series*, 2002)

After forming teams to work on different aspects of teaching and learning in your school, teams will establish protocols. Ideally, decisions should be written down and signed by each team member. Some of the questions may appear to impose an unnatural formality on friends and colleagues who have long worked casually together, but deciding these issues in advance will help to avoid future problems. *(Note: See the implementation guidelines in Chapter 5 and Appendix D before proceeding. This section assumes an understanding of the material presented there.)*

1. *Team Organization.*
   - What should the team organization be?
   - Will there be a chair? If so, who? What responsibilities will he or she have?
   - If there is no chair, how will operational decisions be made? Consider such details as time and place of successive

meetings, responsibility for minutes or other team records, and so on.

- Who will be responsible for acting as spokesperson for the team?

2. *Decision Making.*
   - Will the team's decisions be made by democratic vote? By consensus? How will conflicts be resolved?
   - What commitment can be made to team members who may end up on the losing side of a debate or in a minority position?

3. *Managing Meetings.*
   - How will discussions and debates be managed or led?
   - In what way can the team ensure that each member will have a turn to speak, but that no one will be permitted to dominate or divert the members from the task at hand?

4. *Sharing the Workload.*
   - How can the team ensure that all members will share the workload equally, so that no member is overburdened in comparison to the rest?

5. *Commitment of Team Members.*
   - Develop an agreement (preferably written, but at least a clearly articulated verbal statement) in which each member commits to: (1) attending all team meetings, (2) working toward consensus on each matter of difference, (3) speaking openly and candidly with each other while respecting different opinions, (4) ensuring that each team member's input and views are sought and heard, and (5) supporting the team's decisions when a consensus is reached.

6. *Communication Protocols.*
   - As team members work on different tasks, how should they alert other members of problems, situations, events, results, or other matters?
   - If a developing problem requires discussion by the entire team, what is the protocol for calling a meeting?
   - Who will be responsible for keeping and disseminating minutes of each meeting, copies of information gathered, reports of task forces, survey or focus group results, worksheets and planning forms completed jointly, and any other

pertinent documents? These are the basis for the team's communications with the rest of the learning community, and they must be accurately maintained.

7. *Monitoring Team Progress.*
   - At what point and in what way will you, as a team, evaluate your effectiveness in carrying out your mandate?
   - What steps will you contemplate if it appears you are not working very effectively?

When the previous issues are settled, begin to address your assigned task:

1. *Establish goals.*
   - Articulate short-term or intermediate goals within the larger purpose assigned to you.

2. *Prioritize and assign tasks.*
   - Decide whether you will work on the short-term goals in sequence or simultaneously.
   - If the latter, who will work on each?

3. *Decide on sequence and timetable of tasks.*
   - What are the first steps to take toward achieving the first goal(s)?
   - What is the timeline for taking these steps?
   - How soon should the team (or a subgroup of the team) meet again to discuss progress, findings, or results?
   - What task will each member complete before the next meeting?

Challenges

Collaboration is not natural or common in the traditional school environment. For generations, teachers characteristically closed the classroom door behind them and acted as independent monarchs of their own domains, expecting neither oversight nor support from colleagues. One principal, Steve Edwards, commented that one of his teachers went into the classroom and didn't come out for 38 years. Teachers with problems may frequently feel ashamed to ask for help, believing that their plea will be interpreted as confusion or a confession of failure. Such feelings and the traditional school culture have given rise to several identified challenges to collaboration.

Phasing in Collaboration

When Linda Jonaitis, former principal of Clifford Pierce Middle School, moved to Highland High School, in Highland, Indiana, she knew she would be starting all over again in terms of collaborative teaming. While the teachers at her former school had become comfortable with constant collaboration, it was still a new concept to those at Highland. "They didn't know how to do it, and they didn't feel safe or comfortable," she said. "They still felt territorial."

Linda realized that she would have to move slowly and carefully, in order to avoid "scaring" off her new staff. Her solution was to seek out those teachers who were most likely to try something new and draw them into teaming first. "I identified teachers who felt safe, who appeared as though they might be willing to take risks. I did that by talking with people in the district and by forming relationships with the teachers either through committee work or one on one," she explains. "I'm working with them first, and then will use them as role models to encourage risk-taking and build that climate of safety."

Building truly collaborative teams is a difficult but necessary component of school success. This chapter illuminated four types of cultures relative to collaboration. Brief examples of productive collaboration in schools throughout North America were also provided.

The next chapter addresses gathering and using the essential fuel for productive collaboration: meaningful data tied to results for *all* students. Chapter 8 will go into detail on how to collect, analyze, discuss, and put such data into action on behalf of student achievement.

CHAPTER EIGHT
_____

Principle #4—Using Data to Guide Decision Making and Continuous Improvement

> The most obvious impediment to a results orientation is the failure at the beginning of the year, or as early in the year as possible, to put the data in front of the teachers, have them look at it, and then generate a manageable number of measurable goals based on the previous year's scores. That should be job one for administrators.
>
> —Mike Schmoker (quoted in HOPE Foundation, *FNO Video Series,* 2002)

Does the following sound familiar?

Principal: As you can see from the report, our reading scores from last year are down. So let's take about 15 minutes and brainstorm some ideas for what we can do to raise those scores.

Teacher: Can we see in what areas the scores are down, so we'll know where to focus?

Principal: If you look at the left side of the chart, I think you'll see
              that scores have dropped in almost every single area. So
              we really need to brainstorm ideas for the whole program.

How many times have you tried to use test scores or other
student data as a tool for school improvement and found that the data
were inadequate?

Both effective assessment procedures and effective use of the
associated data are fundamental to a school's continuing achievement
and improvement. With good data, teachers can tell which groups of
students are struggling and where their problems lie. With such data,
teachers can (1) determine whether their students are learning more
or achieving at a higher level than they did in the past, (2) compare
their outcomes with those of other teachers, and (3) evaluate whether
existing curriculum and instruction adequately prepare students to
demonstrate proficiency.

Data are not only important to teachers and administrators.
Students and their families also need a timely means of determining
their level of success in each subject area. Stakeholders in the community also need to know that their schools are improving over time.

COLLECTING AND USING DATA

To successfully use data to drive continuous improvement, a school
will need to answer three important questions:

- What data should be collected?
- How should data be used?
- Who should be involved?

Each of these points will be discussed in the sections that follow.

What Data Should Be Collected?

Many schools rely on state and national standardized test scores
as the primary indicator of student learning. These scores can provide some evidence of system-wide and school-wide achievement,
but they cannot paint a complete, accurate, and timely picture of
learning for all students. For example, a school with an extremely
high socioeconomic profile may have excellent test scores, on the

whole. Those test scores, however, may not reflect trends of scores for the entire student body. In fact, the overall average may mask the low performance of specific subgroups. It is important to disaggregate the test data to focus more closely on student subgroups needing additional support. This is also a key step to building a pyramid of interventions, as outlined in Chapter 6.

In addition to disaggregating test data, schools need to track different types of data to more fully assess their progress. Those sources include:

Academic Outcomes

- Grade spread on unit tests or semester exams, compared with previous results
- Course and curriculum analysis to measure alignment with state and national standards
- Graduation rates for high schools
- Continuing education levels, such as the percentages of graduating students pursuing higher education or the percentage of students entering regular or honors high school classes (after junior high or middle school)
- Outcomes on state achievement tests compared with previous years and with other schools of similar demographics
- Outcomes on nationally normed tests

Correlates to Student Achievement

- Engagement levels of students in extracurricular activities
- Attendance numbers, including enrollments and dropouts during the course of a year and hour-by-hour or class-by-class attendance figures
- Discipline actions, such as the number of in- or out-of-school suspensions and the number of repeat cases

Specific Targeted Areas

- Census, enrollment, and lunch subsidy applications, to profile the demographics of the whole school
- Observations of daily activities, occurrences, and situations that would not appear in any type of formal record-keeping
- Surveys of students, staff, and parents to gauge satisfaction and attitudes toward the school

Think It Through . . .

In your school or district, what data besides state test scores have guided recent decisions and planning? Can you think of other data sources that would have provided you with helpful information to make better decisions?

How Should Data Be Used?

Information from achievement data is ideally the foundation of constructive, collective decisions regarding issues such as goals, curricular emphases, unit plans, programs or policies, and planning for prevention and intervention systems. (See the implementation guidelines in this chapter for a detailed example.) According to Jay McTighe (FNO Video Series, 2002), one of the most powerful and effective ways of working with data is to provide teachers with the opportunity to meet in grade-level or departmental teams and analyze student work together, with all faculty members sharing equally in the responsibility for success. The results-oriented analysis should focus on the following questions:

- What criteria will be used to determine proficiency?
- Does this piece of work show proficiency?
- What are students doing particularly well?
- What are the areas for growth?
- What should be done to assure this growth?

Note that teachers may require training and encouragement when it comes to this last point. Many educators have become accustomed to using data strictly as an evaluative device—to determine whether students did or did not learn what was required. These teachers may not automatically understand how to use data as a tool to guide day-to-day decision making.

Using Data to Identify and Bolster Weak Areas

One Illinois school district used data analysis to pinpoint an easily resolved problem area. The approach of DuPage District

88 to analyzing test scores involved looking at individual test items to discover areas of weakness. Nancy Sindelar, former assistant superintendent for curriculum, instruction, and development, explained, "When you get the assessment results, there are a number of things that you can change: curriculum, instruction, or assessment. In the course of one of our analyses, we discovered that our high-scoring students were struggling with measurement—so we researched the issue further to see why." In that particular case, the school opted to change the curriculum. "It turned out that when our students were in sixth grade, they learned both standard and metric measurements simultaneously, and they were confused," Nancy said. "We changed the curriculum so that it had more material on measurement, and we purchased rulers that had both kinds of measurements. After that, we saw an improvement in measurement-related assessment items."

As trust among teachers grows and meeting protocols are well established, data revealing distinctions between results of various teachers' classrooms can be shared. This is always done with the intent of collegial sharing of internal "best practices." It is never used to rank or blame individual teachers for poor performance.

Who Should Be Involved?

Often, data are collected too far from the source to be useful to those who need the information. To be most effective, the use of data is best determined at least in part by those most responsible for learning. For example, teachers should be involved in determining which data most closely measure the current level of achievement and which data will be used to gauge and monitor improvement.

Data Collection at the Source

Sometimes data collected by teachers can provide unexpected insights into what's going on in the classroom. This was the case recently at Edison Middle School in Milwaukee,

Wisconsin, when the eighth-grade math teachers began analyzing results from a special assessment they'd designed. As part of the assessment, they had included questions that tested both pure content knowledge and questions, and the application of that knowledge. In reviewing assessment data, the teachers were surprised to discover that students were not struggling with the math concepts being taught, as they had suspected. They *were* struggling, however, with how to apply those concepts to solving problems. With this finding, the teachers were able to respond quickly, changing their instructional focus to emphasize problem solving.

Think It Through . . .

Who, in your experience, usually collects the data for your school or district? Who controls access to the data that are available?

GUIDELINES FOR DATA QUALITY

A school's ability to make improvement plans is directly tied to the quality of its data. Without clear, quantifiable information about the school's current status, leaders will find it very difficult to create focused improvement plans.

Data from diverse sources guide each step of planning and implementing initiatives for academic improvement. The characteristics of useful data are shown in the following box:

Data Should Be . . .

- Multisourced
- Relevant
- Timely
- Consistent over time
- Disaggregated

MULTISOURCED DATA

The data collected should be drawn from a variety of sources in order to give a complete picture of a school's progress. Many of those sources are discussed in the first section of this chapter, titled "What Data Should Be Collected?" Data should include demographic and socioeconomic information, absentee rates, dropout rates, suspension and disciplinary rates, report card grades, and, of course, scores on state and nationally normed tests.

A school is more than a set of numbers, however, and student, teacher, and parent perceptions of their learning community are an essential part of its achievement. Uncovering and recording these perceptions is a fundamental part of the improvement process. Doing so requires a variety of "soft" data and the use of information-gathering strategies such as surveys, questionnaires, interviews, focus groups, brainstorming, or round table discussions.

Gathering and Using Anecdotal Data

Although external and internal assessment data are extremely important, they are by no means the only types of available or useful information. Linda Jonaitis, principal of Highland High School in Highland, Indiana, says that a wealth of data is available in the perspectives and opinions of students and families. Yet these too must be collected and organized systematically. Even "soft" data can be quantified and turned into unbiased information.

"When I sat down with students in the process of developing a vision statement, the information I got from them was data," Jonaitis says. "I got a lot of things that weren't necessarily vision things, but that were important, and hearing what they had to say has affected decisions I've made."

Recognizing the value of student perceptions, Jonaitis instituted a Student Issues Committee. Members were responsible for gathering information from their peers and bringing it back to the administration in monthly meetings. This information is incorporated into the school improvement planning process as data.

"It's really important in the framework of school improvement that we have a means of communication, a way to share information," Jonaitis says. "If I had not been in a position to listen to the students, I might have drawn some wrong conclusions about where their heads were." Ultimately, these "soft" data will be systematically collected and tabulated to eliminate biases and provide a more complete picture of the school.

Relevant Data

To be useful, data must be relevant to the school's goals. Schools revamping their curriculum to align more closely with state standards, for example, will want to look closely at the results on state tests. Schools that have adopted a goal of improving writing skills through a program of writing across the curriculum may find that samples of current student work provide the best indicators of progress.

Relevant assessment data:

- Align with the curriculum and the overarching SMART goals of the school
- Are disaggregated sufficiently to show achievement and progress of all groups of students and to drive constructive decisions about finding solutions to problems
- Reveal problem areas

Think It Through . . .

What data are most relevant to teachers designing curricula and developing lesson plans? When should they receive such data?

Timely Assessments

Since large proportions of student populations turn over annually, outcomes of last year's tests may not reflect the strengths and weaknesses of this year's enrollment. Curricular goals and emphases also change, and they do not always correspond to state test standards. The most useful data for teachers and students, therefore, are the more immediate feedback from formative assessments.

In many schools, the timeliest data are generated by internal assessments and measurements. According to Fredrika Harper (quoted in HOPE Foundation, *FNO Video Series,* 2002), teachers cannot rely solely on state or district test results to guide their daily decision making. The data on which they base their day-to-day instructional decisions must be more immediately derived from classroom tests and observations.

Another important data source for teachers is administrator feedback, according to Gary Burgess (quoted in HOPE Foundation, *FNO Video Series,* 2002):

> When people don't get feedback, they begin to think the worst of a situation, of themselves and what they're involved in. When people can say immediately "This is good" or "I like the way you're doing this" or "Have you thought about that," it reinforces what the teacher is doing—or it may suggest an alternative approach.

ASSESSMENTS THAT ARE CONSISTENT OVER TIME

In order for assessments to indicate trend lines, outcomes from the same assessment instruments are viewed at different points in time. Data from this year—whether test scores, absentee rates, or average numbers of writing exercises completed per student—need to be compared with similarly collected data from previous years to be meaningful. Only a comparison of results from several years will indicate the trend line of the school.

Struggling with Data Consistency

Over the course of 12 years, the state of Illinois cycled through three different tests: the Illinois Goal Assessment Program, the Illinois State Assessment Test, and the Prairie State Achievement Exam. "There wasn't anything wrong with any of those tests," explained Nancy Sindelar, former assistant superintendent for curriculum, instruction, and development for DuPage District 88. "But the fact that the state kept changing them meant I wasn't able to track scores over time as a district. Every time we changed tests, I was back to score one." While there was little the district could do about the state-level tests, it was able to partially solve the problem by maintaining as much consistency as possible in its local assessments, and also by giving an additional district-wide standardized test.

DISAGGREGATING DATA

Data represent all groups within a school. Overall averages can hide persistent problems that do not reveal themselves until the data are disaggregated in order to describe each group that makes up part of the student population. A school can take pride in the fact that its mean eighth-grade reading score is at the 72nd percentile, but that figure may hide evidence that although 10% of the class reads at the 99th percentile, a troubling 15% are reading below the 40th percentile. Unless this school examines disaggregated data, the needs of 15% of its students may be overlooked.

Disaggregating Data

Teachers in Newport News, Virginia, have grown accustomed to disaggregating data over the past several years. Data are disaggregated by race, socioeconomic status, language, all levels of disability, gender, and content strands. Each school is also required to compile seven different data displays as part of its improvement plan as well as a five-year trend analysis for each grade level and content area. Each school in Newport News also develops a graphic description of its data in relation to district and state norms for the entire population, as well as for each disaggregated subgroup. Principals and teachers on the data committees attend a three-day training session on the process of disaggregating data, ensuring that they are prepared.

All data should be analyzed in terms of the identifiable ethnic and socioeconomic groups in the school. Although district-level enrollment information available from the central office may not reveal a child's cultural, ethnic, linguistic, or socioeconomic status, creative improvement teams can develop the information by correlating test results, grades, and other outcomes with subsidized lunch lists, ESL class enrollments, residential addresses, and other recorded information. They can also require teachers to correlate the children in their classes with preestablished categories (e.g., limited English proficient, newcomer to the community, and living in public housing), then compare the scores of these subgroups with those of the school as a whole. Such analysis allows schools to set goals and prioritize prevention and intervention strategies for the children who need them most.

Disaggregating Data

When Gary Burgess served as principal of Pendleton High School in Pendleton, South Carolina, he and his staff dug deep into the data to look at various groups within the overall population. "We met with teachers to discuss the data. We asked, Are the males doing better in this area than the females? Are the African American kids doing as well as the white kids? Are kids on free or reduced lunch doing as well as kids who are not?"

In the course of the analysis, Burgess and his staff discovered that ninth-grade students appeared to be struggling with the transition into high school. Within that group, ninth-grade African American males were performing especially poorly.

Responding to what the data indicated, the school developed a mentoring program called "Generations." Initially, the program paired African American males with junior and senior male mentors, who were required to keep logs of their contacts with the ninth-graders. Reviewing these contact logs, along with disciplinary data, Burgess and his staff saw that the program was only working moderately well. "There seemed to be a tendency for the juniors and seniors to start acting like ninth-graders instead of serving as more mature role models," Burgess explained.

To make the program stronger in its second year, he added a new layer of mentors: adult males in the community. While the upperclassmen continued to mentor the incoming ninth-graders, the adult males mentored the mentors themselves. The program was also expanded to include Caucasian males.

Since it began incorporating adult mentors, the program has been successful at reducing dropout rates among ninth-grade boys. Its success has also led to the creation of a parallel program for ninth-grade girls, called "No Limitations."

Think It Through ...

How do you respond to the notion that high average test scores may mask the fact that a significant percentage of students are not sharing in the high achievement?

GUIDELINES FOR USING DATA

Once you have collected, disaggregated, and analyzed data, findings from the data analysis can be used. Administrators and teachers can now find ways to apply the results of their data explorations to their day-to-day efforts with students. Below are some ways in which data can be effectively used.

Using Data to Drive Decisions and Set Goals

The selection of goals, instructional practices, materials, programs, and policies in a school should be directed by good information that clearly identifies both the locus and nature of problems that need to be addressed and the strengths on which to build. If a school's disaggregated data reveal a strong correlation between low reading scores and students for whom English is a second language, for example, then the staff may decide to target its initial improvement efforts on the improvement of ESL teaching strategies. Wholesale changes in the reading curriculum and teaching strategies may not be necessary.

Data can be used first to determine what kinds of goals need to be established, then to determine whether a goal is achieved.

A measurement must be chosen to indicate whether progress has occurred. For example, a school that is determined to raise students' math performance needs to decide how to measure improved performance: What test or observable performance demonstrates how well students are doing? How will the school know when the goal is attained? The selection of the measure and a target score are best established at the outset and articulated as part of the goal.

Using Data to Target Interventions

The more current the data are, the better they can be used to create on-the-spot interventions for struggling groups of students. Taking a big-picture view of three levels of assessment—the state, district, and classroom levels—allows teachers and administrators to design effective and timely intervention strategies. State testing enables schools to make benchmarks for themselves against state standards and to align curriculum accordingly. Unfortunately, the delay between such higher-level tests and the receipt of results renders them virtually useless for informing immediate academic interventions. District testing assures consistency across school levels and provides more timely feedback for teachers. For this type of testing to be most useful, districts must maintain a high level of consistency in curriculum, instruction, and pacing, in order to ensure that all students are equally prepared for their assessments.

Using Data to Prescribe Interventions

The New Berlin Public School District, just outside Milwaukee, Wisconsin, incorporates data collected throughout the year to plan its Summer Extended Learning Opportunity program—a program that provides additional direct instruction and learning time for students who have not reached mastery in one or more of the four core curricular areas. "As students are assessed through the year, those data go into designing their diagnostic/prescriptive plan for the summer," says Fredrika Harper, the district's director of teaching and learning. "We really rely on our principals, resource teachers, and classroom teachers to gather and use assessment information to develop the most effective intervention strategy."

Use Data Regularly in Collaborative Teams

However, it is classroom testing that offers the best inputs for creating just-in-time interventions. "The information you get from state testing is less usable than what you get from district testing—which is less usable than what you get from classroom testing," Harper says. "Teachers use data from classroom assessments to tailor day-to-day instructional planning . . . to evaluate whether they should go back and reteach a concept or skill."

When it comes to actually using the collected data to design interventions, there are a number of approaches. Jay McTighe (2002) suggests having teachers from across the district meet monthly in teams by grade level or content area to review and examine results of periodic testing. This approach presupposes a district-wide unified assessment plan, in which all same-grade students are given the same test or assignment at pre-specified points in the school year.

Using Data to Support Change Initiatives

Negative outcomes, combined with proposals for improvement, may inspire commitment to change. Positive outcomes reward those who work to turn things around and inspire broader support for change. Reports that are clearly explained and accompanied by credible data can respond to demands for accountability with facts. It is in the interest of school leaders to use relevant, appropriate data in support of all arguments for change and improvement.

Using Data to Guide Continuous Improvement and Redefine Success

Although it may seem that data can most effectively be used to identify problem areas within a school, it can also be used to discover areas of strength that could be made even stronger.

Continuous improvement can play out at the school level in various ways. One way to improve is through periodic evaluation of teaching plans, lessons, unit designs, and assessments by using a set of design standards. Such an approach compels administrators and teachers to apply these same standards to their own work:

If we critically look at our plans, our designs, against design standards, often we see ways in which they can be improved. What this implies, however, is a collegial model that has teachers sharing lessons, units, and assessments with each other, looking at them as critical friends against a set of design standards and giving each other feedback upon which we can make our work better. (Jay McTighe, quoted in HOPE Foundation, *FNO Video Series,* 2002)

Using Data to Monitor Progress

The value of any instructional practice should be judged according to its results. If two-thirds of the third-graders who have been in a school since kindergarten read a year below their grade level, then teachers might immediately question the effectiveness of their teaching approaches. They would begin to explore research-based practices and strategies that are proven for teaching reading. Then, when implementing a new strategy, teachers would use data to monitor outcomes frequently and regularly to determine how well the new practices work.

Using Data to Guide Professional Development

In Frederick County, Maryland, the school district has developed a district-wide Criterion-Referenced Evaluation System, which includes various performance assessments and high school exams based on district and state standards. In addition to providing assessment results to teacher teams, the district uses the results to target staff development efforts.

"Rather than having the flavor of the year, the programs are much more data-driven," says Jay McTighe, an author and consultant who has worked with the district. "If the scores indicate that students are better at creative writing than persuasive writing, that suggests that one of our in-services will focus on strategies for teaching persuasive writing." McTighe goes on to note that this approach is compatible with a sports coaching model. "We don't wait until the game to see how we're doing," he says. "We look for where the problems are, and that's what we work on in our practices."

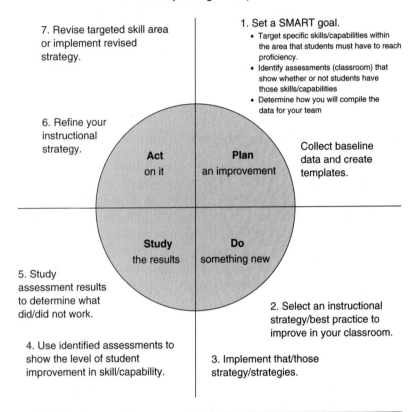

CONTINUOUS IMPROVEMENT MODEL
PDSA (Deming – TQM)

7. Revise targeted skill area or implement revised strategy.

1. Set a SMART goal.
- Target specific skills/capabilities within the area that students must have to reach proficiency.
- Identify assessments (classroom) that show whether or not students have those skills/capabilities
- Determine how you will compile the data for your team

6. Refine your instructional strategy.

Act on it

Plan an improvement

Collect baseline data and create templates.

Study the results

Do something new

5. Study assessment results to determine what did/did not work.

2. Select an instructional strategy/best practice to improve in your classroom.

4. Use identified assessments to show the level of student improvement in skill/capability.

3. Implement that/those strategy/strategies.

Figure 8.1   Collecting and Examining Data in Your School
Source: Linda D'Acquisto, Pat King, and The HOPE Foundation

What Good Looks Like

Teachers in high-performing schools don't view "data" as abstract, out-of-context information that shows whether they're meeting their goals; they interact with data in a much more personal way, using data of various kinds to make daily decisions about teaching.

Consider the following exchanges. Each one illustrates either an effective or ineffective use of data. Can you identify which ones are effective and why? Place an "E" for effective or an "I" for ineffective on the line beside each example, and note why you made that choice.

_____ Exchange 1

Principal: I received our state test results earlier this week, and I've got nothing but good news to share. Our average score is in the 88th percentile—that's the highest it's been in the last 10 years. Congratulations to all you, and keep up the good work.

_____ Exchange 2

Principal: Mr. Grant, we need to schedule an appointment to go over your class's test scores from earlier this year and talk about what we need to be doing in the coming months.

Teacher: I agree—but I already know those test scores don't paint an accurate picture of what's going on in my classroom now. Since my kids took their tests, I've seen a radical improvement in both math and reading skills.

Principal: That's a valid point. In that case, I suggest we augment our test score analysis with some more recent data. Can you pull together some information on your students' unit math and reading test scores throughout the year? Also, let's take a look at how well they're doing on homework—especially in the last three months.

_____ Exchange 3

Principal: We're here to talk about what we can do to ensure learning for all our students.

Teacher 1:   It seems as if we're *already* doing it . . . our test scores are great.

Teacher 2:   It's true that our overall scores are good. But when we look more closely at the scores, it appears that we have a population—about 20 percent of the student body—that isn't doing well. This correlates highly with poor attendance, which makes a lot of sense. A lot of these same children also receive subsidized lunch. We should start thinking about what we can do to ensure *these* students' success.

_____ Exchange 4

Principal: Okay, if you'll look at page two, you'll see that our science scores as a whole took a rather sharp drop this year.

Teacher: I actually have a question about that. I think all the science teachers would agree that we've seen no marked difference in our students' achievement this year as compared to past years—and I wonder if the drop in numbers might be attributed to the redesign of the test rather than to an actual decline in achievement.

Principal: It might be, but there's no way to determine that. So we have to go with what the numbers tell us.

What's your analysis? We think examples 1 and 4 illustrate ineffective use of data, whereas examples 2 and 3 show effective use.

In example 1, we see a principal and staff taking test data "at face value" without disaggregating it to look at areas for continuous improvement. Their *average* score is high, but that doesn't tell what's happening with those students who scored on the low end of the scale. Nor does it provide insights into which grades or which subject areas are performing especially well or poorly. This approach to the data reveals very little that could help guide improvement plans and decisions.

In example 4, the problem is data inconsistency. Because the science test has been redesigned, the data it collects can't be reasonably compared to data collected in previous years. Therefore, the fact that the test scores have dropped *may or may not* mean that student learning has declined. For data to be useful, they must be consistent over time.

In example 2, we see data being used well. Realizing that testing data often arrive too late to be used as a gauge of current achievement, the principal and teacher in this example are going to use more timely data to supplement the test scores. The combination of test scores and classroom data should provide them with a more accurate, up-to-date picture of students' status.

Example 3 also illustrates an effective use of data. In it, we see a school really digging into its test scores to see what's hidden beneath the surface. Although this school's overall scores are good, one teacher realized that they do not show the whole picture. She has disaggregated the data and discovered a problem area, which can now be addressed. Moreover, this professional learning culture makes it possible for her to freely dispute the less complete data analysis of teacher #1.

IMPLEMENTATION GUIDELINES

The following steps are designed to generate a school profile—a foundation of data on which to build. (The following steps were actually used to create the pyramid of interventions in East Hartford High School described in Chapter 6. This was contributed by Steve Edwards, award-winning principal of the school.)

CASE STUDY #3, EAST HARTFORD HIGH SCHOOL, EAST HARTFORD, CONNECTICUT

1. *Identify and list pertinent data and information.* At one of the earliest meetings, principals and members of the leadership teams should list all the information they would like to collect in order to guide school improvement efforts. Possible sources of information are provided earlier in this chapter.

2. *Collect data and information.* Teams would then gather all the information and data that are readily available, ensuring that all data are up-to-date and accurate. Next, teams would plan ways to obtain new, useful information from data that may not yet exist. Surveys, questionnaires, focus groups, and interviews may be useful methods for obtaining information and views on subjects ranging from the amount of time that students typically spend on homework to parents' perception of their role in the school.

3. *Disaggregate and analyze the data.* Once the leadership team has compiled most of the information and data it needs, it disaggregates as much data and as many responses as possible to distinguish outcomes by gender, race or ethnic group, and socio-economic status. In schools where disaggregation occurs routinely, all students will be identified as members of a population group. It

should not be difficult for teams to find the relevant data for their school.

When no disaggregated data are available and students are not listed by gender or as members of any specific racial or ethnic group, teams can develop the information themselves. One way to do this is to ask each grade-level, homeroom, or required subject-area teacher who knows all the students in the class to note the gender and ethnicity of each one. This information can be entered into a data-management software program that permits sorting by various groupings and allows basic statistical tests of the data sets. Schools can also disaggregate school-held records such as attendance and discipline rates, family attendance at school events, and participation in extracurricular activities

Schools may be unable to disaggregate anonymous survey results from parents. However, they can set up round tables, focus groups, forums, or other information-gathering events with well-publicized topics such as "How Can Our School Better Serve Latino Youth?" Such events are likely to attract a self-selected group in the community.

4. *Share data with staff members.* Summaries of analyzed data and findings will be most compelling when presented to the entire faculty as soon as possible after they are available. Data especially relevant to a particular grade level or subject area would be shared in detail with the teachers involved.

5. *Determine how to use data to guide school improvement efforts.* One common approach is to use student grade distribution reports as one piece of data when examining students who fail to meet minimum academic standards. From a quantitative perspective, grade distribution reports can be broken down by the number and percentage of students receiving each grade. Qualitatively, teachers can be interviewed to explain and interpret the grade distribution for the class based on their students and their grading systems.

These data are relevant because they give a breakdown of student achievement in a particular class with a particular teacher. This information can then be compared to other courses of the same subject. Such data are timely because they reflect a student's performance over a set period, comparing performance from one marking period to the next or from year to year.

Teachers, department heads, and administrators are the users and the collectors of the data. Disaggregating the data into different categories such as gender and ethnicity allows teachers and administrators to analyze trends with particular populations. The analysis of grade distribution reports is only one example of how data can be a useful tool in better meeting student needs. Adhering to the criteria listed above provides schools with a solid framework from which they can begin to analyze, interpret, and use the data they collect.

Using data not only allows for the identification of problem areas but also helps to identify strengths. It is important when collecting and analyzing data to focus on both problem areas and strengths. Schools should highlight what they do well while at the same time developing a plan to address areas of concern. Celebrate what is working by focusing on the sustainability of identified strengths, and develop a plan for working on problem areas.

CHALLENGES

Challenge: "Data analysis is just a fancy name for a witch hunt. What the administrators really want is to find out which teachers aren't getting their kids ready for the state tests." The idea of slicing data by classroom puts some teachers on the defensive. They may feel that if their students' scores are low, they will be unfairly blamed.

Solution: Use one of the following approaches:

(1) Have teachers collaborate to look at data that have been "depersonalized" in such a fashion that teachers aren't able to focus on students' specific classroom, level, or teachers. For example, an administrator might draw a team together to look at students' tests or assignments, using codes in order to avoid connecting the work under evaluation to a specific teacher. Teachers can score anonymous student results, then spend the rest of the meeting looking for patterns and designing appropriate intervention strategies.

(2) Get teachers together in vertical (cross-grade-level) teams to discuss what students are expected to know and be able to do, how to know if they have achieved proficiency, and what must be done to ensure success for all students.

(3) Build general trust among teachers, and back it with specific actions. It is critical that teachers know that administrators will never use student achievement data to rank or evaluate teachers. Nor should this information be used in any public forum. Without making this commitment, it is very difficult to collect accurate data.

Challenge: "I don't have time for this." According to Linda Jonaitis (quoted in HOPE Foundation, *FNO Video Series,* 2002), one of the greatest obstacles to the effective use of data is finding the time to both collect and analyze the information needed.

Solution: Methods for creatively structuring time can be found in Chapter 2 and Appendix B.

Finding Time to Collect and Analyze Data

A few years ago, the DuPage, Illinois, school district underwent a major realignment of its curriculum. After writing local assessments that tested existing curriculum, the administration reviewed the results against state standards, then rewrote the curriculum and local assessments to ensure that they were properly aligned with these standards.

Finding time for such an intensive process was a challenge—one that the district solved by using summer and inservice days. Teachers were paid for the summer work of revising the curriculum, a one-time project. Then, each school year, they spent their inservice days conducting item analyses on test data in order to identify problem areas and calibrate the curriculum and instruction to ensure continued alignment with state objectives.

Challenge: "Our test scores are great. Why mess with success?" Schools can become complacent when their test scores are good in comparison to state and national norms. Yet even high-scoring schools often have a population of students who are not yet proficient—as well as a population of students who, despite good test scores, are not working up to their highest potential.

Solution: Provide data in a meaningful *context.* This usually means comparisons. Looking at test scores from last year to this, for one group of students versus another, or from one district versus another provides a frame of reference that can be unsettling—and productive for change!

Challenge: "Testing data are great for periodically making sure you're on track, but I don't use them to make day-to-day decisions."

Solution: Help teachers understand how to analyze relevant and timely classroom data by providing appropriate staff development to team leaders. Once teams are established, they can watch and learn from one another by visiting other team meetings.

Using Data to Make Instructional Decisions

When Chicago's McCosh School switched to a five-week assessment program, the teachers did not know at first how to effectively use the data that the new program generated. McCosh principal Barbara Eason-Watkins explained: "At the end of the five-week period, at first teachers didn't look at the data—they just filed it, and it didn't make a difference for us."

Accustomed to viewing data as strictly an evaluative tool, teachers had to be taught how best to use the information. "We had to create an environment where it was not such that it was used for evaluation purposes. We had to truly stress that it was used to inform instructional decision making and to help teachers determine whether they needed to change their instructional practices or do some more personalized things with children who were experiencing difficulties."

The school also had to structure opportunities for teachers to come together and give them strategies for analyzing and using the data. Given the appropriate staff development and a new lens through which to look at the data, the teachers began using data to guide their day-to-day decisions.

GETTING STARTED

Table 8.1 (Reeves, 2002a) presents a simplified method of collecting and examining data in your own school. You might want to start by looking at a fairly narrow subset of data, to make the exercise manageable (Table 8.1).

Table 8.1   COLLECTING AND EXAMINING DATA IN YOUR SCHOOL

Find the Data

1. Develop a list of the types of data you want to examine (e.g., reading scores, math scores, writing scores, and free or reduced-cost lunch, Title 1, special ed, attendance, and extracurricular engagement). Note that to show trends, you will need to collect data from more than just one school year.
2. Determine how you want to categorize and disaggregate the data (e.g., by grade level, by classroom, or by gender).
3. Design a graphic organizer that will help you get the best picture of your school's overall data (e.g., a simple table or graph, with types of data across the top and disaggregation categories down the side).
4. Search for and record the data on your chart.

Analyze the Data

1. Use the data to answer the following questions:
   - In which content areas has improvement been made?
   - Which content areas still need improvement?
   - Which are the areas of greatest potential growth?
   - Which student groups need the most assistance?
   - Where are the same students alternately weak and strong?

2. Draw conclusions. Record your findings and observations. Note that general statements like "Math scores are low" or "Fifth and sixth grade reading scores are the lowest" may not be specific enough. Better statements might be "Math achievement of students taking the bus is disproportionately low" or "Reading achievement of high-mobility students is low."

Reflect

Review your findings. Did you learn something new by charting the data? Below, list three facts that are new to you or that stand out more clearly than before:

1. _____

2. _____

3. _____

Based on the data you collected, what are your school's three greatest causes for celebration? Its three greatest areas of concern?

Celebration:

1. _____

2. _____

3. _____

Concern:

1. _____

2. _____

3. _____

Source: Adapted from Reeves, D. B. (2002a). Making Standards Work (3rd ed.). Denver, Co: Advanced Learning Press. Used with permission.

CONCLUSION

In this chapter, you have learned important guidelines for the productive use of data by instructional teams focused on enhancing student achievement. The next chapter shows how successful schools grapple with bringing about meaningful family and community engagement.

CHAPTER NINE

Principle #5—Gaining Active Engagement From Family and Community

> The research is abundantly clear: Nothing motivates a child more than when learning is valued by schools and families/community working together in partnership. . . . These forms of involvement do not happen by accident or even by invitation. They happen by explicit strategic intervention.
>
> —Michael Fullan (1997)

D oes the following exchange sound familiar?

Teacher #1: "How's it going?"

Teacher #2: "Not good. I just gave my first test. Over half the class failed. They seem to have no language skills, they're not eating breakfast, so they're starving when they finally get to class—that is, if they get to class at all. What are the parents doing?"

Educational research clearly shows that the support and involvement of students' families and the community at large is fundamental to achievement in schools. The most comprehensive study on the topic (Henderson, 1987; Henderson & Berla, 1995) concludes that greater parental involvement leads to greater student achievement, irrespective of such factors as socioeconomic status or ethnic background. That same research shows that the most accurate predictor of student academic achievement is the ability of the student's family to create a home environment that encourages learning; to communicate high, yet reasonable, expectations for achievement; and to become involved in the student's education.

These findings and others like them have captured the attention of U.S. policymakers. In 1994 Congress added a goal focusing on parental involvement to the National Educational Goals. Goal 8 states: "By the year 2000, every school will promote partnerships that will increase parental involvement and participation in promoting the social, emotional, and academic growth of children" (National Education Goals Panel, 1995).

This added goal presents a significant set of challenges. Relations between school, family, and community can often be minimal or even rocky—rife with misunderstandings, misinterpretations, and disagreements. (Note that, four years after this goal was to have been achieved, we're still a long way from reaching it.) Few educators feel that parents have a genuine interest in being involved in their children's schooling (Center on Families, Communities, Schools, and Children's Learning, 1994), and teachers everywhere complain that parents send children to school late or sporadically, sometimes unfed, unrested, and unprepared for their classes. Parents, on the other hand, frequently feel that school officials have no grasp of the problems they face and the difficulty of providing support for their children's attendance and continuing progress.

There is no consensus on where the responsibility rests for ensuring parental involvement in schools. According to a 1994 survey (Center on Families, Communities, Schools, and Children's Learning), 90 percent of teachers surveyed felt that parental involvement was needed in schools and supported the idea of parent volunteers. However, only 32 percent felt that it was their responsibility to initiate such involvement, and 50 percent indicated that they did not have enough time to do so. Given those statistics, it is perhaps unsurprising that 70 percent of parents surveyed said they had never been invited to volunteer in their children's schools.

The trends shown in these studies, which are nearly a decade old, are still evident today. In fact, the pressure on parents is greater than ever, and nowhere is this more true than for children in so-called failing schools. Parents of children in these schools must investigate alternate schools and make daunting logistical arrangements in so doing. Many find this task virtually impossible. Parents are given greater responsibility under current educational legislation but not given greater resources or support to exercise those responsibilities. It falls to school leaders who genuinely value learning communities to find ways to include and support the parents of every child in their school.

Think It Through . . .

How would you characterize your school's relationships with parents? With local business and political leaders? With the local media? If any of these relationships are not as good as they could be, what causes would you cite?

Some schools surmount these obstacles and forge close, productive relationships with parents and community members alike. In this chapter, we'll look at some of the approaches and principles these schools have in common.

BUILDING POSITIVE FAMILY AND COMMUNITY RELATIONSHIPS

Schools that have become true professional learning communities have addressed the school/community gap, and closed it, by employing three key principles to positive family relationships:

- Building mutual understanding and empathy
- Effective involvement of family and community
- Reaching out to family and community

Mutual Understanding and Empathy

The first step toward building or repairing home/school relationships is to gain a common understanding, with empathy for students' families. This means that school staff must be aware of the specific conditions that affect many families and make it difficult for them to support their children's learning. This includes recognizing that many parents have had negative experiences with school and are afraid to become involved. They may be intimidated by feelings of ignorance and uncertainty. Instead of penalizing children and their parents for lapses and failures in attendance or preparation, teachers in high-performing schools work with families to help them overcome problems and barriers.

Empathetic Decision Making

Nancy Brantley, principal of Pelham Road Elementary School in Greenville, South Carolina, tells a story that illustrates how the challenges of a child's home life can spill over into life at school. On the first day of state testing at Pelham Road, school buses were late arriving from an outlying neighborhood. When the buses finally arrived, the students on them were visibly upset and agitated. There had been a shooting in the neighborhood the night before.

One little girl, in particular, was extremely upset, so Brantley took her aside for a private talk. The student explained that the shooting had occurred in her apartment building. Without a phone to call the police, she and her family were powerless to do anything other than "hide and cry."

The little girl wanted to know if she had to take the test that day. Recognizing that the student faced personal issues that far superseded academic ones, Brantley readily excused her from the testing. "While testing is important, on that particular day, that child was lucky to even get to school," Brantley said. "Children should never ever have to live in situations like that—something that we hope we'll never have to experience."

Brantley's decision in this case was very much in keeping with other Pelham Road policies, such as its policy on tardiness. When a student arrives late to school, he or she is not penalized. In most cases, the child simply receives a pass and is sent on to class. Even with a chronically tardy student, the school does not seek to punish or reprimand. Rather, it looks for ways to help parents resolve the problem. Brantley says, "If it's a real big problem, although it rarely is, we call the parents in to see if we can help. Because sometimes they simply cannot get an old car started, they don't have a way to school, they've missed the bus—so that's where we step in as a community school, to help."

Schools that are committed to student success are creative in accommodating the difficulties that students face. Some areas in which schools can extend understanding and support include:

- Replacing punitive processes with ones that seek to understand and improve a child's situation
- Creating schedules, policies, and programs that take into account students' home-life challenges
- Providing translators or speakers who can communicate with non-English-speaking families
- Producing versions of important school announcements and communications in the language of many families
- Arranging for transportation of students to after-school activities, and for families to school events
- Setting up alternatives to telephone communication for families who lack telephones
- Working with local agencies (e.g., public libraries and public housing authorities) to provide quiet areas for homework and tutoring

Creative Scheduling

D.R. Hill Middle School in Duncan, South Carolina, has found an effective way to both reduce tardiness and provide students with a "decompression" period between home and school. Every day at D.R. Hill starts with Tiger Advisory Program (TAP) Time. During TAP Time, faculty advisors work with small groups of students to teach life skills, such as cooperation and collaboration, through hands-on activities and exercises. Every student is involved, including those in special education, and students are grouped heterogeneously, with no segregation of any sort.

Principal Steve Gambrell says that the program has become an invaluable part of the day for both students and teachers. "We feel like it's almost a sacred time," Gambrell says. "It's a time when those kids who bring baggage to school are able to get rid of that baggage, so that when they go to their academic classes, they're ready to learn—and teachers are able to teach." A side benefit of TAP Time is that it has virtually eliminated tardiness to academic classes. Because of the experimental and active nature of TAP, students come early to ensure they can participate.

Working with Local Agencies

Newport News School District in Newport News, Virginia, has worked with local agencies to create "Homework Clubs" for latchkey children. In 12 different locations throughout the city—including housing projects, shelters, and other community centers—the district has established quiet, safe places for studying after school. Each Homework Club is equipped with computers and classroom materials and staffed by a teacher and a parent who has been trained as a teacher's assistant.

The district has also worked with housing projects in disadvantaged neighborhoods to create four computer labs for both parent and student use. In the evenings, the computers are available for student use. During the day, while students are at school, the labs are used to train adults in computer skills, with paid trainers teaching everything from computer maintenance to software design. These community resources, funded in part by a federal grant, serve both to prepare parents for the workforce and to help them become better teachers for their children.

Think It Through . . .

Can you think of some recent efforts your school has made to reach out to the community? If so, how were those efforts received?

EFFECTIVE INVOLVEMENT
OF FAMILIES IN THE SCHOOL

According to Barbara Eason-Watkins (quoted in HOPE Foundation, *FNO Video Series,* 2002), the best way to ensure parental and community involvement in a school is to welcome people into the school. Although this may seem obvious, it is actually a common stumbling block in community/school relationships. Eason-Watkins says, "In many conversations I've had with parents and members of the community, they felt that most schools didn't want them to participate, didn't want them to be part of the school" (quoted in HOPE Foundation, *FNO Video Series,* 2002). This feeling of being unwanted and shut out sometimes stems from parents' own experiences in school. Those parents who struggled in their own academic careers may feel resentment, distaste, or even anxiety about interacting with school authorities.

In other cases, language and cultural differences create a barrier to parental involvement in schools. In some districts, many parents speak and read English imperfectly or not at all, making meaningful involvement in the school difficult, if not impossible. These same parents may be extremely hesitant to contact the schools. In many cultures, educators are imbued with an authority and status that makes families unwilling to ask questions or voice complaints.

Barriers like the ones above make it obvious that family involvement in the schools is not something that occurs naturally or easily. It must be purposely cultivated. Professional learning communities cultivate such involvement by bringing parents and other adults in to share their expertise and talents in meaningful ways and by creating parent-to-parent support networks. These schools recognize the value of the contributions that family members can make to the achievement of the school's educational mission.

Ways of encouraging meaningful parent involvement include:

- Establishing a Parent-to-Parent Outreach that contacts all parents to see what they can contribute to student learning
- Inviting parents and community members in to provide lessons in the language and/or culture of ethnic groups that are represented in the school community
- Inviting parents and community members in to provide leadership for extracurricular clubs based on special interests

Using Parents' Unique Abilities

At Pelham Road Elementary, parents use their abilities and experiences to enrich the lives of students through special-interest groups and clubs. Two bilingual parents volunteer their time twice a week to meet with the after-school Spanish Club. Other parents, who have literary interests, work with the school's Authors' Club, to guide students through the process of writing and publishing a book.

Parents or community members can serve as translators to facilitate communication between the school and non-English-speaking families. They can also make presentations—talks, slide shows, and/or videotapes relevant to current events, areas, or subjects being studied.

Engaging Parents in Their Child's Curriculum

One way to involve parents in the school is to keep them informed about what their children are learning—even to the point of offering parent workshops. The Chicago Public Schools tackles this objective in a number of ways. One way is to send home a syllabus at the beginning of every quarter, so parents can track exactly what students are learning each week. Another way is to provide workshops in which parents can themselves learn about the subjects their children are studying—and thereby reinforce them at home.

Other school districts are taking similar approaches. Thornton Township High Schools District 205, of Illinois, has established a "Parent Academy" in each of its buildings to offer adult classes on a range of topics. Thornton Township's Associate Superintendent Gwen Lee says that the district started the academies after conducting a needs assessment with local parents to see what sort of instruction would help them better support their children in school, as well as enhance their personal and professional lives. The result was a broad roster of classes ranging from word processing to Spanish language to swimming. Not only are the courses *attended* by parents and community members, but many courses are also *taught* by parent volunteers. Lee says that the "Parent Academies" have gone a long way toward bringing parents into the schools and increasing their comfort level.

Parents or community members can:

- Mentor and/or tutor students who need extra help
- Assist with classroom writing projects, science experiments, and so forth
- Direct or assist with dramatic productions
- Present performances of puppet shows, musicals, drama, or dramatic readings

Think It Through . . .

What are some kinds of things your school typically asks parents to do? How essential to the teaching and learning process are their contributions? What are some kinds of contributions parents or community members could make that would be especially useful?

Parent Volunteers

Bringing parents into the school as volunteers ensures that they feel welcome, involved, and needed. It is important to actively seek the involvement of all parents. A Parent-to-Parent Network in which each parent volunteer reaches out to get another family involved is a very effective way to break down barriers that may exist between some parents and the school.

Schools can use parents as volunteers on a daily basis in many ways. Both Pelham Road Elementary and Pendleton High School actively seek out parents who don't work during the day to assist as volunteers—doing everything from answering phones to making copies to helping in the classroom. Thornton Township High Schools, in Illinois, also use parent volunteers during every school day. According to Associate Superintendent Gwen Lee, volunteers serve as greeters at school entrances, tutor students, attend field trips, and help in the cafeteria.

Reaching out to parents and inviting them into the school—and especially into the classroom—can inspire a cultural change for teachers. Teachers are often accustomed to teaching in isolation and may be uncomfortable or wary with other adults in their classroom. Gary Burgess (quoted in HOPE Foundation, *FNO Video Series,* 2002) notes that changing the school's culture to embrace and value in-class volunteers is a prerequisite for an effective parent volunteer program. If the teachers don't accept the idea of having parents in the classroom, it won't work.

REACHING OUT TO FAMILY AND COMMUNITY

In effective schools, teachers and administrators go the extra mile to reach those children and families whose problems stand in the way of their full involvement in schooling. Part of reaching out is simply making staff members visible in the neighborhood fast-food restaurants, malls, and other places students and families are likely to visit. Gary Burgess (ibid.) says that *wherever* you meet parents—whether at the barbershop, the gym, the church, or the community center— becomes the locus of your campaign to get them into the school. In other words, recruiting parents is not an activity restricted to specific hours at specific places; it is a constant, ongoing process that encompasses every interaction with every parent.

Think It Through . . .

Can you think of situations or events in your community where the presence of someone from the school could be a significant gesture of reaching out?

Burgess also suggests a "bring the mountain to Mohammed" approach for providing information about school activities and efforts to the community. In his district, school principals hold periodic informational meetings at local churches and other public meeting places. He notes that these meetings are sometimes better attended than those held at the school because parents and community members perceive them as less threatening and more convenient. Burgess also uses a teacher log to record all parent contacts and then evaluates the information with teachers. By formalizing, valuing, and monitoring these contacts, he has been able to change teachers' behavior.

Other ways for the school to reach out to the community might include a variety of supportive programs conducted off-campus—in libraries, community centers, religious centers, and so on. These programs can include initiatives such as homework tutoring, book drives to provide books for common rooms of housing projects, and even transportation of children to and from after-school activities.

At D.R. Hill Middle School, faculty and staff reach out to families in many different ways. The school holds dances at which each student's "price of admission" is simply to bring a parent. It also holds a yearly "March Math Madness" night, which involves a math treasure hunt, complete with prizes for winners. This activity is especially popular among the school's dads.

Although they vary greatly in focus and theme, virtually all of the school's family activities have one thing in common: food. According to Principal Steve Gambrell, D.R. Hill operates on the premise that "if you feed them, they will come"—so snacks or meals are a staple of event planning (*Failure Is Not an Option Video Series*, 2002).

Recognizing that many obstacles to academic achievement are caused by family problems and community breakdown, strong school leaders create and maintain close ties with law enforcement and service agencies to minimize the disruption of children's academic progress. For example, programs might be devised to ensure that children in homeless families moved to temporary shelters need not transfer to new schools. Counselors and other school officials can work closely with probation officers to ensure that adjudicated youth receive the full complement of prevention and intervention programs offered by the school.

Finally, professional learning communities need to reach out to their local business community. Local businesses have a considerable stake in the quality of graduates that the schools produce—and they are often quite willing to contribute time, expertise, guidance, and funding.

What Good Looks Like

Each of the following scenarios offers an example of how schools can interact with parents and community members. Can you identify which illustrate a positive, relationship-building interaction and which do not, and why?

Scenario 1

Teacher: Marissa, this is the third time this week that you
             haven't had your homework done. The last two

	times I gave you second chances—but you just don't seem to be trying.
Marissa:	I'm sorry. I didn't have time again last night because I have to help take care of my brother on the nights my mom works.
Teacher:	I understand that you have a responsibility, but I can't continue to overlook the fact that you aren't completing your work. From now on, if you don't turn in homework when it's due, I'm going to have to give you a zero for it.

Scenario 2

Parent:	We're new to the district, and I understand that my daughter will be attending this school in the fall. I wondered if you'd mind giving us a tour?
Principal:	I would love to give you a tour because this is the best school in the county!
Parent:	We've certainly heard some wonderful things about it.
Principal:	Well, we've really been blessed with wonderful kids and wonderful staff. But the most wonderful thing is that the staff has such a close relationship with the community—and we need you as a volunteer, too, by the way, if you're interested.

Scenario 3

Teacher:	Miguel, I've noticed that your mother has not been signing your weekly assignment sheets. Have you been showing them to her and asking her to help you check your work, as I asked?
Miguel:	I did ask her, Mrs. Torphy, but she says her English isn't good enough to check my work. She says she doesn't understand most of my homework at all.
Teacher:	I'm sorry, Miguel. I didn't realize that. You know what? Mr. Manors in the other fourth-grade class speaks Spanish very well. Why don't I invite your

mother in to meet with Mr. Manors and myself, and we'll see what we can do to help your mother understand what we're doing in class.

Scenario 4

Parent: I'm Rob Gillian, Marcus Gillian's father. Marcus is giving a social studies report tomorrow, and he'd like me to come and watch. I was just calling to make sure it was okay.

School secretary: Mr. Gillian, we leave those decisions up to the individual teacher. Sometimes they prefer to have parents visit only on certain days, so as not to distract the students when they really need to be concentrating. Do you know the name of your son's social studies teacher? I could give you his or her voice mail and you could check to make sure tomorrow's a good day.

Scenario 5

Principal: Hello there, Mr. Burton, it's good to see you.

Community member: Good to see you too, Dr. Combs. How are things going over at the high school?

Principal: Very well. We're very pleased with the results we're seeing from some of our new programs—especially our school-to-work program. Actually, we could really use *your* expertise on that program.

Community member: Oh?

Principal: Absolutely. In order to get these kids ready to enter the workforce, we need the perspective of local employers on what skills they value in employees. In fact, the program steering committee meets this coming Tuesday evening. Would you be willing to attend and share your thoughts?

What are your thoughts about each of these scenarios? We've provided our analysis in past chapters; now we're taking off the "training wheels." Have fun with this!

IMPLEMENTATION GUIDELINES

The National PTA lists six national standards for family involvement programs, along with associated practices (1997). These standards and practices are:

Standard 1: *Communication*

Communication between home and school is regular, two-way, and meaningful. Associated practices include:

- Using a variety of communication tools on a regular basis, seeking to facilitate two-way interaction through each type of medium
- Establishing opportunities for parents and educators to share partnering information such as student strengths and learning preferences
- Providing clear information regarding course expectations and offerings, student placement, school activities, student services, and optional programs
- Mailing report cards and regular progress reports to parents; providing support services and follow-up conferences as needed
- Disseminating information on school reforms, policies, disciplinary procedures, assessment tools, and school goals, and including parents in any related decision-making process
- Conducting conferences with parents at least twice a year, with follow-up as needed; conferences should accommodate the varied schedules of parents, language barriers, and the need for child care
- Encouraging immediate contact between parents and teachers when concerns arise
- Distributing student work for parental comment and review on a regular basis
- Translating communications to assist non-English-speaking parents
- Communicating with parents regarding positive student behavior and achievement, not just misbehavior or failure
- Providing opportunities for parents to communicate with principals and other administrative staff

- Promoting informal activities at which parents, staff, and community members can interact
- Providing staff development regarding effective communication techniques and the importance of regular two-way communication between the school and the family

Standard 2: *Parenting*

Parenting skills are promoted and supported. Associated practices include:

- Communicating the importance of positive relationships between parents and their children
- Linking parents to programs and resources within the community that provide support services to families
- Reaching out to all families, not just those who attend parent meetings
- Establishing policies that support and respect family responsibilities, recognizing the variety of parenting traditions and practices within the community's cultural and religious diversity
- Providing an accessible parent/family information and resource center to support parents and families with training, resources, and other services
- Encouraging staff members to demonstrate respect for families and the family's primary role in the rearing of children to become responsible adults

Standard 3: *Student Learning*

Parents play an integral role in assisting student learning. Associated practices include:

- Seeking and encouraging parental participation in decision making that affects students
- Informing parents of the expectations for students in each subject at each grade level
- Providing information regarding how parents can foster learning at home, give appropriate assistance, monitor homework, and give feedback to teachers

- Regularly assigning interactive homework that will require students to discuss and interact with their parents about what they are learning in class
- Sponsoring workshops or distributing information to assist parents in understanding how students can improve skills, get help when needed, meet class expectations, and perform well on assessments
- Involving parents in setting student goals each year and in planning for postsecondary education and careers; encouraging the development of an individualized educational plan for each student, in which parents are full partners
- Providing opportunities for staff members to learn and share successful approaches to engaging parents in their child's education

Standard 4: *Volunteering*

Parents are welcome in the school, and their support and assistance are sought. Associated practices include:

- Ensuring that office staff greetings, signs near the entrances, and any other interactions with parents create a climate in which parents feel valued and welcome
- Surveying parents regarding their interests, talents, and availability, then coordinating the parent resources with those that exist within the school and among the faculty
- Ensuring that parents who are unable to volunteer in the school building are given the options for helping in other ways, at their home or workplace
- Organizing an easy, accessible program for using parent volunteers, providing ample training on volunteer procedures and school protocol
- Developing a system for contacting all parents to assist as the year progresses
- Designing opportunities for those with limited time and resources to participate by addressing child care, transportation, work schedule needs, and so forth
- Showing appreciation for parents' participation, and valuing their diverse contributions

- Educating and assisting staff members in creating an inviting climate and effectively using volunteer resources
- Ensuring that volunteer activities are meaningful and built on volunteer interests and abilities

Standard 5: *School Decision Making and Advocacy*

Parents are full partners in decisions that affect children and families. Associated practices include:

- Providing understandable, accessible, well-publicized processes for influencing decisions, raising issues or concerns, appealing decisions, and resolving problems
- Encouraging the formation of PTAs or other parent groups to identify and respond to issues of interest to parents
- Including parents on all decision-making and advisory committees, and ensuring adequate training for such areas as policy, curriculum, budget, school reform initiatives, safety, and personnel; where site governance bodies exist, giving equal representation to parents
- Providing parents with current information regarding school policies, practices, and both student and school performance data
- Enabling parents to participate as partners when setting school goals, developing or evaluating programs and policies, or responding to performance data
- Encouraging and facilitating active parent participation in decisions that affect students, such as student placement, course selection, and individualized educational plans
- Treating parental concerns with respect and demonstrating genuine interest in developing solutions
- Promoting parent participation on school district, state, and national committees and issues
- Providing training for staff and parents on collaborative partnering and shared decision making

Standard 6: *Collaborating With Community*

Community resources are used to strengthen schools, families, and student learning. Associated practices include:

- Distributing information regarding cultural, recreational, academic, health, social, and other resources that serve families within the community
- Developing partnerships with local business and service groups to advance student learning and to assist schools and families
- Encouraging employers to adopt policies and practices that promote and support adult participation in children's education
- Fostering student participation in community service
- Involving community members in school volunteer programs
- Disseminating information to the school community, including those without school-age children, regarding school programs and performance
- Collaborating with community agencies to provide family support services and adult learning opportunities, enabling parents to more fully participate in activities that support education
- Informing staff members of the resources available in the community and strategies for using those resources

CHALLENGES

Teachers and administrators face numerous challenges as they work to strengthen school/community ties. Below are some of those challenges—and some of our suggestions for resolving them.

Challenge: "*I've* tried *to reach out to the parents of my students . . . but most of them don't seem to care, and some are downright hostile. The ones who* do *care are so overly involved that they second-guess my every move.*" There are few educators with even a few years' experience who haven't had negative experiences with parent/school relationships. Such negative experiences can quickly cause teachers to avoid parental involvement rather than to embrace it.

Solution: Parents and administrators, and designated parent coordinators, need to actively reach out to parents and families not connected to the school. In those situations in which parents have negative feelings about school and teachers, it is better not to place teachers in a position of possible conflict with the parents.

Challenge: "*Our school has no problem communicating with parents! In addition to the full binder of material we send home with every student at the beginning of the year, we send weekly newsletters and calendars of upcoming events. Every teacher maintains a current 'homework hotline,' so parents can call in and check their children's assignments. And we post everything on our Web site and update it every two weeks."* Many schools mistakenly believe that communication flows in only one direction—that as long as they're getting information to parents, they're doing their part. Meaningful communication, however, must be *two-way*, constantly alternating between informing and listening.

Solution: Look into interactive modes of communication—including, but not limited to, voice mailboxes, suggestion boxes located both in the school office and in key locations around the community, parent surveys, and direct phone calls to ask for parent feedback and input.

Challenge: "We have some great parents, and I know they want to be involved in their kids' education—but they just don't seem to have a clue how to go about it." Clearly achievement is enhanced when students receive help with schoolwork at home. However, not all parents know how to help, and they may not feel qualified to offer guidance on subject matter they themselves are unfamiliar with.

Solution: Set up community-based homework support. Use students in the National Honor Society, students earning community service credit, and other peer-tutors. Set up tutoring after school and during the weekends at the school, community center, or local library. Invite parents in and show them how best to help their children with homework. Remember that the children who most need the help often have parents who are not well prepared to provide the needed assistance.

Challenge: "I'd be happy to have parents help out . . . as long as they don't try to tell us how to do our jobs." DuFour (1991) notes that there is a strong tendency for teachers and administrators to define parent/school relationships in very strict terms—that is, schools should *make* the decisions, and parents should support those decisions unquestioningly. Yet such a one-sided "partnership" is not only less appealing to parents—it is also less beneficial to the school. Research shows that schools enjoy higher levels of both public support and student achievement when they involve parents in the decision-making process (National PTA, 1997).

Solution: This is tricky. Partnerships are easy to talk about and difficult to establish. A school that is serious about creating partnerships with parents will reach out to bring parents in and will engage parents in conversations about what a partnership might look like. Parent needs must be taken into consideration along with the needs of the child and the teacher.

GETTING STARTED

As you begin preparing to open the lines of communication with parents and other community members, first take a moment to evaluate where your school currently stands with regard to community and parental involvement.

- How many community members participate as members of teams for various improvement activities in your school?
- How many parent volunteers does your school have?
- In what capacities are those volunteers used?
- Of the ethnic and cultural groups forming significant parts of the school population, how many are represented on school teams? As parent volunteers?
- What outreach initiatives have been undertaken to recruit community members?
- What forums or meetings have been organized to explain school-related issues and answer families' questions?

Consider these strategies for engaging parents in genuine partnerships:

- Change middle and high school handbooks so that they emphasize the positive, identity-building opportunities awaiting students. Feature interviews and stories with graduates. Place less emphasis on disciplinary infractions, but do present school rules that contribute to the positive identity of the school.
- Develop positive feedback systems to show appreciation of social-emotional intelligence, small amounts of progress, and academic success. Create progress reports about progress of all kinds, and change report cards to include indicators of life skills that parents will understand and appreciate.

- Provide parents with multimedia-formatted guidance with regard to how parents should support at home the work of the school.
- Create forums for dialogue about cultural and ethnic differences; create networks of parent liaisons comprised of educators, parents, and community residents who can help new families of different ethnic groups adapt to the neighborhood.
- Create opportunities for community service and more meaningful, widely participatory student government. Publicize what happens in these contexts so parents can see what the school is doing and gain a better understanding of the interests and competencies of their teenagers.
- Provide forums for parent discussions and mutual support around the various developmental issues, familial stressors, and parent/child communication concerns that can be expected during the adolescent years. (Elias et al., 2003)

CONCLUSION

This chapter has provided scores of strategies and a framework for productively engaging family and community in the school. We have included many examples of what successful schools are doing to engender broad-based support and to strengthen their entire school community in the process.

The next and final chapter addresses an issue that is crucial to sustaining the successes that arise from following the practices described in this and preceding chapters. Building sustainable leadership capacity at all levels has enabled school communities to maintain focus and continue to improve even while withstanding massive changes. Chapter 10 explains how this can be accomplished.

CHAPTER TEN

Principle #6—Building Sustainable Leadership Capacity

by Alan M. Blankstein with
Andy Hargreaves and Dean Fink

> It took about five years before I felt we had really turned a corner; that kids were beginning to think and say that the system was working for them. But the process never ends. There is no single mountain to climb. At the top of one peak is another just beyond.
>
> —Richard DeLorenzo, Superintendent,
> Chugan School District, Anchorage,
> Alaska (quoted in LaFee, 2003)

T his final chapter focuses on three key words for long-term school success: leadership, capacity, and sustainability. Taken together, these words emphasize the importance of continually developing the human resources of the school community so that success lasts well beyond the initial implementation of school improvement efforts.

This chapter includes text that has been adapted with permission from "Sustaining Leadership" by Andy Hargreaves and Dean Fink, *Phi Delta Kappan* 84(9), May 2003, pp. 693–700.

This implies a steadfast depth of commitment to change—a depth that comes from the commitment of the entire school community to a compelling *long-term* vision that encompasses the entire culture of the school. When developed with care and forethought, sustainable leadership capacity enables school cultures to thrive despite challenges, including transition of the leadership.

The following section addresses the "why" question—specifically, why should we build leadership capacity in our teaching staff? The current realities for principals and teachers are included here, as are obstacles to change and the means of addressing each.

This is followed by a definition of "leadership." The summary of research leads us to propose a form of leadership that is enduring and outlasts any single *leader.*

Next we address the issue of "capacity." Although building leadership capacity at all levels—including students, family, and the community—is the ideal, here we focus on teachers as leaders. What does this mean? What roles would a teacher leader play? What examples exist? How can teacher leadership be instituted systematically? All of these questions are addressed in this section.

Finally, Hargreaves and Fink address sustainability using three case studies from their five-year-long school improvement program involving six secondary schools in Ontario, Canada. Particular focus is paid to "leadership of learning," "distributed leadership," and "leadership succession."

WHY BUILD LEADERSHIP CAPACITY

The Job Is Too Big

Our proposed purpose of education—*sustained success for all students in which failure is not an option*—is a big job. Making the statement that all children will succeed (or learn to high levels) can be energizing. Trying to operationalize it as the sole leader of the school can be depleting. The distance between the ideal and the reality for building leaders is often great, as evidenced in this NASSP survey of principals (*Priorities and Barriers in High School Leadership: A Survey of Principals,* 2001):

Principals feel the most important aspects of their job are establishing a learning climate, dealing with personnel issues like hiring and evaluations, and providing curricular leadership. Yet of the average 62 hours a week they work, only about 23 are spent on these activities. The rest are spent on parent issues, discipline, community relations, and school management. (Adapted from Schiff, 2002)

Regarding the chasm between the demands on educational leaders and what they are actually able to do, Richard Elmore (1999–2000) writes:

Instructional leadership is the equivalent of the Holy Grail in educational administration. Most programs that prepare super-intendents and principals claim to be in the business of training the next generation of instructional leaders. . . . This is mainly just talk. In fact few administrators of any kind or at any level are directly involved with instruction. (p. 9)

The principal's job is too big and too complex to be done alone. Moreover, principals who try to "fly solo" often feel isolated and tend to burn out. It can be lonely at the top!

Yet giving up control and the traditional roles and views of authority is difficult, and not often accomplished (Elmore, 1999–2000). This task requires the courage, described in Chapter 3, to take the risk of letting go of some control, trusting staff members to lead in major areas of decision making, admitting that you don't know everything, and becoming a learner alongside your staff, as did Principal Nancy Duden (see Chapter 2).

According to Principal Gary Burgess (quoted in HOPE Foundation, *FNO Video Series,* 2002), this is the most effective way to be a strong leader. "When you keep power, people will not work with you," he says. "When you invest power in other people, it always, inevitably comes back to you." Redefining "strong leadership" in terms of being a developer and facilitator of other leaders requires courage within oneself, and the *en*couragement of others.

Shared Leadership Develops Commitment and Yields Higher Student Achievement

As indicated in Chapter 4, a *collective* commitment to student achievement on the part of teachers is correlated with increased scores in literacy, math, and other subjects (Kruse and Louis, 1995; Ovando, 1994; Newmann and Wehlage, 1995). Increasingly, shared or distributed leadership is defined as a vital ingredient to creating a successful learning community (Cuttance, 2001; Hord, 1997b; Huffman and Hipp, 2004; King and Newmann, 2000, 2001).

Other benefits of teacher leadership include teacher efficacy (Hipp, 1997; Short, 1994), retention of good teachers (Gordon, 1991; Hart and Murphy, 1990), commitment to change efforts (Firestone, 1996; Fullan, 1993; Rosenholtz, 1989), and increased accountability for results (Hammond, 1990). One teacher from a high-performing school noted, "When they [administrators] listen to you, you have some ownership of the school, instead of just following orders. So that is going to motivate you and keep you working hard to try new things" (Hipp, 1997).

Although experience and the research clearly support the notion of teachers as leaders, the reality is that many teachers are reluctant to play that role. Their hesitancy arises from two reasons: First, they don't feel *able* to be a "leader." Their training has not been in this arena, and they have never considered themselves in that role. The legitimate question these teachers may ask is, "What *exactly* do you want me to do, and how am I supposed to do *that*?" The request for very specific information on what to do and how to do it puts the teacher again in a role of follower and seems to minimize the risk of failure. This teacher may feel unable to meet the challenge.

Teachers feeling unable to rise to the challenge need two things: (1) to understand the positive impact they will have on student achievement by assuming an active role in the school; and (2) support and encouragement in taking on leadership roles.

Talking with teachers about the important role they can play *outside* their classroom to affect student achievement is one strategy. Specifically, principals can use the data provided above and that which was used to build the organizational mission, vision, and values. Encouraging teachers to witness other teachers playing these roles in similar school settings is another strategy. Seeing is believing. Calling on early adopters within the school to model the leadership role that can be played is perhaps the most powerful strategy for persuading others of its feasibility. A five-year research project by Hord and Associates found a correlation between successful schools and their display of "high readiness" for change (Hord, 1997a and b). The initial fear and hesitancy among teachers in one of these high-readiness schools was overcome in the following manner:

Teachers teach teachers. [W]e have our computer liaison and our building computer person who train here on campus, and we have the other elementary schools that come here for training from our teachers. . . . Our teachers are great at what they do. Others see this and say, "I'd like to try that!" (Huffman and Hipp, 2004)

Any one or a combination of the above approaches may be effective in addressing teachers' fears of assuming new roles within their school. (Additional means of overcoming obstacles are listed in Chapter 2.) Most important to success, however, is the issue of relational trust (see Chapter 4) and belief in the teachers, as described in Chapters 1 and 3. There is a high correlation between the trust and confidence in teachers displayed by the leaders and the amount of risk those teachers will take.

The second challenge facing teachers is in rethinking their traditional role as followers. The new and unaccustomed role of making and being responsible for decisions requires a major shift in thinking.

Our principal gives us responsibility, so that we feel a valued part of what's happening. Before, I just did what I was told. . . . I just stayed in my classroom . . . but I didn't feel like I had any impact at the school level. Now I feel more involved. (Huffman and Hipp, 2004)

Moreover, many teachers don't want to be leaders, at least not as leadership is traditionally defined. The charismatic, dynamic, highly public concept of a leader is much less appealing to many teachers than would be a role of humble yet courageous leader focused on curriculum and instruction. These are areas in which many teachers would pursue the opportunity to play a leadership role and make meaningful decisions. Many professionals with whom we work say, "I would like to be a part of deciding what we teach and how we teach it!" This desire is understandable, and it provides a good entry point for developing leadership and responsibility.

In addition to the strategies mentioned above, a new definition of leadership would be helpful for many of these teachers—one in which they could see themselves and thus feel impassioned. Many appealing leadership roles for teachers are listed in the section below on "Building Capacity." First, however, let us provide a brief summary of some recent leadership literature, as well as an operational definition of "leader."

DEFINING LEADERSHIP

Traditionally, the role of the leader has been that of a bold, action-oriented figure who solves most of the problems and draws others to his side in the effort. John Wayne did it in the old West, just as Bruce Willis and countless others do it in today's movie shoot-em-ups.

Although there may be some call for such a style of leadership today, particularly in life-threatening crises, a growing body of research calls for a more participative approach in our schools (Cuttance, 2001; Hord, 1997b; Huffman and Hipp, 2004; King and Newmann, 2000; Newmann and Wehlage, 1995). Dan Goleman (2000) defines six styles of leadership. The two styles most closely associated with the "traditional" model are the least effective (Figure 10.1).

The highest level of leadership, according to Jim Collins (2001), is a "Level Five" leader. In addition to being able to create a compelling vision and galvanize people to implement it (Level Four leaders do this also), the Level Five leader has intense professional will and deep humility. This enables submergence of the ego to the greater purpose of the organization. Leaders who "begin with their core" (see Chapters 1 and 3) make a point of clarifying that greater purpose and thus make "Level Five" leadership possible. Ultimately this allows the organization to survive and even thrive, even after that leader's departure. Ego-driven "charismatic" leaders, according to Collins, often leave a large hole in their wake, and their organizations falter.

Thus the most effective school leaders are able to collaboratively create and sustain changes that *continually* enhance student achievement. They display the following characteristics:

(1) They start by building in themselves and others the Courageous Leadership Imperative, focused on sustaining success for *all* students, creating a culture in which failure is not an option.

(2) They work collectively with all staff to assure the resources and support necessary to bring about this mission of achievement for all students.

(3) They do this with a long-term view of sustainability so that internal capacity will continually thrive and enhance student outcomes, even in the face of external threats and their own departure.

LEADING IN A CULTURE OF CHANGE

Leadership Styles	• Visionary
	• Coaching
	• Affiliative
	• Democratic
	• Pacesetting
	• Commanding *Goleman, 2002*

Goleman's Leadership Styles

	How it Builds Resonance	*Impact on Climate*	*When Appropriate*
Visionary	Moves people toward shared dreams	Most strongly positive	When changes require a new vision, or when a clear direction is needed
Coaching	Connects what a person wants with the organization's goals	Highly positive	To help an employee improve performance by building long-term capabilities
Affiliative	Creates harmony by connecting people to each other	Positive	To heal rifts in a team, motivate during stressful times, or strengthen connections
Democratic	Values people's input and gets commitment through participation	Positive	To build buy-in or consensus, or to get valuable input from employees
Pacesetting	Meets challenging and exciting goals	Because too frequently poorly executed, often highly negative	To get high-quality results from a motivated and competent team
Commanding	Soothes fears by giving clear direction in an emergency	Because so often misused, highly negative	In a crisis, to kick-start a turnaround, or with problem employees

Figure 10.1

Source: Adapted and reprinted by permission of Harvard Business School Press. From *Primal Leadership: Realizing the Power of Emotional Intelligence* by D. Goleman, R. Boyatzis, and A. McKee. Boston, MA: 2002, p. 55. Copyright © 2002 by Daniel Goleman; all rights reserved.

The above definition of leadership allows for the development of leaders at every level of the organization. The responsibility for success shifts from one or two people to the entire learning community. This does not imply that everyone plays the same role, but that every role is important and that most entail some level of leadership. The next section of this chapter focuses on specific leadership roles played by teachers in high-performing schools.

BUILDING CAPACITY

As mentioned above, we are witnessing a small but growing shift today toward teachers as leaders. Among the obstacles to this much-needed change is the narrow definition of leadership and the minimal number of roles that comprise it. Districts that work with teachers to define various leadership roles have begun to systematically invite new teachers to select one of these roles to pursue once hired. They then provide support throughout the process of new teachers taking on leadership roles. These schools and districts are well on their way to building vital leadership capacity.

> Some districts are enlisting teachers to create home-grown instructional policies and tools. . . . A number of them are going beyond conventional activities and are using teachers to develop performance-based assessments, scoring rubrics, curriculum, and standards. Teachers in one Colorado district, for example, run a summer institute based on the construction of curriculum units aligned to their local standards. These initiatives are seen not only as strategies for building the knowledge and skills of the teaching staff, but as ways for districts to expand their own capacity to accomplish major policy goals. (CPRE Policy briefs, p. 4)

Staff development has traditionally been delivered by outside experts. In a growing number of school districts, it is coming into line with the recommendations of the National Staff Development Council that leadership be embedded in the school culture (Bradley, 1993; Clark and Clark, 1996). This has included teachers taking on the role of teaching other teachers. This happens through teacher mentors; teachers being recognized as content-area specialists; master teachers; teachers leading curriculum writing teams, standards development teams, and professional development programs.

The San Francisco school district relies heavily on Teachers on Special Assignment. These professionals make a three- to five-year commitment to coordinate and facilitate professional development for the district. They also help schools implement site-based plans. The TSA's work with Teacher Leaders, who in turn lead instructional content areas and assist individual schools in implementing professional development. These Teacher Leaders also mentor and do peer training, coaching, and team-building in schools throughout the district.

Beyond this, teachers in high-performing schools may engage in a particular intellectual pursuit. This has included teachers who wrote and received grants for more intensive study on teacher self-efficacy, for example. This fit neatly with their school's interest, so they became a resource to the school while enhancing their own knowledge base. This, in turn, furthered their commitment to the school. One school formalized this process by creating a "Scholar of the Year" program.

This approach can be expanded in many ways. Teachers on special assignment, for example, may take a year off to do intensive research and/or speaking in a way that builds school capacity.

Most important, perhaps, are the informal roles that teachers can play. Schools with strong learning cultures expect that when a teacher attends a professional development workshop offsite, it is with an eye toward how what is learned can be transmitted and used to enhance learning in the school. The follow-up to such an activity could include speaking at a teacher luncheon, sharing during weekly team meetings, posting summaries on the bulletin board (or school Web site), or calling colleagues on the phone to discuss possible implications for implementation at the school.

Teacher Leadership

At Adlai Stevenson High School, opportunities abound for teachers to assume leadership roles. At Stevenson, the faculty are divided into subject-area divisions, each led by a teacher who serves as director. Each director, assisted by a core leadership team of four to five other teachers, is responsible for monitoring virtually every aspect of his or her division—including curriculum, budget, and policies.

Within each division are a number of teacher teams, and each team is headed by a team leader. The team leaders' main responsibility is to keep the team operating as a collaborative, productive unit. Toward that end, leaders schedule meetings, set agendas, and ensure that any necessary tasks get done. They are accountable to either the division director or one of the members of the core leadership team.

Giving teachers the opportunity to lead results in many positive outcomes, according to Dan Galloway, Stevenson's principal. "It gives them an opportunity to do something outside the classroom. It gives them more responsibility with their peers and with the school as a whole. It gives them a broader perspective of what needs to be done," he says. Leadership opportunities can even lead to greater commitment and prevent teacher burnout. "It gives teachers more ownership in the school," says Galloway. "I think it's a source of renewal for them."

It is helpful to institutionalize and systematize capacity-building approaches. Once this is done, they can become both a means of screening and recruiting prospective job applicants. New employees would also be given both the expectation and the support necessary to become a part of a learning team and a project or endeavor that taps both their passions and interests in leadership.

In the next section, Hargreaves and Fink define "sustainability" and provide case studies that demonstrate how some schools build it into their culture.

SUSTAINABLE LEADERSHIP
BY ANDY HARGREAVES AND DEAN FINK

In this section, we connect the concept of sustainability to the leadership literature in education and outline different interrelated principles that underpin the ideas and practices of "sustaining leadership." We draw on a five-year program of school improvement involving six secondary schools in Ontario, Canada. We use three positive and negative sets of "case stories" to illustrate our analysis of sustainability in leadership. Specifically, we focus on: (1) leadership of learning, (2) "distributed" leadership, and (3) leadership succession.

Background of Sustainability

For many years, change theorists and change agents have been concerned with the problem of how to move beyond the *implementation* phase of change, in which new ideas and practices are tried for the first time, to the *institutionalization* phase, when new practices are integrated into teachers' repertoires and begin to affect many teachers, not just a few (Stiegelbauer and Anderson, 1992). "Institutionalization means a change is taken as a normal, taken for granted part of organizational life; and has unquestioned resources of time, personnel, and money available" (Miles, 1998, p. 59). Many longstanding practices—the graded school; the compartmentalized, hierarchical, bureaucratized secondary school; tracking or streaming according to students' abilities; and didactic, teacher-centered teaching—are examples of policies and practices that have been institutionalized over long periods of time and that have become part of the "grammar" of schooling (Tyack and Tobin, 1994). The persistence of this grammar and of everyone's ideas of how schools should really work as institutions have repeatedly made it exceptionally difficult to institutionalize other changes, innovations, and reforms that challenge accepted practice, that imply a different and even deviant institutional appearance and way of operating for schooling (Meyer and Rowan, 1977).

Innovations that challenge the traditional grammar of schooling often arouse intense enthusiasm. They prosper and flourish in well-supported pilot projects, in specially staffed and charismatically led schools, or among an atypical minority of teachers and schools whose teaching careers and identities are characterized by risk and change (Fink, 2000a; Fletcher et al., 1985; Riley, 1998; Smith et al., 1987). But typically innovations fade, lighthouse schools lose their luster, and attempts to spread initiatives across a wider, more skeptical system—to scale them up—meet with little success (Elmore, 1995). Even those few innovative settings that survive often serve as outlier exceptions—giving the system a safety valve where all its most critical and questioning educators and their clients can be congregated together in one site (Lortie, 1975; Sarason, 1990).

In the face of the traditional grammar of schooling, and those whose interests are served by its abstract academic orientations, the vast majority of educational change that deepens learning and allows everyone to benefit from it neither spreads nor lasts. Sustainability, in the deeper sense, raises questions about the preoccupation of policymakers with short-term success over long-term improvement, statistical appearances that make them look good over sustained changes that ensure students learn well, and timelines for change that address electoral cycles of popularity rather than change cycles of durability.

Contemporary discussions of sustainability in educational change in some ways repeat these traditional preoccupations with how to keep change going over time. In doing so, however, they often trivialize the idea of sustainability (Barber, 2001). They reduce it to *maintainability*—to the question of how to make change last—and add little to our understanding of change.

The Meaning of Sustainability

Sustainability is about more than endurance. It concerns more than the life and death of a change. Sustainability is also a spatial issue. As we have argued elsewhere,

> Sustainability does not simply mean whether something can last. It addresses how particular initiatives can be developed without compromising the development of others in the surrounding environment, now and in the future. (Hargreaves and Fink, 2000, p. 32)

Specifically, this implies several things. First, sustainable improvement is enduring, not fleeting. It does not put its investment dollars in the high-profile launch of an initiative, then withdraw them when the glamor has gone. Sustainable improvement demands committed relationships, not fickle infatuations. It is change for keeps, change meant to last. Sustainable improvement contributes to the growth and the good of everyone, instead of fostering the fortunes of the few at the expense of the rest. It does not promote model schools, magnet schools, or schools with special emphases that raid scarce resources from the rest.

Second, sustainable improvement develops and draws on resources and support at a rate that can match the pace of change. It does not let change outrun its resource base and deplete reserves that are needed by others. Sustainable policies do not lavish resources on computer hardware when long-term spending commitments cannot support continuing maintenance or updates in software. Sustainable educational policies don't squander all the resource on pilot projects, leaving little for everyone else, or invest improvement funds in coordinators who disappear once the money has dried up. Sustainable improvement requires investment in building long-term capacity for improvement, such as the development of teachers' skills, which will stay with them long after the project money is spent (Stoll, 1999).

Finally, promoters of sustainability cultivate and re-create an educational environment that possesses the capacity to stimulate ongoing improvement on a broad front. They enable people to adapt to and prosper in their increasingly complex environment. Rational, standardized scientific efficiency is the enemy of healthy and creative diversity. It produces overly simple systems that are too specialized to allow the learning and cross-fertilization that are necessary for healthy development. The evidence of research that we have undertaken with our colleagues on the long-term impact of educational reform in Ontario is that standardized reform is destroying diversity and seriously endangering the lives and futures of the weakest members of the school system, that is, the poor, the marginalized, those who are learning through a new language, and those with special educational needs. Standardization is endangering these students to the point of educational extinction, where failure to meet the regimented standards is denying severely disadvantaged students the right to graduate (Hargreaves et al., 2001). Similarly, high-pressure improvements in test results in the short run are being bought at the expense of a long-term recruitment and retention crisis in teaching—since teaching driven by short-term results is not the kind of teaching that teachers want to do (Hargreaves, 2003).

In education, one important addition to this definition of sustainability is that not anything or everything is worth keeping. In education, it matters that what is sustained is what, in terms of teaching and learning, is itself sustaining. To sustain is to keep alive in every sense; sustenance is nourishment. Sound education, good teaching and learning are inherently sustaining processes. Supporting and maintaining those aspects of teaching and learning that are deep and that endure, that foster sophisticated understanding and lifelong learning for all, defines the core of sustainable education. This includes not just knowing what, but knowing *why* (deep understanding), knowing *how* (application), and knowing *who* (building social networks and social capital; Organization for Economic Cooperation and Development, 2001). Merely maintaining practices that raise test scores or produce easily measurable results does not sustain these deeper aspects of teaching and learning.

To sum up, sustainability in educational change comprises six key and interrelated characteristics. These are:

- improvement that sustains learning, not merely change that alters schooling
- improvement that endures over time
- improvement that can be supported by available or achievable resources
- improvement that is a shared responsibility
- improvement that doesn't impact negatively on the surrounding environment of other schools and systems
- improvement that promotes ecological diversity and capacity throughout the educational and community environment

Method

What contribution can leaders make to sustainable improvement according to the sense of sustainability we have outlined? In our view, leaders develop sustainability by how they approach, commit to, and protect deep learning in their schools; by how they sustain others around them to promote and support that learning; by how they sustain themselves in doing so, so that they can persist with their vision and avoid burning out (see Chapters 1 and 3 also on sustaining your vision and yourself); and by how they try to ensure that the improvements they bring about last over time, especially after they themselves have gone. We will now look at three particular aspects of what we call *sustainable leadership* that illustrate the different components of sustainability (and nonsustainability) that we have outlined: leading learning, distributed leadership, and leadership succession.

The examples are drawn from our research and experience of working with four, then six, secondary schools over five years (1997–2002) to help them implement a major set of legislated changes in Secondary School Reform in ways that were consistent with principles of successful school improvement and with their own professional values as educators. All schools were located in a large urban and suburban school district in Ontario, Canada, which funded the project in partnership with the Ontario Ministry of Education and Training.

The project design generated relationships of trust and candid disclosure among the schools, between the schools and the project team, and accordingly built an authentic understanding of how teachers and leaders were experiencing and coping with reforms over a relatively long five-year period when other major changes were also affecting their schools.

Examples of Sustainability and Nonsustainability

Let's look now at the three paired examples of sustainability and failed sustainability in our project schools.

Leading Learning

The prime responsibility of all school leaders is to sustain learning. Leaders of learning put learning at the center of everything they do: student learning first, then everyone else's learning in support of it (Glickman, 2002; Stoll, Fink, & Earl, 2002). The leader's role as a leader of learning is put to the strongest test when his or her school faces demanding measures or policies that seem to undermine true learning or distract people's energies and attention away from it.

High-stakes testing can push teachers to deliver improved results but not necessarily to produce better learning. What educators do in this situation depends on their commitment to student learning and on their attitudes to their own learning. In 2001, the Canadian province of Ontario introduced a high-stakes literacy test in Grade 10. It was applied to virtually all students who were required to pass in order to graduate. High stakes, high pressure!

Two Approaches to High-Stakes Testing

Ivor Megson was the new principal at Talisman Park Secondary School. Promoted from being assistant principal at the school, Megson was dedicated to his work as a leader but did not like to rock the boat too much. Most of his staff had been at the school a long time. They liked being innovative in their own academic subjects but were skeptical and often cynical about larger-scale reform agendas. A coffee circle of embittered staff members met every morning before school to complain about the government's latest (almost daily) initiatives and announcements. Like many principals, Megson saw his responsibility as being to protect his staff from the deluge of reforms that descended on the school. This, he felt, was the best way he could help them.

With his staff, Megson therefore figured out the most minimal and least disruptive school response to the Grade 10 test—one that would produce the best results with the least amount of effort. Quickly, Megson and his staff began identifying a group of students who, on pretests, indicated they would fall just below the pass mark. The school then coached or "prepped" these students intensively in literacy learning, so they would perform acceptably when taking the real test. Technically, the strategy worked. The school's results looked good. But teachers' energies are finite, and as staff concentrated on those students near the cut-off point, the ones who really needed help with literacy, and had little chance of passing the test, were ignored. At Talisman Park, authentic literacy and learning for all—especially for the most needy—were sacrificed to appearances and results.

Charmaine Williams was the principal of Wayvern High School, just up the road from Talisman Park. Wayvern was a culturally and ethnically diverse school and had a high number of students for whom English was their second language. Wayvern had a lot to lose on the literacy test. Yet Williams's school made literacy, not the literacy *test*, one of their key improvement goals. Williams engaged her staff in inquiry about how to improve literacy so it would benefit all students in the long term, instead of focusing on how to manipulate the short-term scores on the test. Working with large staff teams, across disciplines, and with workshop training support, Wayvern undertook an audit of existing literacy practices in classrooms, researched effective literacy strategies that might be helpful, and undertook a "gap" analysis to see what improvements would be necessary. Teachers shared their literacy strategies across subjects, then dedicated a whole month to a high-profile focus on literacy learning in the school and with the community. They also continued a successful literacy initiative they had already made where everyone in the school read together for 15 minutes each day. Williams harnessed her staff's learning in support of student learning. The immediate results were not spectacular (as is usual with more sustainable change), but together the staff and parents were confident that long-term improvement mattered the most. Wayvern teachers were convinced that, in future years, scores would increase as genuine reflections of learning and achievement, rather than because of cynical manipulations of the testing process (Talbert and MacLaughlin, 1994).

One reform; two principals; two schools—but different outcomes! Especially in the most adverse circumstances, those principals who are leaders of learning make the most lasting and inclusive improvements for their students in their schools.

Distributed Leadership

Different Leader Styles; Different Outcomes

Outstanding leadership is not just the province of individual icons and heroes (Saul, 1993). In a complex, fast-paced world, leadership cannot rest on the shoulders of the few. The burden is too great. In highly complex, knowledge-based organizations, everyone's intelligence is needed to help the organization to flex, respond, regroup, and retool in the face of unpredictable and sometimes overwhelming demands. Locking intelligence up in the individual leader creates inflexibility and increases the likelihood of mistakes.

But when we use what Brown and Lauder (2001) call "collective intelligence"—intelligence that is infinite rather than fixed, multifaceted rather than singular, and that belongs to everyone, not just a few—the capacity for learning improvement is magnified greatly. For these reasons, more and more efforts are being made to replace individual leaders with more distributed or distributive leadership (Institute for Educational Leadership, 2000, 2001; Spillane et al., 2001). In a distributed system, leadership becomes a network of relationships among people, structures, and cultures (both within and across organizational boundaries), not just a role-based function assigned to, or acquired by, a person in an organization, who then uses his or her power to influence the actions of others. Leadership is viewed as an organic activity, dependent on interrelationships and connections (Riley, 2000).

Mark Warne was the principal of North Ridge High School. Three years from retirement, Warne has a keen intellect and a deep knowledge about imposed change and its effects; he valued and was skilled at seeing the "big picture" of reform. When legislated reforms were announced, Warne produced detailed, thoughtful written and projected timelines for implementation responses that he circulated to staff members for comment. The response was disappointing, though, and Warne confided that his staff was generally apathetic about getting involved with change. His strength was his great intellectual clarity, but he could not develop the capacity among his staff to share his vision. The big-picture change belonged to Warne alone, not to everyone. His office was packed with policy statements, resources, and materials that might better have been distributed around the school.

Warne controlled the directions of his school through the line management of the department heads. The department heads were quite autonomous in their areas; staff involvement, therefore, depended on the leadership style of each head. One of his assistant principals (also close to retirement) performed traditional discipline and administrative roles. The other was battling with what sadly turned out to be a terminal illness.

Warne delegated to his subordinate department heads and accepted their advice in areas where they were more expert than he. The department heads generally described him as "support-ive," "compassionate," and "well-intentioned." Yet the larger staff was excluded from decisions and ill-informed on important issues. They considered their principal to be "indecisive," "inconsistent," and "lacking a personal vision." At a school improvement workshop we ran with the whole staff, they were the only school of the six to identify themselves as "cruising" (Stoll and Fink, 1996)—their mainly affluent students were get-ting good results, but the school lacked purpose and direction. The chief problem the staff chose to address at the workshop was "communications with the administration."

Soon after this, the school began to change dramatically, but not through a change of principal. In 1998, two new assistant principals were appointed. Together they infused the school's administration with renewed enthusiasm, optimism, and focus. Diane Grant's athletic bearing and infectiously energetic style brought her sophisticated knowledge of curriculum and class-room assessment to the problem of reform. Before long she was skillfully leading the staff in curriculum gap analysis or having them share successful experiences in classroom assessment by seating them in cross-disciplinary tables at the staff picnic, where they scribbled their ideas as graffiti on paper tablecloths. Meanwhile, Bill Johnson, the other deputy, drew on his counseling skills to develop effective communications and relationships with and among the staff. Grant aroused teachers' passions, and Johnson calmed them; as a team, they were able to set a common vision for the school and a more open style of communication. In this new style, the staff focused on collaborative learning, inquiry, and problem solving. Warne's strength was having the good sense to "distribute" the leadership of important classroom-related changes to his assistant principals, who in turn redistributed much of the leadership among the staff, who learned to be critical filters for government mandates rather than mere pipelines for implementing them.

Leadership Succession

Sustainable leadership outlives particular individuals. It does not disappear when the leaders leave. There is evidence that the departure of the initiating principal or a critical mass of early leaders from model or beacon schools is the first symptom of decline (Fink, 2000b; Sarason, 1972). MacMillan (1996, 2000) has observed that the practice in some school districts of regularly rotating leaders between schools can harden teachers against change because they come to see the school's principalship as little more than a revolving door in a building where they are the permanent residents. Whether principal rotation is formalized or not, leadership succession always poses a threat to sustainable improvement.

How Two Schools Dealt with Leadership Succession

Bill Mathews was a tall, commanding figure who brought vision, energy, and intellectual rigor to his role. The son of a police officer, he believed strongly that students came first and pursued this belief with a sense of clear expectation and relentless determination. Some staff respected his commitment to children and his willingness to take action and put himself on the line for their sake. Prior experience of principalship buttressed his self-confidence, and in a teacher culture that reveled in argument and debate, his somewhat adversarial style (Blase and Anderson, 1995), which encouraged and entertained well-reasoned and supported opposition to his ideas, suited a sizable number of staff very well. It also stimulated some extremely lively staff meetings. Mathews led Stewart Heights School with firm expectations and clear example, accompanied by lively argument and considerable humor. The most outstanding instance of leading by example was when he personally solved the scheduling problems of 80 students to demonstrate that better service for students was indeed possible.

Mathews was quick to move to action by getting staff members to analyze data consciously and to make action plans on the basis of what they learned. He integrated several improvement teams to permit far greater voice and participation for teachers in the work of the school compared to the previous dominance of the department heads' council. In this culturally diverse school, Mathews encouraged the staff to initiate a range of changes that made students feel more included and parents feel more welcome. Structures, planning, and initiation, backed by his own personal interactions with people and his visibility around the school, were the ways in which Mathews brought about change. Many staff members, including most of those on the School Success team, warmed to his decisiveness and sense of direction. Staff referred to him as a "visionary," "change agent," and "efficient manager." Others, however—especially women—indicated they respected him but questioned his somewhat "authoritarian" style.

The two assistant principals offered complementary, indeed dramatically contrasting, approaches within Mathews's administrative team. One presented a quieter, more restrained, and more procedural version of masculinity in leadership than his more "up-front" principal. The other took a more relationship-centered approach to students, curriculum, and staff development, in which caring coupled with hard work and high expectations played an important role. With their contrasting styles, they too fostered greater teacher participation in the work of the school.

Bill Matthews felt it had been a struggle to change the school culture to provide "a service to kids and the community."

Yet, when he presented the staff with survey data showing that 95% of staff were satisfied with the school, but only 35% of students and 25% of parents were, this created a common problem that the staff had to work together to solve.

With more time to help staff members work through their doubts and difficulties, Matthews and his team may well have been able to convert the temporary success of short-term innovation into sustainable improvement. But by the end of his third year, changing circumstances within the school system resulted in his moving to a superintendency, one of the assistant principals to his first principalship, and the other to her second deputy principalship. Stewart Heights' new principal was new to the school and to the role; he had to feel his way carefully into both of them. Meanwhile, the mandated reform agenda was quickly gathering pace. The result of these converging forces was that the staff and their new principal turned their attention to implementation more than improvement. Observations at the school climate meetings indicated that with the previous principal's departure, student-centered policies now gave way to more conventional behavior-code initiatives. The early achievements of school improvement at Stewart Heights quickly began to fade. If school improvement is to be sustainable, one essential factor is continuity of tenure or at least longer tenure for the initial principal, as well as consistency in philosophy among those who come after.

By comparison, Blue Mountain School, an innovative model school established in 1994, planned its own leadership succession from the outset. The fate of most innovative schools is to fade once their founding principals have left. Blue Mountain's principal anticipated his own departure and worked hard to create a school structure that would survive his departure and "perpetuate what we are doing." He was especially alert to the threats posed by leadership succession (Fink, 2000b; Hargreaves and Fink, 2000; MacMillan, 2000), in which an ensuing principal might import a different philosophy. He therefore "negotiated very strongly [with the district] to have my deputy principal appointed principal." After four years, the system moved the principal who founded the school to a large "high profile" school in the system and promoted his deputy in his place. In her words:

> We talked about [this move] and we talked about how we could preserve the direction that the school is moving in, and we were afraid that if a new administrator came in as principal that if he or she had a different philosophy, a different set of beliefs, then it would be quite easy to simply move things in that particular direction and we didn't want that to happen.

Blue Mountain is a rarity. In general, planned succession is one of the most neglected aspects of leadership theory and practice in our schools, and one of the most persistently missing pieces in the efforts to secure sustainability of school improvement.

DISCUSSION AND CONCLUSION

Our definition and dimensions of sustainability in education and our case illustrations carry a number of implications for what it might mean to develop sustainable leadership.

1. *The future of leadership must be embedded in the hearts and minds of the many, and not rest on the shoulders of a heroic few.* We want dedicated and committed professionals in school leadership, not martyrs to management—severed heads whose all-consuming devotion to their work comes at the cost of their families, their lives, their health, and themselves.

School leadership is not the sum of its individual leaders, still less its separate principals. School leadership is a system, a culture. Schools are places where principals, teachers, students, and parents all lead. To sustain quality leadership, school systems must apply systems thinking to their mandate of leadership quality, qualifications, and development—not just by setting common standards and criteria, but by applying systems thinking to all initiatives. Leadership must be a culture of integrated qualities rather than merely an aggregate of common characteristics.

School jurisdictions should see leadership as a horizontal system across space, where leaders can learn from each other within and across their schools through peer support groups, online dialogue, pairing of schools and their principals (Stoll and Fink, 1996), joint research and development projects, etc. As we experienced in our school improvement project, one of the components most consistently valued by school leaders is the regular opportunity to meet and converse with each other to talk openly about shared professional, and sometimes personal, concerns.

2. *Educational systems should see leadership as a vertical system over time.* The efforts of all leaders are influenced by the impact of their predecessors and have implications for their successors. No leader is an island in time.

Principals and their systems tend to put all their energy into what is called inbound knowledge—the knowledge needed to change a school, improve it, make one's mark on it, turn it around. Little or no attention is devoted to outbound knowledge—the knowledge needed to preserve past successes, or keep initiatives going once the originating leader has left. The moment that head teachers/principals get new appointments, they immediately start to focus on their new school, their next challenge, or on how to ensure that their present achievements live on after their departure.

Few things in education are more fragile than leadership succession. Heroic heads do not plan for their own obsolescence. The emphasis on change has obliterated the importance of continuity. In inner-city schools, teachers see their principals come and go constantly; they learn quickly how to resist and ignore each new leader's efforts (MacMillan, 2000). The result is that school improvement becomes like a set of bobbing corks; many schools rise under one set of leaders, only to sink under the next. If we want *sustainable* as well as successful leadership, we must pay serious attention to leadership succession (Fink, 2000b). Leaders must be asked, and must ask themselves, these questions: What will be my legacy? How will my influence live on after my departure? The time for leaders to ask such questions is at the very beginning, not when their tenure is drawing to a close.

3. *The promise of sustainable success in education lies in creating cultures of distributed leadership throughout the school community, not in training and developing a tiny leadership elite.* Amid today's contextual realities—sky-high expectations, rapid change, and a youthful profession in the first decades of the 21st century—teachers cannot be the mere targets of other people's leadership, but must see themselves as being, and *encouraged* to be, leaders of classrooms and of colleagues from the moment they begin their

careers. Distributed leadership means more than delegation. Delegation involves passing on lesser and often unwanted tasks to others. The individual leader decides what will be delegated and to whom. Distributed leadership means creating a culture of initiative and opportunity, in which teachers of all kinds propose new directions, start innovations—perhaps sometimes even challenging and creating difficulties for their leaders in the higher interests of the pupils and the school. In its fullest development, distributed leadership extends beyond the staff to pupils and parents. Distributed leadership gives depth and breadth to the idea and practice of leadership.

4. *Recruiting and developing future educational leaders will require focusing on their potential rather than recycling their existing proficiencies.* The recruitment and development of leaders in the public service in most Western countries has become a major concern as the "baby boom" generation moves into retirement (Government of Western Australia, 2001; Jackson, 2000; Langford et al., 2000; National Academy of Public Administration, 1997). For example, by 2005, 70% of the senior managers in the U.S. public service will be eligible for retirement, "causing unique challenges for numerous agencies in maintaining leadership continuity, institutional memory, and workforce experience" (Financial Executive International, 2001). In education, after years of top-down, market-driven reforms, many existing leaders are retiring at their first opportunity, creating a crisis of "recruitment and retention" (Bowser, 2001; Early et al., 2002; Goldstein, 2001; Johnson, 2001; National Association of Secondary School Principals, 2001). Education has much to learn from the private sector about planning for succession.

The "best" private sector organizations consider investing in the development of leaders as an "asset" to the organization, not a "cost." These forward-looking organizations look at the long term to determine the kinds of leadership skills and aptitudes that will be needed in the future (Jackson, 2000). Rather than focusing on existing competencies based on existing roles, they recruit and develop people who have "learned how to learn" and are sufficiently flexible to adjust to changing circumstances (Stoll, Fink, and Earl, 2002). We need to prepare leaders for their future, rather than "polishing yesterday's leadership paradigm" (Peters, 1999).

Schools that sustain "deep" learning experiences for all pupils should address the breadth of school leadership in supporting and promoting the learning of present and future leaders themselves.

They should address the length and sustainability of school leadership over time, helping leaders to plan for their own professional obsolescence and to think about the school's needs for continuity as well as change. School systems will have to acknowledge and create conditions that distribute leadership far beyond the head teacher's office to the entire culture of the school, and even to the larger community. And they will need to concentrate on the leadership skills and qualities that will sustain leaders into the future rather than merely help them manage and survive in the present. Successful leadership is sustainable leadership—nothing simpler, nothing less.

CONCLUSION

I began *Failure Is Not an Option* with a dedication recognizing its simple history: a grandmother who was unwilling to give up on her grandson. This is similar to the untold story of so many of our successes with students in schools. One teacher, one principal, one cafeteria worker or janitor is unwilling to give up on a young person, who then succeeds as a result.

Taken independently, each of these courageous acts—these acts of the heart—are extraordinary. They have ripple effects that continue for generations. Creating a collective culture in which such courageousness is the norm—places in which the entire school community can realistically expect sustained success for themselves and for all of their students—is what this book is about.

As demonstrated throughout this book, success is at hand! Schools and districts throughout North America are overcoming real and perceived obstacles, using their moral outrage and courageous leadership to tackle both fears and traditions of failure.

This book has provided examples from Bristol, England, to Toronto, Canada, from Baltimore, Maryland, to Pixley, California. Every example illuminates the precious "how to's," but, even more important, the *who* and the *why* of success. Eventually these small islands of possibility became oceans of hope, creating communities where failure is no longer an option.

With a clear focus on why we are in this profession, the development of our Courageous Leadership Imperative, and some information about how to create sustainable communities of learning, there is little that can stand in the way of our success. Grandma wouldn't have had it any other way!

Appendix A

SELF-ASSESSMENT

Do the Cultural Norms of Your School
Promote School Improvement?

	Never	Rarely	Sometimes	Often	Always
1. Shared goals ("We know where we are going")	1	2	3	4	5
2. Responsibility for success ("We must succeed")	1	2	3	4	5
3. Collegiality ("We're working on it together")	1	2	3	4	5
4. Continuous improvement ("We can get better")	1	2	3	4	5
5. Lifelong learning ("Learning is for everyone")	1	2	3	4	5
6. Risk taking ("We learn by trying something new")	1	2	3	4	5
7. Support ("There's always someone there to help")	1	2	3	4	5
8. Mutual support ("Everyone has something to offer")	1	2	3	4	5
9. Openness ("We can discuss our differences")	1	2	3	4	5
10. Celebration and humor ("We feel good about ourselves")	1	2	3	4	5

ADD THE 4'S AND 5'S

Source: Stoll and Fink, *Changing Our Schools* (1996). Used with permission.

How Effective Is Your School?

	Never	Rarely	Sometimes	Often	Always
1. Instructional leadership (firm and purposeful, a participative approach, the leading professional)	1	2	3	4	5
2. Shared vision and clear goals (unity of purpose, consistency of practice)	1	2	3	4	5
3. Shared values and beliefs	1	2	3	4	5
4. A learning environment (an orderly atmosphere, an attractive working environment)	1	2	3	4	5
5. Teaching and curriculum focus (maximization of learning time, academic emphasis, focus on achievement)	1	2	3	4	5
6. High expectations (for all, communications of expectations, intellectual challenge for all)	1	2	3	4	5
7. Positive student behavior (clear and fair discipline and feedback)	1	2	3	4	5
8. Frequent monitoring of student progress (ongoing monitoring, evaluating school performance)	1	2	3	4	5
9. Student involvement and responsibility (high student self-esteem, positions of responsibility, control of work)	1	2	3	4	5
10. Climate for learning (positive physical environment, recognition, incentives)	1	2	3	4	5

Source: Halton Board of Education (1988). Used with permission.

School Typology

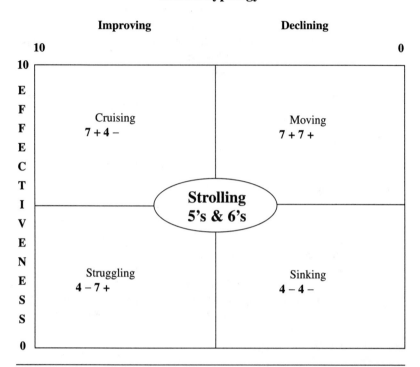

Source: Stoll and Fink, *Changing Our Schools* (1996). Used with permission.

Three Strategies of School Development

III. Good Schools ────▶ **II. Moderately** ────▶ **I. Failing Schools**
                          Effective
                          Schools

Keeping good schools effective and stimulated		
Becoming more effective		
✓ Build capacity ✓ Focus on teaching and learning ✓ Mainly work with existing leadership & support ✓ Some outside pressure/support ✓ Larger lesson periods to promote classroom creativity ✓ Broaden teacher leadership ✓ Listen & respond to students ✓ Motivate disillusioned staff ✓ Staff focused on purposes	✓ Extensive intervention & support ✓ Usually new leadership ✓ Target priorities for visible improvement, i.e., dress codes, attendance, etc. ✓ Building teacher competence & confidence in teaching strategies	✓ External partnerships ✓ Access to networks ✓ Exposure to new ideas/practices ✓ Consolidating collaboration ✓ Celebrating success ✓ Minimal external pressure

Source: D. Hopkins, *School Improvement for Real* (2001). New York: Routledge/ Falmer. Used with permission from Thomson Publishing Services.

Appendix B

STRATEGIES FOR MAKING TIME

- Shared classrooms. Plan and schedule team teaching and multidisciplinary class time.
- Adjust daily schedule. Teachers agree to arrive sufficiently in advance of classes starting to allow for meeting time. Classes can also be started late one day a week to add 15–20 extra minutes to regular early meeting time.
- Bring classes together. Have classes exchange visits on a reciprocal basis (e.g., fifth-graders visit first-grade classes to read or work with younger children, and first-graders visit fifth-graders on alternate weeks), and be supervised by one teacher, freeing up the other one.
- Use assemblies to free up time. Schedule building-wide or school-wide events (movies, assemblies, and so on) during which class-room teachers can meet while students are supervised by counselors, paraprofessionals, or administrators.
- Give common assignments. Several classrooms of students at the same grade level (or taking the same course) are given the same assignment or project simultaneously. Videos, library time, or other related activities are scheduled for all the classes at once, freeing their teachers to meet together while aides, volunteers, or others supervise.
- Use parent or business volunteers. Involve parents as aides or chaperones for appropriate activities. Invite local business representatives to share their particular expertise as they supervise classes.
- Free up the fifth day. Schedule all academic classes to take place four days each week, leaving the fifth day free for team meetings while students rotate to art, music, P.E., technology, the library, and so on.

- Reduce the number of all-staff meetings, and replace them with smaller team meetings where the topics under discussion can be tailored to the needs of the group. (Pardini, 1999)
- Use paraprofessionals, student teachers, and aides to cover classes on a regular basis.
- Allocate more staff positions to classroom teaching than to pull-out teaching and/or support roles. (Darling-Hammond, 1999)
- Implement schedules that engage students with fewer teachers each day for longer periods of time. (Darling-Hammond, 1999)
- Free teachers from nonprofessional activities (e.g., playground, bus duty, and so on).
- Use professional development funding and time allocation for teamwork.

Appendix C

STRATEGIES FOR DEALING
WITH RESISTANCE

When faced with resistance, most people feel challenged. They feel that they must "overcome" the resistance in order to win their point. This instinct to "overcome" can actually lead to counterproductive behaviors. Some of these ineffective behaviors include:

- Use of power—meeting force with force to overcome the resistance
- Manipulating those who oppose—finding subtle ways to apply pressure, or giving false impressions or partial information
- Applying force of reason—overwhelming opponents with facts, figures, and flowcharts
- Ignoring the resistance—failing to address it in the hopes that it will go away on its own
- Playing off relationships—using friendships as leverage to get others to agree
- Making deals—offering something in exchange for agreement (e.g., tradeoffs)
- Killing the messenger—getting rid of or bypassing the resistor
- Giving in too soon—ceding your position before exploring the true level of resistance or the possibility of common understanding (OISE/UT, 2001)

According to research from the University of Toronto, these common responses actually increase people's resistance. Even if they are effective in the short term, the win may not be worth the long-term costs of sabotage, compliance versus commitment, and/or people opting out of the implementation phase.

We can better deal with resistance by remembering a set of core behaviors, or touchstones. As we develop strategies for dealing with resistors, each strategy should be consistent with these touchstones:

- *Maintain clear focus.* Don't let the "fog" of resistance obscure your vision of your original goal. Yet while never losing sight of the long-range goal, you must also keep an eye on the work of the moment. By maintaining a clear focus, you can switch your attention back and forth between what is going on at the moment and what you are ultimately trying to accomplish.
- *Embrace resistance.* Although it may seem counterintuitive, resistance can actually serve a positive purpose in your efforts to build consensus. If you are to overcome objections, you must know what they *are*—and resistance provides you with that information.
- *Respect those who resist.* Listen to what your resistors have to say with an open mind; do not automatically assume that they are uninformed, unjustified, or motivated purely by self-interest. Treat them with respect and dignity and be completely truthful.
- *Relax.* When someone pushes against us, it is instinctive for us to push back. It is that instinct, however, that prevents us from relaxing and embracing resistance. By relaxing—and not pushing back—you can allow your resistors to talk and tell you their thoughts. And once you understand their thoughts, you can use them to begin seeking common ground.
- *Join with the resistance.* By listening with an open mind and exploring the ideas of the resistors, you can begin to identify areas you have in common. Building support for your idea happens when you find this common ground—this merging of interests and concerns.

Source: Adapted from *Dealing with Resistance,* OISE/UT, 2001.

Appendix D

RUNNING RIVER ELEMENTARY
SCHOOL MISSION STATEMENT

The mission of Running River Elementary School is to provide an opportunity for every student to master grade-level skills regardless of previous academic performance, family background, socioeconomic status, race, or gender. It is our purpose to educate all students to high levels of academic performance, while fostering positive growth in social/emotional behaviors and attitudes. The entire staff pledges itself to these student outcomes.

Appendix E

DEVELOPMENT PROCESS FOR
MISSION, VISION, VALUES, AND GOALS

The first step in the collaborative process of developing your school's mission, vision, values, and goals is identifying the underlying beliefs and priorities of all stakeholders and seeing what personal obstacles may prevent them from acting on those beliefs. The steps below will help you begin developing the four pillars of your own professional learning community.

DEVELOPING THE MISSION

The development of a mission statement should be the first step in the mission, vision, values, and goals axiom. As soon as a leadership team is formed, a timeline should be developed with "no later than" dates entered for each activity below. The process should begin early in the school year, and it should take three to four months to complete. In a two-semester year, you may want to try to complete the mission development by the end of the first semester.

The process is as follows:

- *Plan the questioning, drafting, review, and adoption process.* Planning the process that leads to the adoption of the mission statement is the job of the leadership team, or a task force composed of some of its members, under the supervision of the principal. They should draw up a written plan for developing the mission statement that includes ample time for the crucial first step—questioning, discussion, and debate.

The plan should include timelines for each step and should ensure that all constituencies of the school community have an opportunity to review the draft and participate in the approval process.

- *Review and critique your existing statement and examine current attitudes and beliefs.* The first step in drafting a mission statement is to involve all school staff—and parents and students as appropriate—in a serious and ongoing dialogue about the purpose of the school and the responsibility of educators. The principal and members of the leadership team facilitate the dialogue so that all voices receive a respectful hearing. All participants should ask themselves and each other the three essential questions about the school's mission, and all stakeholders should have a chance to enter the debate. Ultimately, the goal of the discussion is to reach a consensus about the answers to each of the three questions.

At many schools, there may be broad agreement that the answer to the first question—"What do we expect students to learn?"—is "To become contributing members of society," "To become lifelong learners," or "To realize their full potential." It may require considerable discussion, however, to lead members of the community to a consensus that schools were founded and continue to exist to teach academic and social skills, that many standards for expected achievement levels exist, and that schools are mandated by society to help students reach these levels. There is likely to be even greater debate over the next two questions, which require participants to examine their attitudes about various kinds of assessments, their expectations for their students, and their attitudes toward their own ability and responsibility to turn around student failure.

Because these issues are so contentious, it may be necessary to continue the period of discussion and debate for several weeks or even a couple of months. During this period, however, the leadership team should begin drafting possible mission statements. These drafts can become focuses for the ongoing debate. The principal and members of the leadership team should facilitate the discussion, which can take place in open meetings, focus groups, interviews, and through the use of surveys and questionnaires.

- *Draft the statement.* Although the actual drafting of the mission statement can be done by a small (two- to three-person) task force, members of the leadership team should be actively involved in each stage of the process. They should discuss the views articulated during the questioning and discussion activities and decide on desirable content and language before anything is written.
- *Submit the draft for review by all appropriate stakeholders and revise it in accordance with their suggestions.* The draft document should first be submitted to all members of the faculty. When their comments and suggestions have been incorporated, the revised document can be submitted to students and families for comment. After reviewing responses and making any necessary revisions, the final version should be prepared for approval by all stakeholders.
- *Adopt and disseminate the mission statement.* The final draft of the mission statement should first be submitted to the faculty as a whole for approval and adoption. The principal or another school leader should impress upon staff that the statement is not just words on a piece of paper; it is a solemn commitment of the entire school community to develop an organizational culture dedicated to high-quality student learning. It is only fair to point out that carrying out the mission will require many changes in the way things are done in the school.

After the faculty have adopted the mission statement, it should be presented to the parent group, older students, and the central administration for approval. After all stakeholders have approved the statement, it should be widely publicized and disseminated—posted on corridor walls, included in newsletters or bulletins, perhaps even posted in each classroom. As soon as possible, it should be incorporated into the school's letterhead, Web site, and any other visible face of the school.

DEVELOPING THE VISION

As soon as the leadership team is formed, a timeline should be developed with "no later than" dates entered for each activity listed below.

In a two-semester year, an attempt could be made to complete work on the vision statement by the end of the first semester. Work on the vision statement will be concurrent with the development of the school profile and either concurrent with or lagging only slightly behind work on the mission statement. The steps for developing a vision are:

- *Plan to gather views about a vision of the school's future and to develop the vision document.* This should be the job of the principal and the leadership team. The plan should include sufficient time for engaging all members of the school community in a dialogue about what the school can and should be—what the end result of the improvement process should look like. This step may involve developing surveys or questionnaires or planning meetings and focus groups. In many cases, these activities can be combined with those that focus on the school's mission.
- *Seek dialogue and ideas from all staff and school community representatives.* Initiating and maintaining a continuing conversation about improving the school is one of the most effective strategies for changing the school's climate. The dialogue can be conducted by the principal or by members of the leadership team. The means may include small meetings and focus groups, surveys and questionnaires, and a series of one-on-one conversations between members of the leadership team and representatives of various constituencies in the school community. In many cases, combinations of all these methods are used.

Even when formal meetings or conversations-by-appointment are completed, the talk is likely to continue—and it can be a valuable way to encourage the collegiality and collaboration that is the basis of an effective school. The principal and leadership team, as a whole, should be closely involved in deciding what kinds of questions or topics should be explored by various constituencies, but a small task force is adequate to collect opinions and draft the document.

- *Draft the vision statement, and submit it for review, revision, and adoption by stakeholders.* As noted earlier, in many schools the vision document contains several different sections. These may refer to topics such as curriculum or school climate, or to groups, such as teaching staff or students. The leadership team decides on the topics for each section of the document. The team may decide to form several task forces, each working on one section, and then all come together to combine the separate sections into a complete document. Alternatively, they may undertake to have a single small group draft the entire document. Whatever method is chosen, the principal and leadership team should review all the sections and merge them into a single document.

- *Communicate the adopted vision statement.* After adoption, the vision statement should be communicated to the entire learning community and should be present as a constant reminder of what the school aims to become. The lead sentences of each section, for example, could be inscribed on a poster placed in a central location.

DEVELOPING THE VALUES STATEMENT

Begin working on a statement of values as your work on the mission and vision winds up. In a two-semester school, the work on the values statement should begin early in the second semester. Work on the values statement may be concurrent with the development of the goals statement and should occur in a context of awareness of the disaggregated data and information gathered in the school profile. The steps for developing the statement of values are:

- *Develop a plan for having each role-group in the school community draft, revise, and adopt a values statement.* The principal and leadership team should work together to decide which groups should contribute statements of their values to the document. Normally, the groups would include administrators, teaching staff, support staff, parents, and students. A plan should be drawn up that includes the designation of task forces or leaders within each group and a timeline for discussion and consensus building, drafting, review, revision, and group approval followed by discussion, review, and adoption of the composite document by all stakeholders.
- *Have each group draft, review, and approve its part of the statement.* Each group (or representative task force of each group)

should review the school's mission and vision statements, then discuss and list the kinds of behaviors and attitudes that can move the school toward the articulated vision. Leaders of each task force should ensure that all members of the constituent group participate in focus groups or brainstorming sessions to help identify the values to be listed.

Examining current assumptions and expectations is the first step in affirming new values based on the belief that all children can perform at a high standard of learning when taught by committed teachers utilizing the best possible instructional practices. Teachers may be willing to commit themselves, in their daily work, to the responsibility of seeing that every child is learning—but unless they truly believe that the child *can* learn and that their teaching can help him or her do so, they will quickly burn out. The corollary to an expressed belief in children's potential for learning is recognition and acceptance of the teachers' primary professional responsibility: to make learning happen. Acceptance of this responsibility should be central to the faculty's values statement, and the values statements of other groups should include a similar recognition of their role and an expression of responsibility to support their efforts.

- *Have all stakeholders review, revise, and adopt the combined statements.* As task forces from each group complete a draft of the values statement, the group as a whole should have the chance to review them and offer comments and suggestions. All groups should be reminded that the values expressed must be consistent with the mission statement and should provide a basis for the vision. In other words, reviewers should ask about each articulated value: "If we behave this way, will our school look more like the ideal we described in our vision statement?" If the answer is no, the value should be revised.

The principal and the leadership team should decide on the best venues and times to distribute the completed, composite values statement to all stakeholder representatives and to collect comments. Representatives of each constituent group should work with the principal to decide on the most appropriate times and means for seeking adoption of the values statements.

- *Disseminate and communicate the values statement throughout the learning community.* The principal, assisted by the process coach, should ensure that the values statement is disseminated throughout the learning community and that the values expressed are communicated frequently and clearly at every opportunity. For example, suppose a particular school's statement included a commitment in the students' section to "work hard to take advantage of the learning opportunities offered to us," and the teachers' values included the statement, "We will use our knowledge and expertise to support student learning and remove impediments to continuing progress."

A parent, enrolling her son in this school, might say, "He works hard, but he can't seem to make much progress in math—he just doesn't seem to understand it." An appropriate response from the counselor might be, "We value hard work, but we want to make sure it's productive. Our staff is committed to seeing that students progress, so we'll find ways to help him overcome his problems with math."

DEVELOPING GOALS

Before a final goals statement can be adopted, teams must have the school profile on hand as well as a large amount of disaggregated data and copies of the mission and vision statements. Schools may find, however, that the adoption of interim goals early in the year can provide direction and impetus to the improvement process. The leadership team and principal should decide, early in the year, on a timetable and plan for developing both interim and long-term goals.

- *Develop a plan for drafting, revising, and adopting a goals statement.* Interim goals, adopted early in the year, may be developed by the principal and the leadership team and presented to the faculty for discussion and review. Such interim goals would be short term, limited to priority improvements that can be implemented fairly quickly, and put in place well before the end of the school year.

A more comprehensive set of short- and long-term goals requires more time and thoughtful analysis of data, establishment of priorities, review, revision, and development of consensus about what is necessary and possible. Under the direction of the principal, the leadership team should create a plan that provides for review of data, an assessment of available resources, sufficient discussion and review by those most affected—the teachers—and an established and consistent means of monitoring progress.

Analyze data as a foundation for establishing priorities and setting realistic goals. Only reliable, up-to-date, carefully disaggregated data can provide teams with the information and direction they need to establish priorities and decide what targets are realistic in the short- and long-term. Much data may already have been included in the school profile. Other necessary data, particularly the performance outcomes of identified subgroups in core curricular subjects, should be fully available and shared among task force and leadership team members. Priorities should reflect hard evidence pointing to areas with the greatest problems. In reviewing data, teams should take note of the assessments used to provide the outcomes they are analyzing and consider specifying their continuing use for monitoring progress. The suggested priorities and goals should be accompanied by a list of assessments deemed most useful and revelatory for gauging learning outcomes.

- *Have all grade-level subject-area staff discuss, refine, limit, and prioritize suggested goals.* The burden of meeting any adopted goal target will fall largely on teaching staff in the area of focus. Such staff should be consulted early in the goal-setting process. They should be able to review all available data and encouraged to comment on the practicality and realism of proposed targets.
- *Draw up a draft goal statement and submit it for review, revision, and adoption.* This activity involves a lot of hard choices, and members of the leadership team may have differing but passionately held views on where the school's primary improvement efforts should be focused. The principal may need to exercise considerable leadership and management

skills to help the team reach consensus. Although the mission, vision, and values statements involved all stakeholders in a direct and personal way, the goals statement, if it focuses as it should on academic skills and outcomes, has the greatest effect on the teaching staff. Consequently, teachers should have the largest opportunity to review and comment on the developing document. Administrators should respond to the teachers' suggestions and comments with a thoughtfulness and respect, but they should not let a faculty member's fear of higher standards or a changed climate turn them aside from insisting on high expectations for progress and improvement.

- *Develop a plan for monitoring progress toward goals.* A goal statement that is adopted and ignored will not move a school one inch nearer its improvement targets. Progress—defined by outcomes on selected assessments—must be monitored regularly, consistently, and frequently. A plan for doing so must be a part of the goal statement and must be adopted simultaneously with the goals themselves.

Such a plan should state at what intervals progress is to be measured, the instruments to be used, and the amount of progress deemed acceptable at each occasion. Although state achievement tests may be the monitoring instrument of most interest to the state and the public, the outcomes tend to be too delayed and too late for prompt corrective action. Schools must have other assessments that are easily administered and scored, that are relevant to what is being taught in the classrooms at the time, and that provide more immediate feedback. Ideally, schools will choose to use a combination of objective tests and performance assessments. Whatever monitoring plan is adopted, it should provide for revision of interim goals or modifications of teaching strategies whenever outcomes indicate a change is necessary.

Appendix F

WORKSHEET FOR DEVELOPING A STUDENT IMPROVEMENT PLAN

Work either singly or in small groups to answer the following questions.

1. List all prevention and intervention strategies already in place at your school, grouping them in the following categories, which correspond to the ones in the pyramid below.
   A. Strategies for Identified Underachievers (entering ninth-graders)
   B. Strategies for All Ninth-graders
   C. Strategies for Persistent Underachievers
   D. Strategies for Fewer Than 5 Percent of Underachievers

2. Evaluate each strategy carefully to determine whether it? fits with your school's philosophical structure (i.e., mission, vision, values, and goals).
   A. Place a check mark beside those that are already philosophically sound and do not need to be changed.

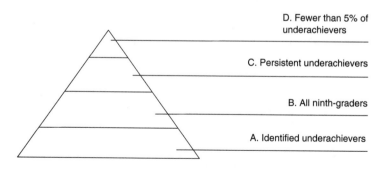

Figure F.1   Adlai Stevenson High School Pyramid of Interventions, *Failure Is Not an Option Video Series*, 2002.

B. Place a *C* beside those strategies that will need to be modified to better fit into your school's philosophical structure.

3. Now, looking at your pyramid of interventions as a whole, identify any gaps in the structure that need to be filled (e.g., strategies to support specific subgroups). Add those strategies to your earlier list in question 1, placing an *N* beside them to mark them as new.

Appendix G

DEVELOPING A SYSTEM OF
PREVENTION AND INTERVENTION

Begin the process by working with your colleagues to sketch plans or procedures on separate sheets of paper for (1) identifying students in need of extra support and attention; (2) monitoring such students intensively; (3) providing mentors, "good friends," or other adult support to these students; and (4) establishing intervention programs. List programs that already exist and note whether they need to be modified or expanded and, if so, in what ways. For new programs, state the specific goal and then address the following questions.

1. Identification
   - What criteria, data, or information will we use to identify incoming students who need extra attention?
   - Who will be responsible for gathering and evaluating this information?
   - When will this be done?
   - What obstacles need to be confronted?

2. Monitoring
   - What kinds of ongoing information or data about identified students will be collected?
   - How often will the information be gathered?
   - What will be the vehicle for entering and transmitting the information?
   - Who will be asked to provide it?
   - Who will gather and evaluate it?
   - How promptly will it be reviewed?
   - What obstacles need to be confronted?
   - What are some strategies for overcoming these?

3. Mentoring
   - What kind of mentoring program is needed in our school?
   - How can we ensure that every identified student has a "best friend" adult?
   - Who should be recruited to fill such roles: certified personnel only? Clerical staff? Custodial staff? Kitchen workers? Parents and community volunteers? Also, what guidelines, orientation, or training should be provided to them?
   - Who should provide or lead the training?
   - What should be the procedure for pairing students with mentors? Should meetings between students and mentors be structured or allowed to develop naturally?
   - What communication tree should exist for mentors who become aware of problems?
   - What obstacles need to be confronted?
   - What are some strategies for overcoming these?

4. Intervention
   - What is a reasonable and specific goal for each prevention or improvement program that we plan to implement?
   - What resources are available for such programs (money, personnel, space, time, and so on)?
   - What criteria should be established for selecting students for the programs?
   - Should the program be mandatory or optional?
   - What benchmark or standard do we hope to meet with each intervention, and what assessment and evaluation data will determine the program's success?
   - How often will each intervention program be evaluated?
   - What obstacles need to be confronted?
   - What are some strategies for overcoming these?

Appendix H

PYRAMID OF INTERVENTIONS
AS USED IN HARTFORD, CONNECTICUT

Each level of the pyramid represents a specific intervention and is explained in greater detail in the following sections.

The *summer transition program* serves as the base of the pyramid. Prior to entering high school, approximately eighty middle school students are identified as being highly at risk for success at the next level. In cooperation with teachers, counselors, and administrators from the middle school, high school personnel work

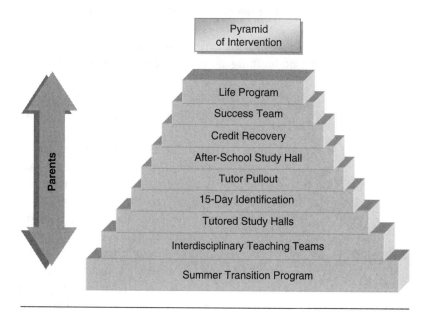

Figure H.1

to identify select students who will benefit from such a program. Academic performance, social/emotional issues, and faculty/administration recommendations provide the criteria for selection. All students selected are non–special education students.

The goals of the summer transition program are to acclimate students to the high school, to begin forging relationships with adults with whom they will be working, and to further assess gaps in the cognitive and affective domains. The program runs for three weeks, three hours per day. Certified teachers, support staff, and peers instruct students. Staff and students establish relationships that help ease the transition for these students entering high school in the fall.

Interdisciplinary teaching teams, the second level of the pyramid, serve as an intervention for all ninth- and tenth-grade students. Students are grouped in heterogeneous teaching teams comprised of approximately 100 students and four teachers. The teachers represent the four core academic areas: English, mathematics, science, and social studies. Students spend two years with the same teachers and are scheduled into a 180-minute teaching block each day. Curriculum is aligned to allow for natural connection between academic areas.

Advantages of teaming impact both cognitive and affective domains. From a cognitive perspective, teachers have greater contact time with students. Because of this, teachers better understand students' learning styles and are able to structure the curriculum to foster the transfer of learning across disciplines. In the affective domain, strong bonds are formed between teachers and students due to the increased contact time between the two groups. This level of contact builds stronger, more lasting relationships between students and teachers.

Tutored study halls are the third level of intervention and a requirement for all ninth-grade students. Replacing the traditional study hall, tutored study halls have an increased academic focus. A tutor is assigned to each interdisciplinary teaching team and is an integral part of all team events and activities. The tutor sits in on team classes, team meetings, and parent conferences. Tutors also oversee the study hall periods for students on their respective teams. Since tutors are fully aware of required homework, exams, and projects, the study period becomes an opportunity to review, clarify, and complete academic assignments. This time serves as a chance to enhance learning that has taken place in the classroom.

The next level of the pyramid of intervention is the *fifteen-day identification* system. After the fifteenth day of school, team teachers are asked to identify all students who are falling behind and not meeting minimum academic expectations. The vast majority of students fall under one or more of four primary causes of failure:

- Attendance and tardiness issues
- Social and/or behavioral issues
- Lack of basic skills
- Failure to complete out-of-class assignments

Based on the cause(s) of failure, the teams are able to provide these students the appropriate additional interventions needed to succeed. Once team teachers identify students according to the above criteria, they are able to develop an individual intervention plan for each student that utilizes internal and external resources.

Identified students will be selected for a *tutor pullout program*, the fifth level of the pyramid. Tutors who are assigned to interdisciplinary teaching teams are afforded a flexible schedule. Flexibility allows for creative scheduling to assist identified students who continue to fall below minimum academic standards. When and where appropriate, selected students are pulled out of team activities for one-on-one or small-group instruction. At times, these students may be pulled from noncore classes for further instruction. In order to best meet the academic needs of the student, the schedule remains flexible. The length of the tutoring is based on each student's individual needs.

After-school study period is the next level in the pyramid of intervention. A one-hour academic study period is a requirement for identified students. Team tutors who monitor the period provide necessary instruction in core academic areas and assist in the development of basis study skills. Faculty and staff work closely with parents to maximize the benefits of the after-school time. With the exception of students who have a preapproved pass to see a core academic teacher, attendance is required at each session. Students remain in this study program until team teachers determine they have reestablished academic stability.

Students who experience academic failure quickly fall farther and farther behind, thus perpetuating their academic problems. A *credit recovery program,* level seven of the pyramid of interventions, affords students the opportunity to earn back lost credit due to course failure. This level of the pyramid provides a mechanism for students to maintain the necessary credits to meet graduation requirements. All ninth- and tenth-grade courses are semesterized, which allows students to earn one half-credit per semester for each course successfully completed. Students who fail a core academic semester course have the opportunity to recover the lost credit through the credit recovery program. For instance, a student who fails the first semester of a core academic course (English, mathematics, science, or social studies) may participate in the credit recovery program during the second semester under the following conditions:

- The student maintains a "C" average in the same course during the present semester.
- The student completes all credit recovery requirements outside the regular school day.
- All requirements are completed during the semester the program began.

The credit recovery course requirements are consistent with the core curriculum for each subject area, and the contact time is equivalent to the time requirement in a summer school program. Grant dollars fund credit recovery, and teachers are paid an hourly rate for participating in the program.

The *success team* was added to the pyramid of intervention to meet the needs of non–special education students who fail to meet minimum academic standards based on multiple variables. Middle and high school teachers identify students who have not responded to any other academic intervention thus far. In essence, the success team is a last resort for these students, as they are placed on the team only after all other interventions have been exhausted. The school must meet with parents and obtain their consent in order to place their child on the team. The success team provides a learning environment with smaller classes, intense tutorial support, and individual/group counseling. Although the same academic curriculum is used, smaller classes and individualized assistance makes learning more manageable for these students. Students enter and exit the program at the beginning of each new marking period. The amount of time a student may be in the program can range from one semester to the full two years. The program provides wraparound services for each child, engaging all necessary internal and external service providers to meet the child's social, emotional, and academic needs. Services also extend to the family to better ensure the student's success.

At the top of the pyramid is the *LIFE program* (lifelong initiatives for education). The LIFE program services the smallest number of students in an offsite location. The three major components of the LIFE program are academics, counseling, and vocational and/or service learning. Students are enrolled in the program at the discretion of the building administrator in consultation with teachers, support staff, parents, and the student. The goal is for the student to reach a point where he or she sees the LIFE program as an opportunity rather than as a punishment. Students who participate in the program are engaged in academics and counseling for four hours per day, and the rest of the day centers around a vocational component or a service learning project.

A contract is established for each student, along with an individualized educational plan that focuses on the specific academic and behavioral needs of the student. Students may return to the high school based on successful completion of the contract.

Appendix I

FAITH, HOPE,
AND INTERVENTION

Alan Boyle, Leannta Education Associates

Two simple questions:

- How do you turn failing schools around?
- Does it always work?

To the first question, I would say you don't—failing schools can only turn themselves around. What you can do is provide support by developing capacity within the school. You may also try to build confidence through encouragement and by recognizing small steps along the way.

And for the second—no. There are no blueprints or checklists that guarantee success. But there are things you can do that will give you a better chance.

Facing up to failure is not a comfortable or easy ride. But for the benefit of students in those schools, it must be the right thing to do. This moral authority should be used with humility and respect for others. Humiliation is a slippery slope to avoid because it actually diminishes capacity even further, just when capability needs to be boosted. Public humiliation provides deep roots for resentment that will delay recovery. The danger in establishing the moral authority to tackle failing schools is to ignore the perils of humiliating those within them, especially the students.

It is a fact that some schools fail to meet certain standards or specifications. Responses to this fact range from denial to school closure. Whilst I might support each of these individual responses in different circumstances, neither gets us very far along the way to transforming a failing school. For turning round failing schools, we need to search between denial and closure. There is lots of fertile ground there.

The term "failing school" became an official category in England after 1993. In 1995, Michael Barber (destined to become the key education adviser to Tony Blair and the new Labour government in 1997) used his Greenwich Lecture to imagine an end to failure in urban education. He called it *The Dark Side of the Moon* (Barber, 1997). Barber proposed four requirements to eradicate failure in schools:

- A means of evaluating the quality of every school in the country and a climate of openness
- Knowledge of what describes a good school
- Knowledge about what a school needs to do to improve itself
- Knowledge about how best to intervene in schools that prove incapable of improving themselves

By 1996 over 200 schools in England and Wales "required special measures," the euphemism used to describe a failing school. These were identified by the new national system of school inspections, point 1 on Barber's list. At the same time, research into school effectiveness around the world provided a surprising consensus about the characteristics of a good school. Knowing how to describe a good school is a long way from understanding how a school can improve itself. For point 3, research into school improvement reflected the complexity of the change process and provided useful ways forward. The challenge was point 4. There was little shared knowledge at that time about intervening in failing schools.

The responsibility for intervention in failing schools was given to Local Education Authorities (LEAs), the equivalent of school districts in the USA. For some LEAs this was nothing new, but others were reluctant to intervene. At that time I was responsible for supporting school improvement in a London LEA, having moved from another urban area of England. With some limited experience of intervention in my former LEA, we set about turning round a rapidly growing number of schools that were failing their inspections in my new LEA. I struggled to make sense of our interventions. There was no predictable outcome. It felt like we were continually flying by the seats of our pants. Action that led to rapid improvement in one school had no impact in another similar situation. We had no faith in our strategy that was built on the best available knowledge of school improvement techniques.

In desperation I reached out to my colleagues in other LEAs. We organized a national conference and invited LEAs to write a case study based on their own experience working with a failing school. Fifteen LEAs contributed their own case studies and these were handed to a researcher who analyzed them. At the conference, our researcher presented some common features that emerged from her analysis. She also identified some key issues for further discussion. Over 100 representatives from LEAs all over the country chose which working groups they were interested in and through the conference the groups shared experiences about these key issues.

The following points emerged from our collective endeavor (Riley and Rowles, 1997):

Failing schools are not the antithesis to effective schools.

Failing schools have special characteristics of their own that include:

- Isolation from other schools and little involvement in any forms of professional development
- Poor professional and social relationships between staff in the school with frequent conflicts in the staffroom
- Problems recruiting and/or retaining good teachers
- A culture that denies responsibility for the situation in the school, often blaming it on the students
- A "death wish" mentality demonstrated by unwillingness or inability by staff in the school to do anything about it

There is a distinction between recovery and improvement.

We agreed that techniques used to improve effective schools often had limited impact in failing schools. The title of our conference was *From Intensive Care to Recovery.* And it quickly emerged that what we were dealing with was helping schools to reach a point where they were no longer failing. We called this "recovery" and shared successful strategies that we had used to help failing schools reach this stage in their development. From that point, "normal" school improvement techniques were successful.

Naming and shaming was counterproductive.

Back in 1993 the national press broke like a storm around the first schools identified as failing. Media interest was extreme and this caused shock and psychological damage to staff and students. Blaming followed the naming and shaming and this only delayed recovery. Here is an extract from a typical case study:

> Everybody blamed someone else. The governors blamed the LEA for not telling them that the school was failing. The LEA blamed the Principal for not responding to the issues that they raised with him. The Principal blamed his staff because they would not co-operate with him. The staff blamed the students because most of them did not speak English. Nobody asked the students who they blamed. (Boyle, 2001)

Key Questions For Moving Forward

The distillation of our shared information and experiences produced two key questions. The answers to these questions are the keys to deciding the most effective action that would help a failing school to improve.

- How much capacity does the school have to improve itself?
- To what extent is the school willing to change?

At first sight these questions seem unremarkable, but I will describe how they were to form the basis of an intervention strategy in our LEA that provided the faith we needed to help turn around eight failing schools in the following two years.

Prevention Is Better Than Cure

We were all agreed that early action to prevent schools from failing was the best solution. We discussed the principles of early warning systems that would lead to smarter and more cost-effective intervention. Some LEAs went on to build databases, using key performance indicators, which would generate a green, amber, or red light for each school. Successful early intervention on the amber should prevent it failing and turning red.

Two years later, about 200 failing schools distributed throughout the LEAs that participated in this conference, and its follow-up, had been turned around. I am not suggesting any cause and effect between the conference and this remarkable turnaround. What I do claim is that some of the expertise that was used in those schools and LEAs was drawn into the conference and shared among all who participated. The conference provided more evidence to support the view that the benefits of cooperation exceed those of competition.

Before moving on to describe how our intervention strategy evolved, it is worth reflecting on the conference as a pioneering event. It was designed to share and draw on the collective expertise of practitioners in LEAs. Our researcher provided rigor and impartiality to the analysis of our case studies. This first learning loop generated key issues for work groups at the conference. A second learning loop came at the conference when the working groups took the key issues, shared their expertise, and developed their collective knowledge. Similar structured collaboration provides a way of tapping into the extensive experience and information among practitioners about other issues. Participation in similar events has potential for the rapid development of leadership capacity.

In his Romanes lecture at Oxford University in 2000, Tony Blair discussed the reluctance of the UK government in the past to confront issues in education such as: an average performance that was far too low; an inadequate momentum to improve it; and an inadequate system of accountability and responsibility, from the center outwards. In making explicit his views about the role of national government, he said,

> First, government must take national responsibility for investing in raising standards. Its intervention should be in inverse proportion to the success of schools and colleges—decisive action to tackle failure, but trust and reward for success. (Blair, 2000)

The phrase "intervention in inverse proportion to success" was used as a slogan for government education policy following the election of the new Labour government in 1997. Intervention in failing schools is first the responsibility of the LEA, with national government watchdogs ready to intervene if things do not work out as desired.

By 1998 I was leading a team that had five years' experience dealing with failing schools. We were able to draw on our experience to articulate a local policy to support continuous improvement in all schools in our LEA. Following consultation with schools, the policy was published in 1999. It contains a section about dealing with failing schools that attempts to use our tacit knowledge, gained from experience of turning these schools around. It turns the slogan "intervention in inverse proportion to success" into a strategy.

The policy assumes that schools are responsible for their own improvement and that they have effective self-evaluation systems. It also includes an intervention strategy built on the two key questions that emerged from the conference. The key questions to ask are:

- What is the school's capacity for improvement?
- How willing is the school to make major changes?

The different levels of LEA intervention in schools causing concern are illustrated in the diagram below, based on the responses to the questions above. This was our interpretation of "intervention in inverse proportion to success." Using this strategy, we considered the level of intervention carefully and then explained to the school how, and why, we were intervening.

TAKE OVER

Radical action is necessary for schools with low capacity for improvement that are also unwilling to change. We used our additional powers to withdraw the school's delegated powers, including the budget, and took over the governance of the school. This gives the LEA responsibility for action to improve the capability of staff rather than the governing body. We installed staff, usually an experienced principal or deputy, to take over management of the school until the school's own capacity is improved sufficiently. This assumes that the school's principal has already gone or is suspended.

LEAs compiled lists of "step-in" principals who could be moved quickly into a failing school for a short period. Securing the release of a principal from his or her existing school for a short time requires sensitivity and diplomacy. A step-in principal should not

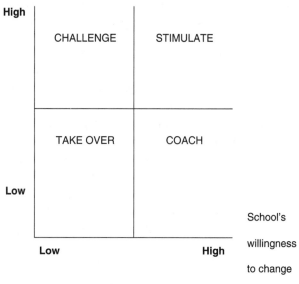

Figure I.1   Intervention strategy in schools causing concern

be needed for more than two terms. This gives the governing body enough time to appoint a new permanent principal. A good appointment will improve the capacity of the school.

Meanwhile the step-in principal will work on the school's reluctance to change. It's about dealing with resistance and winning hearts and minds. At the same time, it's also about taking firm action where capability is questioned. This is a crucial time. The school needs to prepare its action plan and make some quick wins to gain momentum. In failing schools quick wins are easy because so much is wrong. When the new principal takes up post, the momentum is increased and willingness to change should be secure.

Using a step-in principal does work, but it's like carrying a basketful of snakes—one slip and you've had it. There are some cautionary tales (OFSTED, 1998). The removal of the step-in principal leaves the failing school in a position to improve itself. Our intervention strategy now shifts to the lower right-hand quadrant.

COACH

Intervention in schools, or with staff, that are willing to change is different. External consultants can coach the staff to develop the skills they need to improve. This is most successful as school-based support, to strengthen the management of the school and/or improve the quality of teaching and learning.

Learning and teaching are always weaknesses in a failing school. Understanding why is important and that requires a clear analysis. Whatever the weaknesses are, it eventually comes down to lesson planning. In the classroom, advisory teachers will work alongside staff in the school. They will plan jointly with the teachers, team-teach, or demonstrate different techniques in real situations. Teachers in the failing school can try out new ideas, in their own working situations, with immediate feedback. This is what Elmore describes as learning in context (Elmore, 2000).

In this part of the strategy we assume that teachers are willing to change. However, there will be times when the teacher does not respond immediately, not because they don't want to but because they find it too difficult. In these cases the staff must be given the intensive support provided by capability procedures. For most teachers this works, or they find a job elsewhere. For a small minority, these procedures will result in dismissal. OFSTED make this point in the report about the first 250 failing schools to be turned around (OFSTED, 1999).

Action to improve teaching relies on effective management. Depending on the size of the school, this will involve both senior and distributed management. It follows that if the learning and teaching have weaknesses then there are also problems with management. Management consultants can provide the school managers with on-the-job support, advice, and feedback following actions taken. It is always easier for a new principal, or a step-in principal, to tackle issues that have been ignored in the past.

The school's capacity may also be increased by problem solving. Instead of advising managers about what to do, as their capacity increases, the approach should be through problem solving with the external consultants becoming less "hands on." As the school's capacity increases, intervention becomes less intensive until we reach the top right-hand quadrant.

STIMULATE

In this quadrant schools are no longer failing. The recovery process is complete and the school is now able to improve itself. However, it will not be a good school yet. That will take longer but that process can begin. Our intervention strategy at this stage involves a much lighter touch. The school-based consultants will have been withdrawn as the school's capacity increased. However, the school will still be fragile and the intervention should ensure that the school does not slip back.

Staff in the school will still need advice from external consultants about a whole range of issues, depending on the nature of the school's weaknesses. In providing this advice, consultants need to:

- Ask searching questions about progress in the school
- Give constructive feedback about what has been achieved
- Be readily available to provide advice when staff try out new ideas

Our strategy helps because schools realize that the intervention has been progressively reduced as the school's capacity has grown.

The strategy works by shifting the levels of intervention according to the response in the school. Within the timescales allowed to improve failing schools, it is reasonable to expect that "takeover" should last no longer than six months. Twelve months can be allowed for "coaching" followed by six months when the school is in the "stimulate" situation. For most failing schools, the school failure should continue for no more than two years.

CHALLENGE

The fourth quadrant of the diagram that represents our intervention strategy concerns schools that have the capacity to change but are not willing to do so. This is sometimes known as the "coasting school." Some of these schools hold powerful ideological views about teaching and learning that cannot be shaken, even when confronted with evidence that shows it isn't working. They may be politicized to some extent and they hold political views that are in opposition to the locally, or nationally, elected government. When that government attempts any education reform, these schools will oppose any change on principle, without even considering the relative merits or possible reasons for the change. Such schools present the greatest challenge of all to change. That challenge needs to be turned back onto the school itself.

These schools should be informed clearly how they are perceived. They must also be listened to. Their views and reasons for opposition need to be carefully explored. As long as there is dialogue then there is the possibility of making progress. Taking a rational adult approach, they should be set targets for improving standards and the quality of education that are in line with targets set by other schools. How they might achieve those targets is up to them, but as long as there is a dialogue going about their ways of working then it may be possible to develop a creative response that will allow progress.

However, there have to be limits to how long the failure can be tolerated. My rule of thumb would be six months, about the same length of time spent in takeover. So what if the school still won't move after six months? The national policy framework allows for closure or Fresh Start.

Our intervention strategy, developed from collaboration with colleagues in other LEAs, gave us a framework for action that restored faith in our schools and our own abilities. This was crucial, as faith in our strategy enabled us to create hope in desperate circumstances. Hope is a key personal attribute of successful leaders (Fullan, 2001) and in a failing school it is an essential virtue. Without hope, actions lack belief and are rarely successful. Faith, hope and intervention form a virtuous circle that can help failing schools to turn themselves around.

REFERENCES

Barber, M. (1997). *The Learning Game*. London: Indigo.

Blair, T. (2000). Education: The story so far. *Prospect*, February 2000, 50–53.

Boyle, A. (2001) *Turning failing schools around: Intervention in inverse proportion to success*. London: Leannta Education Associates.

Elmore, R. F. (2000). *Building a new structure for school leadership*. Washington, D.C.: Albert Shanker Institute.

Fullan, M. (2001). *Leading in a Culture of Change*. San Francisco: Jossey-Bass.

Office for Standards in Education (OFSTED). (1998). *Making headway.* London: Office for Standards in Education.

Office for Standards in Education (OFSTED). (1999). *Lessons learned from special measures.* London: Office for Standards in Education.

Riley, K., and Rowles, D. (1997). *Learning from failure.* London: Haringey Council Education Services.

Appendix J

TEACHER-PRINCIPAL TRUST ITEM

- It's OK in this school to discuss feelings, worries, and frustrations with the principal.
- The principal looks out for the personal welfare of the faculty members.
- I trust the principal at his or her word.
- The principal at this school is an effective manager who makes the school run smoothly.
- The principal places the needs of the children ahead of his or her personal and political interests.
- The principal has confidence in the expertise of the teachers.
- The principal takes a personal interest in the professional development of teachers.
- I really respect my principal as an educator.
- To what extent do you feel respected by your principal?

Bibliography

Ackerman, R.H., & Maslin-Ostrowski, P. (2002). *The wounded leader.* San Francisco: Jossey-Bass.

Adams, P. (2002, September 5). Personal communication. Arlington, Virginia.

Anthony, E. J. (1982). The preventive approach to children at high risk for psychopathology and psychosis. *Journal of Children in Contemporary Society, 15*(1).

———. (1987). Risk, vulnerability, and resilience: An overview. In E. J. Anthony & B. J. Cohler (Eds.), *The invulnerable child* (pp. 3–48). New York: Guilford Press.

Attachment and Belonging. (Fall, 1998). *Journal of Emotional and Behavioral Problems, 7*(3).

Bandura, A. (1986). *Social foundations of thought and action: A social cognitive theory.* Englewood Cliffs, NJ: Prentice-Hall.

Barber, M. (2001). High expectations and standards for all, no matter what: Creating a world class educational service in England. In Michael Fielding (Ed.), *Taking education really seriously: Three years of hard labour.* London: Routledge/Falmer.

Bardwick, J. (1996). Peacetime management and wartime leadership. In F. Hesselbein, M. Goldsmith, & R. Beckhard (Eds.), *The leader of the future* (pp. 131–140). San Francisco: Jossey-Bass.

Barth, R. S. (2001). *Learning by heart.* San Francisco: Jossey-Bass.

Bennis, W. G. (1989). *On becoming a leader.* New York: Addison-Wesley Publishing Company.

Blankstein, A. M. (1992). Lessons from enlightened corporations. *Educational Leadership, 49*(6), 71.

———. (1997). Fighting for success. *Reaching Today's Youth: The Community Circle of Caring Journal, 1*(2), 2–3.

Blankstein, A. M., DuFour, R., & Little, M. (1997). *Reaching today's students.* Bloomington, IN: National Educational Service.

Blankstein, A. M., & Swain, H. (February, 1994). Is TQM right for schools? *The Executive Educator,* 51.

Blase, J., & Anderson, G. (1995). *The micropolitics of educational leadership: From control to empowerment.* New York: Teachers College Press.

Block, P. (2002). *The answer to how is yes: Acting on what matters.* San Francisco: Barrett-Koehler.

Bolman, L. G., & Deal, T. E. (1991). *Reframing organizations: Artistry, choice, and leadership.* San Francisco: Jossey-Bass.

Bower, E.M. (1964). The modification, mediation, and utilization of stress during the school years. *American Journal of Orthopsychiatry, 34,* 667–674.

Bowser, B. A. (2001). Principal shortage. *Online NewsHour,* Public Broadcasting System. Accessed online June 29, 2003, at www.pbs.org/newshour

Brendtro, L. K., Brokenleg, M., & Bockern S. V. (1990). *Reclaiming youth at risk: Our hope for the future.* Bloomington, IN: National Educational Services.

Brown, P., & Lauder, H. (2001). *Capitalism and social progress: The future of society in a global economy.* New York: Palgrave.

Bryk, A., Camburn, E., & Louis, K. S. (1999). Professional community in Chicago elementary schools: Facilitating factors and organizational consequences. *Educational Administration Quarterly, 35* (special issue), 751–781.

Bryk, A. S., & Driscoll, M. E. (1998). *The school as community: Theoretical foundation, contextual influences, and consequences for teachers and students.* Madison, WI: National Center for Effective Secondary Schools.

Bryk, A. S., Easton, J. Q., Kerbow, D., Rollow, S. G., & Sebring, P. A. (1994). The state of Chicago school reform. *Phi Delta Kappan, 76*(1), 74–78.

Bryk, A. S., Lee, V. E., & Holland, P. B. (1993). *Catholic schools and the common good.* Cambridge, MA: Harvard University Press.

Bryk, A. S., & Schneider, B. (2002). *Trust in schools: A core resource for improvement.* New York: Russell Sage Foundation.

Bryk, A. S., & Thum, Y. M. (1989). The effects of high school organization on dropping out: An exploratory investigation. *American Educational Research Journal.*

Buckingham, M., & Coffman, C. (1999). *First, break all the rules: What the world's greatest managers do differently.* New York: Simon & Schuster.

Champy, J. (1995). *Reengineering management.* New York: HarperCollins.

Clarizio, H. F., & McCoy, G. F. (1970). *Behavior disorders in school-aged children.* Scranton, PA: Chandler.

Clark, C. M. (1988). Asking the right questions about teacher preparation: Contributions of research on teaching thinking. *Educational Researcher, 17*(2), 5–12.

Cole, A. L. (1989, April). *Making explicit implicit theories of teaching: Starting points in preservice programs.* Paper presented at the Annual Meeting of the American Educational Research Association, San Francisco.

Collins, J. (1996). Aligning action and values. *Leader to Leader, 1*(1).

————. (2001). *Good to great.* New York: HarperCollins.

Combs, A. W., Miser, A. B., & Whitaker, K. S. (1999). *On becoming a school leader: A person-centered challenge.* Alexandria, VA: Association for Supervision and Curriculum Development.

Cooperrider, D. L. (1990). Positive image, positive action: The affirmative basis of organizing. In S. Srivastva, D. L. Cooperrider, and Associates (Eds.), *Appreciative management and leadership: The power of positive thought and action in organizations.* San Francisco: Jossey-Bass.

Costa, A. L., & Kallick, B. (Eds.). (2000). *Discovering & exploring habits of mind.* Alexandria, VA: Association for Supervision and Curriculum Development.

Covey, S. R. (1989). *The 7 habits of highly effective people.* New York: Simon & Schuster.

Darling-Hammond, L. (1996). The quiet revolution: Rethinking teacher development. *Educational Leadership, 53*(6), 4–10.

————. (1997). *The right to learn: A blueprint for creating schools that work.* San Francisco: Jossey-Bass.

————. (1999). Target time toward teachers. *Journal of Staff Development, 20*(2).

Datnow, A., & Castellano, M. (2000). *An "inside look" at success for all: A qualitative study of implementation and teaching and learning.* Baltimore: Johns Hopkins University, Center for Research on the Education of Students Placed at Risk.

Deal, T. E., & Peterson, K. D. (1999). *Shaping school culture: The heart of leadership.* San Francisco: Jossey-Bass.

Deming, W. E. (1986). *Out of the crisis.* Cambridge, MA: MIT Center for Advanced Engineering Study.

————. (1989, February 3). Personal communication. New York, New York.

Dewey, J. (1927). *The public and its problems.* New York: Holt.

Donaldson, G., Jr. (2001). *Cultivating leadership in school: Connecting people, purpose, and practice.* New York: Teachers College Press.

Drucker, P. (1992). *Managing for the future: The 1990's and beyond.* New York: Truman Talley Books.

DuFour, R. P. (1991). *The principal as staff developer.* Bloomington, IN: National Educational Service.

DuFour, R. (Winter, 2003). Leading edge. *National Staff Development Council, 24*(1).

DuFour, R., & Eaker, R. (1992). *Creating the new American school.* Bloomington, IN: National Educational Service.

DuFour, R., & Eaker, R. (1998). *Professional learning communities at work: Best practices for enhancing student achievement.* Bloomington, IN: National Educational Service.

Duke, D. (1988). Why principals consider quitting. *Phi Delta Kappan, 70*(4), 308–313.

Eaker, R., DuFour, R., & Burnette, R. (2002). *Getting started: Reculturing schools to become professional learning communities.* Bloomington, IN: National Educational Service.

Early, P., Evans, J., Collarbone, P., Gold, A., & Halpin, D. (2002). *Establishing the current state of leadership in England.* London: Department for Education and Skills.

Eastman, C. (1902). *Indian boyhood.* New York: McClure, Phillips & Co.

Edmonds, R. R. (1979). Effective schools for the urban poor. *Educational Leadership, 37*(10), 15–24.

Education Trust. (1999). *Dispelling the myth: High poverty schools exceeding expectations.* Washington, DC: Author.

———. (2002). *Dispelling the myth revisited.* Washington, DC: Author.

Elias, M. J., Arnold, H., & Hussey, C. S. (Eds.). (2003). *EQ + IQ = Best leadership practices for caring and successful schools.* Thousand Oaks, CA: Corwin Press.

Elias, M. J., Bryan, K., Patrikakou, E. N., & Weissberg, R. P. (2003). *Challenges in creating effective home-school partnerships in adolescence: Promising paths for collaboration.* Chicago: Collaborative for Academic, Social, and Emotional Learning.

Elias, M. J., Frey, K. S., Greenberg, M. T., Haynes, N. M., Kessler, R., Schwab-Stone, M. E., et al. (1997). *Promoting social and emotional learning: Guidelines for educators.* Alexandria, VA: Association for Supervision and Curriculum Development.

Elias, M. J., Friedlander, B. S., & Tobias, S. E. (1999). *Emotionally intelligent parenting: How to raise a self-disciplined, responsible, socially skilled child.* New York: Three Rivers Press.

Elias, M. J., Kress, J. S., & Novick, B. (2002). *Building learning communities with character: How to integrate academic, social, and emotional learning.* Alexandria, VA: Association for Supervision and Curriculum Development.

Elmore, R. (2002). Hard questions about practice. *Educational Leadership, 59*(8), 22–25.

Elmore, R. F. (1995). Structural reform in educational practice. *Educational Researcher, 24*(9), 23–26.

———. (1999–2000, Winter). Building a new structure for school leadership. *American Educator, 23*(4), 6–13.

Evans, R. (1996). *The human side of school change.* San Francisco: Jossey-Bass.

Ewing Marion Kauffman Foundation. (2002). *Set for success: Building a strong foundation for school readiness based on the social-emotional development of young children.* Kansas City, MO: Author.

Fenstermacher, G. D. (1986). Philosophy of research on teaching: Three aspects. In M.C. Wittrock (Ed.), *Handbook of research on teaching* (3rd ed., pp. 37–49). New York: Macmillan.

Financial Executive International (FEI). (2001). *Building human capital: The public sector's 21st century challenge.* Accessed online June 19, 2003, at www.fei.org

Fink, D. (2000a). The attrition of educational change over time: The case of an innovative, "model," "lighthouse" school. In N. Bascia & A. Hargreaves (Eds.), *The sharp edge of educational change.* London: Routledge/Falmer.

———. (2000b). *Good schools/real schools: Why school reform doesn't last.* New York: Teachers College Press.

Fletcher, C., Caron, M., & Williams, W. (1985). *Schools on trial.* Milton Keynes, UK: Open University Press.

Frankl, V. (1959, 2000). *Create organizational meaning.* In *Man's search for meaning.* Boston: Beacon Press.

———. (1997). *Recollections.* New York: Plenum Press.

Fullan, M. G. (1991). *The new meaning of educational change.* New York: Teachers College Press.

———. (1993). *Change forces.* New York: The Falmer Press.

———. (2001a). *Leading in a culture of change.* San Francisco: Jossey-Bass.

———. (2001b). *The new meaning of educational change* (3rd ed.). New York: Teachers College Press.

———. (2003a). *Change forces with a vengeance.* New York: Routledge/Falmer.

———. (2003b). *The moral imperative of school leadership.* Thousand Oaks, CA: Corwin Press.

———. (1996). *What's worth fighting for in your school?* New York: Teachers College Press.

———. (1997). *What's worth fighting for in the principalship?* New York: Teachers College Press.

Fullan, M., & Hargreaves, A. (1998). *What's worth fighting for out there?* New York: Teachers College Press.

Galton, M. (2000). "Dumbing down" on classroom standards: The perils of a technician's approach to pedagogy. *Journal of Educational Change, 1*(2), 199–204.

Gardner, J. (1988). *Leadership: An overview.* Washington, DC: Independent Sector.

———. (1991). *Building community.* Washington, DC: Independent Sector.

Garmezy, N. (1983). Stressors of childhood. In N. Garmezy & M. Rutter (Eds.), *Stress, coping, and the development in children.* New York: McGraw-Hill.

———. (1994). Reflections and commentary on risk, resilience, and development. In R. J. Haggarty, L. R. Sherrod, N. Garmezy, & M. Rutter (Eds.), *Stress, risk, and resilience in children and adolescents: Processes, mechanisms, and interventions* (pp. 1–18). Cambridge: Cambridge University Press.

Glasser, W. (1992). *The quality school: Managing students without coercion.* New York: HarperPerennial.

Glickman, C. (2002). *Leadership for learning: How to help teachers succeed.* Arlington, VA: Association for Supervision and Curriculum Development.

———. (2003). *Holding sacred ground: Essays on leadership, courage, and endurance in our schools.* San Francisco: Jossey-Bass.

Goldstein, A. (2001, June 21). How to fix the coming principals' shortage. *Time.* Accessed online June 19, 2003, at www.time.com/time/columnist

Goleman, D. (1995). *Emotional intelligence.* New York: Bantam Books.

Goleman, D. Boyatzis, R., & McKee, A. (2002). *Primal leadership: Realizing the power of emotional intelligence.* Boston: Harvard Business School Press.

Goodlad, J. I., McMannon, T. J., & Soder, R. (Eds.). (2001). *Developing democratic character in the young.* San Francisco: Jossey-Bass.

Goodlad, S. J. (Ed.). (2001). *The last best hope.* San Francisco: Jossey-Bass.

Government of Western Australia. (2001). *Managing succession in the Western Australia public sector.* Accessed online June 29, 2003, at www.mpc.wa.-gov.au

Gregory, T. (2001). Fear of success? Ten ways alternative schools pull their punches. *Phi Delta Kappan, 82*(8), 577–581.

Guetzloe, E. (Summer, 1994). Risk, resilience, and protection. *Journal of Emotional and Behavioral Problems, 2.*

Hallowell, B. (1997). My nonnegotiables. In G. A. Donaldson (Ed.), *On being a principal: The rewards and challenges of school leadership.* San Francisco: Jossey-Bass.

Hargreaves, A. (2001). Beyond anxiety and nostalgia. *Phi Delta Kappan, 82*(5), 373.

———. (2003). *Teaching in the knowledge society.* New York: Teachers College Press.

Hargreaves, A., Earl, L., Moore, S., & Manning, S. (2001). *Learning to change: Teaching beyond subjects and standards.* San Francisco: Jossey-Bass.

Hargreaves, A., & Fink, D. (2000). The three dimensions of reform. *Educational Leadership, 57*(7), 30–34.

Hargreaves, A., & Fink, D. (2003). Sustaining leadership. *Phi Delta Kappan 84*(9), 693–700.

Hargreaves, A., Shaw, P., Fink, D., Retallick, J., Giles, C., Moore, S., Schmidt, M., & James-Wilson, S. (2000). *Change frames: Supporting secondary teachers in interpreting and integrating secondary school reform.* Toronto: Ontario Institute for Studies in Education/University of Toronto.

Haynes, N. M., Emmons, C. L., & Woodruff, D. W. (1998). School development program effects: Linking implementation to outcomes. *Journal of Education for Students Placed at Risk, 3*(1), 71–85.

Heifetz, R. (1999). *Leadership without easy answers.* Cambridge, MA: Belknap Press of Harvard University Press.

Heifetz, R., & Linsky, M. (2002). *Leadership on the line: Staying alive through the dangers of leading.* Boston: Harvard Business School Press.

Henderson, A. (1987). *The evidence continues to grow.* Columbia, MD: National Committee for Citizens in Education.

Henderson, A., & Berla, N. (1995). *A new generation of evidence: The family is critical to student achievement.* Washington, DC: Center for Law and Education.

Higgins, G. (1994). *Resilient adults: Overcoming a cruel past.* San Francisco: Jossey-Bass.

Hoffer, E., (1972) *Reflections on the human condition.* New York: HarperCollins.

HOPE Foundation. (2002). *Failure is not an option* [video series]. Bloomington, IN: Author.

Hopkins, D. (2001). *School improvement for real.* New York: Routledge/Falmer.

Hord, S. M. (1997a). *Professional learning communities: Communities of continuous inquiry and improvement.* Austin, TX: Southwest Educational Development Laboratory.

———. (1997b). *Professional learning communities: What are they and why are they important?* Austin, TX: Southwest Educational Development Laboratory.

Houston, P. D. (1997). *Articles of faith & hope for public education.* Arlington, VA: American Association of School Administrators.

Huffman, J. B., & Hipp, K. K. (2004). *Reculturing schools as professional learning communities.* Lanham, MD: ScarecrowEducation.

Institute for Educational Leadership (2000). *Leadership for student learning: Reinventing the principalship.* Washington, DC: Author.

Jackson, K. (2000). *Building new teams: The next generation.* Paper presented at the Future of Work in the Public Sector conference, organized by the School of Public Administration, University of Victoria, British Columbia, Canada. Accessed online June 19, 2003, at www.futurework.telus.com/proceedings.pdf

Johnson, D. (2001, March 29). Maryland's strategy to lure new principals. *Washington Post,* B–2.

Joyce, B., & Showers, B. (1995, May). Learning experiences in staff development. *The Developer,* p. 3.

Kegan, R., & Lahey, L. L. (2001). *How the way we talk can change the way we work: Seven languages for transformation.* San Francisco: Jossey-Bass.

Kets de Vries, M. (1993). *Leaders, fools, and imposters: Essays on the psychology of leadership.* San Francisco: Jossey-Bass.

King, M. B., & Newmann, F. (2000). Will teacher learning advance school goals? *Phi Delta Kappan, 81*(8), 576–580.

Korczak, J. (1967). *Selected works of Janusz Korczak.* Warsaw, Poland: Central Institute for Scientific, Technical and Economic Information.

———. (1986). *King Matt the first.* New York: Farrar, Straus, and Giroux.

Kotter, J. (1996). *Leading change.* Boston: Harvard Business School Press.

Kouzes, J. M., & Posner, B. Z. (1999). *Encouraging the heart.* San Francisco: Jossey-Bass.

Kozol, J. (2000). *Ordinary resurrection: Children in the years of hope.* New York: Crown.

Kranz, G. (2000). *Failure is not an option: Mission control from* Mercury *to* Apollo 13 *and beyond.* New York: Simon & Schuster.

Kruse, S., Louis, K.S., & Bryk, A. S. (1994). *Building professional community in schools.* Madison, WI: Center on Organization and Restructuring of Schools.

LaFee, S. (2003). Professional learning communities. *The School Administrator, 5*(60), 6–12.

Land, D., & Stringfield, S. (Eds.). (2002). *Educating at-risk students.* Chicago: National Society for the Study of Education.

Langford, J., Vakii, T., & Lindquist, E. A. (2000). *Tough challenges and practical solutions: A report on conference proceedings.* Victoria, British Columbia, Canada: School of Public Administration, University of Victoria. Accessed online at www.futurework.telus.com/proceedings.pdf

Lewis, A. C. (2000). Listening to adolescents. *Phi Delta Kappan, 81*(9), 643.

Livsey, R. C., & Palmer, P. J. (1999). *The Courage to Teach: A Guide for Reflection and Renewal.* San Francisco: Jossey-Bass.

Lortie, D. C. (1975). *School teacher: A sociological study.* Chicago: University of Chicago Press.

Louis, K. S., & Kruse, S. D. (1995). *Professionalism and community: Perspectives on reforming urban schools.* Thousand Oaks, CA: Corwin Press.

Louis, K. S., Kruse, S. D., & Marks, H. M. (1996). Schoolwide professional community. In F. Newmann and Associates (Eds.), *Authentic achievement: Restructuring schools for intellectual quality.* San Francisco: Jossey-Bass.

Louis, K. S., Kruse, S., & Raywid, M. A. (1996). *Putting teachers at the center of reform. NASSP Bulletin, 80*(580), 9–21.

Machiavelli, N. (1999). *The prince* (G. Bull, Trans.). London/New York: Penguin Books. (Original work published 1532)

MacMillan, R. (1996). *The relationship between school culture and principals' practices during succession.* Unpublished doctoral dissertation, University of Toronto (OISE), Toronto, Ontario, Canada.

———. (2000). Leadership succession, culture of teaching, and educational change. In N. Bascia & A. Hargreaves (Eds.), *The sharp edge of educational change.* London: Falmer Press.

McLaughlin, M. (1993). What matters most in teachers' workplace context. In J. W. Lilly & M. McLaughlin (Eds.), *Teachers' work: Individuals, colleagues, and context.* New York: Teachers College Press.

Meier, D. (1995). *The power of their ideas: Lessons for America from a small school in Harlem.* Boston: Beacon Press.

Meyer, J. W., & Rowan, B. (1977). Institutional organizations: Formal structures as myth and ceremony. *American Journal of Sociology, 83,* 340–363.

Miles, M. (1998). Finding keys to school change. In A. Hargreaves, A. Lieberman, M. Fullan, & D. Hopkins (Eds.), *International handbook of educational change* (pp. 37–69). Dordrecht, The Netherlands: Kluwer Press.

Montgomery, A. F., & Rossi, R. J. (1994). Becoming at risk of failure in America's schools. In R. J. Rossi (Ed.), *Schools and students at risk: Context and framework for positive change.* New York: Teachers College Press.

Murphy, J., Jost, J., & Shipman, N. (2000). Implementation of the interstate school leaders licensure consortium standards. *International Journal of Leadership in Education, 3*(1), 17–39.

Nanus, B. (1992). *Visionary leadership.* San Francisco: Jossey-Bass.

National Academy of Public Administration. (1997). *Managing succession and developing leadership: Growing the next generation of public service leaders.* Washington, DC: Author.

National Association of Secondary School Principals. (2001). *The principals shortage.* Accessed online June 19, 2003, at www.nassp.org/publications/shortage

National Education Goals Panel. (1995). *National education goals report executive summary.* Washington, DC: Author.

National Parent Teacher Association. (1997). Accessed online June 18, 2003, from www.pta.org/parentinvolvement/standards/index.asp

Nespor, J. (1987). The roles of beliefs in the practice of teaching. *Journal of Curriculum Studies, 19,* 317–328.

Newmann, F. M., & Wehlage, G. (1995). *Successful school restructuring.* Madison: Center on Organization and Restructuring of Schools, School of education, University of Wisconsin–Madison.

Noer, D. M. (1993). *Healing the wounds.* San Francisco: Jossey-Bass.

Novick, B., Kress, J. S., & Elias, M. J. (2002). *Building learning communities with character.* Alexandria, VA: Association for Supervision and Curriculum Development.

Organization for Economic Cooperation and Development (OECD). (2001). *Schooling for tomorrow: What schools for the future?* Paris: Author.

Ovando, M. N. (1994). *Effects of teachers' leadership on their teaching practices.* Paper presented at the Annual Conference of the University Council of Educational Administration, Philadelphia.

Palmer, P. J. (1998). *The courage to teach: Exploring the inner landscape of a teacher's life.* San Francisco: Jossey-Bass.

Pardini, P. (1999). Making time for adult learning. *Journal of Staff Development, 20*(2).

Pascale, R. Conversations with change practice consulting teams of Price Waterhouse Coopers and Anderson Consulting, Oxford, England, and Colorado Springs, Colorado, 1997–1999.

————. (1998, March). Personal communication with David Schneider, partner, North American Change Practice, Price Waterhouse Coopers, Santa Fe, New Mexico.

Pascale, R. T., Millemann, M., & Gioja, L. (2000). *Surfing the edge of chaos.* New York: Three Rivers Press.

Peters, T. (1999). *The circle of innovation: You can't shrink your way to greatness.* New York: Vintage.

Pintrich, P. R. (1990). Implications of psychological research on student learning and college teaching for teacher education. In W. R. Houston (Ed.), *Handbook of research on teacher education* (pp. 826–857). New York: Macmillan.

Posner, B. Z., & Westwood, R. I. (1995). A cross-cultural investigation of the shared values relationship. *International Journal of Value-Based Management, 11*(4), 1–10.

Purkey, W. W., & Novak, J. M. (1996). *Inviting school success.* Belmont, CA: Wadsworth.

Putnam, R. D. (2000). *Bowling alone: The collapse and revival of American community.* New York: Simon & Schuster.

Putnam, R. D., Leonardi, R., & Nanetti, R. Y. (1993). *Making democracy work: Civic traditions in modern Italy.* Princeton, NJ: Princeton University Press.

Reaching Today's Youth, 1(1). Bloomington, IN: National Educational Service.

Reaching Today's Youth, 2(1). Bloomington, IN: National Educational Service.

Reaching Today's Youth, 2(3). Bloomington, IN: National Educational Service.

Reaching Today's Youth, 4(4). Bloomington, IN: National Educational Service.

Reeves, D. B. (2000). *Accountability in action.* Denver, CO: Advanced Learning Press.

————. (2002a). *Making standards work* (3rd ed.). Denver, CO: Advanced Learning Press.

————. (2002b). *The leader's guide to standards: A blueprint for educational equity and excellence.* San Francisco: Jossey-Bass.

Riley, K (1998). *Whose school is it anyway.* London: Falmer Press.

————. (2000). Leadership, learning and systemic change. *Journal of Educational Change, 1*(1), 57–75.

Rossi, R. J., & Stringfield, S. C. (1997). *Education reform and students at risk.* Washington, DC: Office of Educational Research and Improvement, U.S. Department of Education.

Sanders, L. (2003, March 16). Medicine's progress, one setback at a time. *New York Times Magazine,* 29.

Sarason, S. (1972). *The creation of settings and the future societies.* San Francisco: Jossey Bass.

————. (1990). *The predictable failure of educational reform.* San Francisco: Jossey-Bass.

Saul J. R. (1993). *Voltaire's bastards.* Toronto: Penguin Books.

Schiff, T. (2002, January). Principals' readiness for reform: A comprehensive approach. *Principal Leadership, 2*(5).

Schlechty, P. C. (1992). *Schools for the 21st Century: Leadership Imperatives for Educational Reform.* San Francisco: Jossey-Bass.

Schorr, L. B. (1988). *Within our reach: Breaking the cycle of disadvantage.* New York: Anchor Press/Doubleday.

————. (1998, Summer). Searchlights on delinquency. *Journal of Emotional and Behavioral Problems, 7*(2).

Senge, P. M. (1990). *The fifth discipline: The art and practice of the learning organization.* New York: Doubleday/Currency.

Senge, P. M., Ross, R., Smith, B., Roberts, C., & Kleiner, A. (1994). *The fifth discipline fieldbook: Strategies and tools for building a learning organization.* New York: Doubleday.

Sergiovanni, T. J. (1992). *Moral leadership: Getting to the heart of school improvement.* San Francisco: Jossey-Bass.

————. (1994). *Building community in schools.* San Francisco: Jossey-Bass.

————. (2000). *The lifeworld of leadership: Creating culture, community, and personal meaning in our schools.* San Francisco: Jossey-Bass.

Smith, L. M., Dwyer, D. C., Prunty, J. J., & Kleine, P. F. (1987). *The fate of an innovative school.* London: Falmer Press.

Soder, R. (2001). *The language of leadership.* San Francisco: Jossey-Bass.

Soder, R., Goodlad, J. I., & McMannon, T. J. (2001). *Developing democratic character in the young.* San Francisco: Jossey-Bass.

Solmo, R. (1995, February). Meetings—management; consensus (social sciences). *Social Policy, 44*(2).

Sparks, D. (2002). *Designing powerful professional development for teachers and principals.* Oxford, OH: National Staff Development Council.

Spillane, J. P., Halverson, R., & Drummond, J. B. (2001). Investigating school leadership practice: A distributed perspective. *Educational Researcher, 30*(3), 23–28.

Springfield, S. C. (1995). Attempts to enhance students' learning: A search for valid programs and highly reliable implementation techniques. *School Effectiveness and School Improvement, 6,* 67–96.

Standing Bear, L. (1933). *Land of the spotted eagle.* New York: Houghton Mifflin.

Sternberg, R. J. (1996). *Successful intelligence: How practical and creative intelligence determine success in life.* New York: Simon & Schuster.

Stiegelbauer, S. M., & Anderson, S. (1992). *Seven years later: Revisiting a restructured school in northern Ontario.* Paper presented at the American Educational Research Association Meetings, San Francisco.

Stoll, L. (1999). Raising our potential: Understanding and developing capacity for lasting improvement. *School Effectiveness and School Improvement, 10*(4), 503–532.

Stoll L., & Fink, D. (1996). *Changing our schools: Linking school effectiveness and school improvement.* Buckingham, UK: Open University Press.

Stoll, L., Fink, D., & Earl, L. (2002). *It's about learning (and it's about time).* London: Routledge/Falmer.

Stringfield, S., & Land, D. (Eds.). (2002). *Educating at-risk students.* Chicago: National Society for the Study of Education.

Talbert, J., & MacLaughlin, M. (1994). Teacher professionalism in local school contexts. *American Journal of Education, 102*, 123–153.

Teddlie, C., & Stringfield, S. (1993). *Schools make a difference: Lessons learned from a 10-year study of school effects.* New York: Teachers College Press.

Tutu, D. M. (2003, February 6). Personal communication. Jacksonville, Florida.

Tyack, D., & Tobin, W. (1994). The grammar of schooling: Why has it been so hard to change? *American Educational Research Journal, 31*(3), 453–480.

Walsh, M. (2002). Supreme court upholds Cleveland voucher program. *Education Week, 21*(42). Accessed online June 18, 2003, at www.edweek.org/ew/newstory.cfm?slug_42voucher_web.h21

Weinstein, C. S. (1989). Teacher education students' preconceptions of teaching. *Journal of Teacher Education, 40*(2), 53–60.

Werner, E. E., & Smith, R. S. (1977). *Kauai's children come of age.* Honolulu: University of Hawaii Press.

———. (1982). *Vulnerable but invincible: A longitudinal study of resilient children and youth.* New York: McGraw-Hill.

Wilker, K. (1983). *The lindenhof* (S. Lhotzky, Trans.). Sioux Falls, SD: Augustana College. (Original work published 1920)

Williams, T. (2001). *Unrecognized exodus, unaccepted accountability: The looming shortage of principals and vice-principals in Ontario public school boards.* Toronto: Ontario Principals' Council.

Woods, E. G. (1995). *School improvement research series, close-up 17: Reducing the drop-out rate.* Portland, OR: Northwest Regional Educational Laboratory.

Index